Without Buddha I Could not be a Christian

"The dialogue between Christianity and Buddhism is one of the most important conversations of our time, and Paul Knitter's new book shows why. If you want to know how religions can help to revitalize each other, this is the place to start."

David Loy – Besl Family Chair for Ethics/Religion and Society at Xavier University

"In this revealing retrospective, Knitter recounts very personally how his encounters with liberation theology and with other religions, especially Buddhism, challenged and transformed his Christian faith. This will be of interest to all who are concerned with religious diversity and social justice."

Leo Lefebure – Professor of Theology, Georgetown University

"Radiates wisdom and warmth. Is it possible to become more fully Christian by taking most seriously the Buddhist path – becoming Buddhist in order to live more fully the Christian life? Agree or not with Paul's answer, we can be most grateful to him for pressing the question and making so very clear the possibilities and risks along the way."

Francis X. Clooney – Professor of Divinity and Professor of Comparative Theology, Harvard Divinity School

"A ground-breaking work of inter-religious dialogue, comparative theology and social ethics. The rarest combination of theological acumen, humility and humor. Like a thrilling mystery, the insights of each section build to the final chapter, a tour de force, in which Knitter rediscovers the very meaning of serving others. A must read for anyone who wants to renew their faith and rediscover their humanity in intimate dialogue with the faiths of others."

Lama John Makransky – Associate Professor of Theology, Boston College

"Paul Knitter has always been uncommonly courageous in his writings about Christianity's relationship with other religions. He has also been able to engage other religions with complete openness and honesty. This unique book is highly recommended as an example of how to do personally engaged, self-reflective theology in a religiously plural world."

Rita Gross – Professor Emerita of Religion, University of Wisconsin-Eau Claire

Without Buddha I Could not be a Christian

PAUL F. KNITTER

ONEWORLD
ACADEMIC

A Oneworld book

Published by Oneworld Publications 2009
Reprinted 2009, 2010 (twice)
This paperback edition published in 2013
Reprinted 2015, 2017

ISBN 978–1–78074–248–9 (ebook)
ISBN 978–1–85168–963–7

Typeset by Jayvee, Trivandrum, India
Cover design by Design Deluxe
Printed and bound in Great Britain by Clays, Ltd St Ives plc

Stay up to date with the latest books,
special offers, and exclusive content from
Oneworld with our monthly newsletter

Sign up on our website
www.oneworld-publications.com

FSC
www.fsc.org
MIX
Paper from
responsible sources
FSC® C018072

For my atheist brother, Don,

Who did his best to keep me honest.

CONTENTS

PREFACE

Am I Still a Christian?

Contrary to much of its message, this is a rather selfish book. I've written it mainly for myself.

For much of my adult life, but especially during the past twenty-five years, I've been struggling with my Christian beliefs. Those beliefs have been with me for a long time. Born in 1939, brought up by hard-working, deep-believing, working-class Roman Catholic parents on the suburban edge of Chicago, educated at St. Joseph's Elementary by the School Sisters of St. Francis, I never for a moment doubted that God was everywhere, that Jesus was his Son, and that if you ate meat on Friday or missed Mass on Sunday you were in deep trouble with God and Jesus. Those beliefs began to be both refined and deepened when, at the age of thirteen, and to the bewilderment and reluctance of my parents, I announced that God was calling me to the priesthood. I went off to what was then called a minor (high school) seminary and spent the next fourteen years of my life studying and preparing to be a priest.

Ordained in Rome in 1966, I was assigned the job of studying, and then teaching, theology. (The study was at the University of Marburg, Germany, and the teaching was at Catholic Theological Union in Chicago.) After I was granted permission to leave the priesthood in 1975 (what had looked easy when I was thirteen became more of a nagging problem at thirty: celibacy), and even after I married the love of my life in 1982, I was able to stay faithful to the other love of my life, theology. Instead of seminarians, I taught undergraduates at Xavier University in Cincinnati for some thirty years.

But as exciting as my job was, it didn't really resolve – indeed it often seemed to amplify – the deeper, persistent questions that life kept throwing at me. When I say "life," I mean the need and the effort to *connect* what I was taught about God and Jesus and heaven and hell with all that I was confronting and feeling and learning as a responsible (I try) and an intelligent (I hope) human being. More and more, I found myself – a Catholic Christian all my life, a theologian by profession – having to ask myself what I really do, or really can, believe.

Do I really believe what I say I believe, or what I'm supposed to believe as a member of the Christian community? I'm not talking about the ethical teachings of Jesus and the New Testament witness. The gospel vision of a society based on honesty, justice, and compassion makes eminent, urgent sense. Nor do I have major problems with the controversial ethical or practical teachings of my church (most of them having to do with what one Catholic theologian has called "the pelvic issues") dealing with matters such as birth control, divorce, the role of women, homosexuality, clerical celibacy, episcopal leadership, and transparency. Certainly, these are matters of grave concern, but with many of my fellow Catholics I've realized that, as has often been the case in the history of our church, on such issues the "sense" or "voice" of the faithful has a few things to teach the pastors. It's a matter of time.

No, when I say I'm struggling, I mean with the big stuff – the stuff that applies to all Christians, not just my own Roman Catholic community. I'm talking about the basic ingredients of the Creed, the beliefs that many Christians proclaim together every Sunday and that are supposed to define who they are in a world of many other religious beliefs and philosophies. I'm talking about "God the Father almighty, Creator of heaven and earth," who as a personal being is active in history and in our individual lives, whom we worship and pray to for help and guidance. I'm talking about "his only-begotten Son" who "died for our sins" and will "come again at the end of time" and who will grant eternal life and personal immortality to the body and souls of all those who answer God's call, while those who reject the call will be dispatched to a hellish punishment that will never, ever end.

Do I really believe – or better, am I *able* to believe – what those statements are claiming and professing? Even when I don't take them literally, even when I remind myself that they are symbols that have to be interpreted seriously and carefully but not always literally, still I have to ask myself: when I peel off the literal layers, what is the inner or deeper meaning that I can affirm? What do I believe when I say that

God is personal (indeed, three Persons!), that Jesus is the only Savior, that because of his death the whole world is different, that he rose bodily from the tomb? The "what" of my beliefs can become so slippery that I find myself asking, in all honesty, whether I believe at all.

Now, as a theologian, I get paid to try to struggle with and answer such questions. My job, as Bernard Lonergan, S.J. taught us back at the Gregorian University in Rome during the early 1960s, is "to mediate between religion and culture." That means to make sense of the world in the light of Christian belief and experience *and* to make sense of Christian belief in the light of our experience and knowledge of the world we live in. That's what I've been trying to do, lo these many years.

It is generally said that Christian theologians have two primary sources with which they carry out this job of mediation between religion and culture. On the side of religion, they draw on Scripture and tradition – that is, the first written witness of the early Christian communities, and then the long history of Christian efforts to comprehend and live that message through different historical and cultural periods. Christians in general, and Christian theologians especially, need to know their Bible and their history.

In order to explore the rich fields of culture, theologians draw on their own experience and that of others under different indicators: literature, movies, the daily news and analysis, the visual arts, the natural and human sciences (especially politics and economics). These two general sources for theology have been termed "the Christian fact" and "human experience." Over the four decades of plying my theological trade, I've tried to make as careful and as intelligent a use of these two sources for theology as I could. But especially over the ups and downs of the last twenty years, I have realized that these two sources aren't enough. At least, they haven't been enough for me. By themselves, they haven't sufficiently equipped me to grapple with the kinds of disconcerting and destabilizing questions that I mentioned above – about the nature of God, the role of Jesus, the meaning of salvation. It was only after I added a third ingredient to my supply room of theological resources that my work became more exciting, more satisfying, and, I think, more fruitful.

Like many of my theological colleagues, I have come to realize that I have to look *beyond* the traditional borderlines of Christianity to find something that is vitally, maybe even essentially, important for the job of understanding and living the Christian faith: *other religions.*

That is, the Scriptures and the traditions, the sacred texts, the past teachings, the living communities of other religious believers. It was only after I began to take seriously and to explore other religious Scriptures and traditions that I was able to more adequately understand my own. Stated more personally: my engagement with other ways of being religious – that is, with what I have studied, discovered, been excited about, or perplexed by in other religions – has turned out to be an unexpected but immense help in my job of trying to figure out what the message of Jesus means in our contemporary world.

In other words, following the examples and the instructions of theological mentors such as Raimon Panikkar, Aloysius Pieris, S.J., Bede Griffiths, and Thomas Merton, I've come to be convinced that I have to do my theology – and live my Christian life – dialogically. Or in current theological jargon: I have to be religious interreligiously. I've tried to practice and understand my Christian life through engagement with the way other people – Jews, Muslims, Hindus, Buddhists, Native Americans – have lived and understood their religious lives.

Though I have found my conversations with *all* the other religious traditions to be fruitful, my deepest, most enjoyable, most difficult, and therefore most rewarding conversations have been with Buddhism and Buddhists. My closest other-religion friends have been Buddhists (I'm married to one!). Over the years, I have realized that this conversation with Buddhism has really been one of the two most helpful – really, indispensable – resources for carrying on my Christian and theological task of trying to mediate between my religious heritage (the Bible and tradition) and the culture that has marked my humanity. The other indispensable resource has been liberation theology and its response to the injustice and resulting suffering that infects so much of our culture: that's what my book *One Earth, Many Religions* is all about.

My conversation with Buddhism has enabled me to do what every theologian must do professionally and what every Christian must do personally – that is, to understand and live our Christian beliefs in such a way that these beliefs are both consistent with *and* a challenge for the world in which we live. Buddhism has enabled me to make sense of my Christian faith so that I can maintain my intellectual integrity and affirm what I see as true and good in my culture; but at the same time, it has aided me to carry out my prophetic–religious responsibility and challenge what I see as false and harmful in my culture.

Right now, as I look back over my life, I can't image being a Christian and a theologian without this engagement with Buddhism. And thus, the title of this book: *Without Buddha I Could not be a Christian.* Though the wording is perhaps provocative, it is definitely true!

NOT JUST FOR ME

But at this point, I have to take a step back and ask: is the last word of the title accurate? Am I still a Christian? That's a question I have heard not only from others (especially some of my fellow theologians, including some in the Vatican) but one I have felt in my own mind and heart. Is what I have learned from Buddhism, or the way I have understood and interpreted my Christian beliefs in the light of Buddhism, still consistent with Christian Scripture and tradition? I might put it this way: has my dialogue with Buddhism made me a Buddhist Christian? Or a Christian Buddhist? Am I a Christian who has understood his own identity more deeply with the help of Buddhism? Or have I become a Buddhist who still retains a stock of Christian leftovers?

I've wanted to write this book in order to find out. That's what I meant when I said at the outset that I'm writing it for myself. I want to lay out as carefully and clearly as I can just how my conversation with Buddhism has enabled me to take another, more creative, more satis-fying look at my Christian beliefs. I want to articulate as lucidly as I can how my efforts to understand and make sense of Buddhist teach-ings and practice have made it possible for me to review, reinterpret, and reaffirm Christian teachings about God (Chapters 1–3), life after death (Chapter 4), Christ as only Son of God and Savior (Chapter 5), prayer and worship (Chapter 6), and efforts to move this world towards the peace and justice of the Reign of God (Chapter 7). These are the topics that make up the contents of the book's seven chapters. All of these chapters have a common architecture: in the first part I state my problems in affirming Christian beliefs, the second describes my efforts to "pass over" to Buddhism, and the third part summarizes what I think I can learn when I "pass back" to my Christian identity and beliefs.

As any good psychologist (or artist) will tell us, we can identify and deal with what we're feeling by "getting it out," by expressing it as clearly as we can. That's what I'm trying to do with this book. I really do think I'm a Buddhist Christian (rather than a Christian Buddhist). But to know, I have to unpack and lay out just what that means.

Yet really to know, I have to hear from my fellow Christians. They'll have to tell me whether what I'm putting forth in this book makes sense to them, whether it enables them to connect (or reconnect) with their Christian identity and tradition. That's the way things work in Christianity; we're a community called church. There's got to be some kind, or degree, of community affirmation if a particular belief or practice is going to be labeled Christian. This means that the new insights of a theologian, or the teachings of a bishop or church leader, have to be, to some degree, received by the community of believers. I'm hoping that there will be other, many other, fellow Christians who will so receive what I'm offering in this book. I'm hoping that Buddhism will help them, as I think it has helped me, to review and retrieve their Christian beliefs and their efforts to understand, affirm, and live the gospel of Jesus. So this isn't such a selfish book after all! To help myself, I have to help others.

But, in this case, the others are primarily my fellow Christians, not my Buddhist friends. Though I hope that Buddhists might find this book interesting, and maybe even helpful, I'm writing it mainly for those Christians who like me are struggling, often painfully, with trying to hold together what they believe personally and intellectually as Christians. So, the "orthodox question" I'm asking in the chapters that follow is directed to the Christian community, not the Buddhist. My central concern is that the theological genes I'm passing on are still Christian, that my reinterpretation of Christian belief, though really different, is not *totally* different from what went before. All good theology is a matter of discontinuity in continuity, creating something new that is rooted in and nourished by the old. In this sense, I hope this book makes for some good Christian theology.

I also hope it's based on good "Buddhist theology." Over the past decades I've studied Buddhism as carefully as I can and I've practiced a form of daily Zen meditation. But I'm not a scholar of Buddhism; I don't know Pali or Chinese or Tibetan. Still, I hope that my understanding of Buddhism and the use I make of it are for the most part accurate and will resonate with what many Buddhists hold. (As is the case with Christians, given the different forms of Buddhism, it's practically impossible for the whole Buddhist choir to sing in one voice: there's always polyphony.)

But Buddhist orthodoxy is not my primary, or crucial, concern. Even if I've misunderstood Buddhism, if that leads me to a new, deeper, more engaged understanding of the Christian message, well, that's how things happen. I bet my Buddhist friends will not be at all unhappy. (They'd probably call it *upaya* – a matter of "skillful means" or playing somewhat loosely with the facts to get your point across.)

A LONG PREGNANCY

Understanding the long process by which the following chapters took shape might provide readers with both patience and guidance in reading them. Actually, in my work as a "dialogical theologian" – in the many courses on Buddhism and Asian religions at Xavier University, through the projects and friendships that are the lifeblood of the Society for Buddhist–Christian Studies, through my own daily practice of Zen meditation, as well as my work as a member of CRISPAZ (Christians for Peace in El Salvador), and of the Interreligious Peace Council – I've been writing this book for the past forty years. In trying to be a faithful disciple of Christ and a fledgling disciple of Buddha in a world both wracked by suffering due to injustice and tantalized by ever-new discoveries of science, I have over these four decades been struggling with new questions and pursuing new insights, and, in the process, taking existential notes for this book.

There's also been a pretty steady, but private, conversation with myself. Over the years, not daily but regularly, I've kept a spiritual journal for myself in which I've tried to find words for the insights or questions that bubbled up from what I had been reading, or teaching, or learning from dialogue or political struggles. (I must admit that many of these insights took shape during my meditation periods, when I wasn't supposed to be thinking!) I've gone back and read through these journals, kept since 1994, and excerpted lots of things that have helped me put this book together. Occasionally, when I found myself surprised by a particularly apt turn of phrase, I quote from them directly.

These pages also took shape within more immediate conversations. As each of these chapters became first drafts on my computer screen, I emailed them around to a circle of friends and colleagues whose candid but always loving comments confirmed, clarified, or corrected what I had sent to them. At the top of this list is my wife, Cathy Cornell, who was a Catholic Christian when we married twenty-five years ago but has since found a Buddhist path to be more clear and comfortable. Because of her "dual belonging," but especially because she knows better than anyone else what I really believe and practice, she has been my most helpful and enjoyable dialogue partner, for this book as for life. Following their mom are my children, John and Moira, who have brought to their comments on this book their lifelong ability to tell me when I wasn't making sense.

The other friends, Buddhists and Christians, who have done their best to help keep me both lucid and accurate are: Michael Atkinson (certified *Dharma* teacher with both patience and appreciation for his Christian friends), Richard Bollman, S.J. (my former pastor at Bellarmine parish who preaches anonymously Buddhist sermons), Joseph Bracken, S.J. (long-time colleague, friend, and critic in Xavier University's Theology Department), Dave Callan (friend and fellow former priest and still-struggling Catholic), Rick Certik (my cousin and fellow Buddhist Christian who has spent almost thirty years as a priest in Japan), Ruth Holtel (peace activist, properly impatient with her Catholic Church), David Loy (friend, internationally valued Buddhist scholar and holder of the Ethics/Religion/Society Chair at Xavier University), and Michael Holleran (former Carthusian monk, New York parish priest, certified Zen teacher, and newly found friend). To all these friends I extend both my gratitude for their help and my apologies for not always using it according to their wishes.

Also, a special, unique word of thanks to Nancy King, who made available to Cathy and me her beautiful home in the secluded paradise of Muriwai Beach, New Zealand. Here I found the sabbatical from retirement that I needed to ponder, feel, and imagine – and so to accomplish what for many of us is the most difficult stage in a writing project: getting started with a sense of direction.

My final thank you is utterly unexpected. I never imagined I would be able to make it. You see, when I arrived in New Zealand in January of 2006 I was happily retired and figuring I would end my life in this blissful cruise-mode. When Cathy and I left New Zealand in May 2006, I had, stunned but excited, accepted the Paul Tillich Chair of Theology, World Religions, and Culture at Union Theological Seminary! And in my second semester at Union, in a course titled "Double Belonging: Christian and Buddhist," I decided to take the first-draft manuscript of this book for a test drive with the bright,

curious, engagingly opinionated Union students. And what a prof-
itable testing it turned out to be. I am deeply grateful for the gracious-
ness and for the sharpness with which the students let me know how
they thought the book might help or hinder both their own spiritual
journeys and their future ministries. A bit battered, I felt fundamentally affirmed. The final draft, I think, is battered but better.

Among these Union students, I am particularly and happily grateful to my doctoral advisee, Mr. Kyeongil Jung. He has been both a
hard-working and meticulous assistant in source-gathering, proof-
reading, and fact-checking, as well as an inspiring, younger fellow
traveler on the path of dialogue and liberation who will carry on after
we old-timers wear out. He has offered me help and hope.

If readers of this book can experience some of the blessings I have
felt in writing it, I will be a very happy author.

Paul F. Knitter
Muriwai Beach, New Zealand, where I began writing
Union Theological Seminary, NYC, where I finished.

1

NIRVANA AND GOD
THE TRANSCENDENT OTHER

It's a universal experience, I suspect, that growing up is not only a wonderful and exciting and rewarding experience; it is also, and often even more so, a painful and bewildering and frustrating ordeal. That's natural. To leave the familiar, to move into the unknown, and to become something we weren't can be scary and demanding.

If this is true of life in general, it should also be true of religious faith. More precisely, if figuring out who we really are as we move from childhood to so-called maturity is for most of us a process in which progress takes place through grappling with confusion, we should expect the same process to operate in figuring out who God is. That has certainly been my experience. As I've grown older, my faith in God has, I trust, grown deeper, but that's because it has been prodded by confusion. No confusion, no deepening.

Just why human growth makes for problems in religious growth has to do with the natural process of growing up. Our spiritual intelligence and maturity have to keep pace with our emotional intelligence and maturity. How that syncopated growth takes place, if it does at all, will be different from person to person. But I think there are some general reasons, especially for people in the United States, why this syncopation lags. For many Christians, while their general academic education matures with their bodies and intelligence, their religious education (if they had any) all too often ends with eighth or twelfth grade. They have to face adult life with an eighth-grade, or teenage-level, religious diploma.

That can make for difficulties, mainly because being a grown-up means taking responsibility and thinking for oneself. That requires finding reasons in one's own experience for affirming, or rejecting, what one took from Mom and Dad with a child's trusting, but often blind, faith. And making connections between an adult's experience and a child's image of a Divine Being up in heaven running the show may be as impossible as fitting into your high-school graduation suit or dress twenty or even ten years later.

Add to such tensions the fact that we live in a world (more vocal in Europe than the U.S.) in which scientists keep answering the questions for which we thought God was the response, or psychologists and political scientists keep pointing out how religion is a more effective tool for manipulation than for maturation, and it becomes even clearer why passing from religious childhood to religious adulthood runs into the kind of problems that either block or terminate the process.

Way back in 1975, the very first graduate theology course I taught (at Catholic Theological Union in Chicago) was titled "The Problem of God." For me, and for many, the problem remains. As I try to sort out and identify the different faces of my God problem – or, the reasons why I so often find myself wincing when I hear or read how we Christians talk about God – I find three discomforting images: God the transcendent Other, God the personal Other, and God the known Other.

In no way can I provide neatly packaged answers to a lineup of questions that have teased and tormented many a mind much more erudite than my own. But I do want to try to explore and better understand – for myself and for others – how Buddhism has helped me grapple with such questions and even to come up with some working answers.

In what follows in this chapter (and in subsequent chapters) I hope to carry on what John Dunne in his wonderful little book from back in the 1970s, *The Way of All the Earth*, called the "spiritual adventure of our time:" the adventure of *passing over* to another religious tradition in as open, as careful, and as personal a way as possible, and then *passing back* to one's own religion to see how walking in someone else's "religious moccasins" can help one to understand and fit into one's own.

That's what I'll be doing in the three segments that make up the structure of each of this book's chapters. First I'll try to sketch as clear a picture as possible of the struggles I'm experiencing in a particular area of Christian belief and practice. Then I'll pass over to how a

Buddhist might deal with these struggles and questions. And finally I'll pass back and try to formulate what I have learned from Buddhism and what I think can make for a retrieval and a deepening of Christian belief.

MY STRUGGLES: THE TRANSCENDENT OTHER

Somewhere, Carl Gustav Jung stated that according to his experience with his clients, when religious people move into the territory of middle-age, they start having problems with a God imaged as a transcendent Other – that is, as a Being who exists "up there" or "out there" in a place called heaven. That certainly describes me and my problems. In fact, though I may have been a late bloomer in many aspects of my life, in this area I was, according to Jung's forecast, quite precocious. By my mid-twenties I had growing difficulties in wrapping my mind as well as my heart around the picture of God as Other. As I have struggled, it's become clearer to me that otherness itself is not the real problem. There have to be others, especially certain "significant others," in our life if it is going to be healthy and fruitful. Wouldn't God merit a place on the top of my list of significant others?

The stumbling stone has to do with the way God is portrayed as different from all the other significant others in my life. He (for the rest of this section it feels appropriate to use the traditional male pronoun for God) is the *transcendent* Other. Or as I was taught during my years of theological studies in Rome back in the 1960s, God is the *totaliter aliter* – the totally Other, infinitely beyond all that we are as human and finite beings. In his transcendence, God is, we were taught, infinitely perfect, infinitely complete, happy unto himself, in need of nothing. "*Ipsum esse subsistens*" was the Latin label we memorized – God is "Self-subsistent Being," Being who originates from himself, who is dependent solely on himself, and could be happy all by himself.

An Other in need of no other

Admittedly, this image of God as Self-subsistent Being is more a legacy of Greek philosophy than biblical narratives (though some Bible scholars see its roots in the declaration of God as "I am who I am" in Exodus 3:14). When I thought about this, I realized that this means that God is an Other who really doesn't need others, and so in his self-sufficiency cannot really be affected by others. In fact, that's pretty standard Christian theology: God does not have any needs that would make him dependent on creatures – needs that would tarnish the perfection and self-sufficiency of God. Theologians through the centuries (conditioned, I might add, by the Greek and very male notion of perfection as self-sufficiency) have acted as bodyguards around God, making sure that no one really touches him. To be touched and changed by something that is not God – that would be, as it were, a weakness that is not permitted by God's infinite otherness.

But wait a minute. This is only half the picture of God in Christian doctrine. The God of Abraham and Moses and Jesus is also a God of love. Christianity affirms that the God who is infinitely other, infinitely perfect and powerful, is also a God who infinitely loves. Creation is the supreme sign and expression of that love, and it is so, theologians explain, precisely because this God, who in his self-sufficiency and perfection didn't have to create, did so! To do something that one doesn't have to do, to give of oneself even when one in no way needs to – that, say the theologians, is love at its finest.

But is it? Here is where I stumbled again. In my thinking as well as in my praying, in my efforts to image and in my efforts to feel the Divine, I could not see how Christian teaching succeeded in holding together God's infinite otherness with God's infinite love, or God's transcendent being beyond this world with God's immanent action in this world.

To start with, if we believe that God is love and that creation is the expression of this love, but then immediately add that God did not have to create, it sounds like God did not have to express his love. But what kind of a love is that? A love that can just exist, without finding expression? *Is* there such a love? Can we imagine a person being full of love but never showing it, or putting it into action? Theologians respond by explaining that God's inherent, infinite love is expressed within himself, between the relations that make up the Trinity. So God's love could be satisfied with being only an internal, self-love? … Hmmm. We have words for such love. I don't mean to be disrespectful, but I have to be honest. A love that doesn't need to be expressed just doesn't make sense – or it's a bit sick.

Creation from scratch

Further problems in reconciling God's love in creation with traditional understanding of God's transcendent otherness arise from the way Christian doctrine has understood creation. I'm supposed to believe in a "creation out of nothing" (*creatio ex nihilo*). God produced the world from scratch; he had nothing to work with. Theologians have insisted on this (it's not that clear in the Bible) for two reasons: to make sure that there was nothing around before creation (because it would have come from somewhere else besides God) and to make sure that God didn't spin out the world from God's self (because that would have put the world on God's level and so undermined the divine transcendence). So there's a clear line of demarcation between God and creation; it's the line between Producer and produced, between the totally Infinite and the totally finite, between the Transcendent and the immanent. For me, the line of demarcation feels and looks like a chasm.

But that, Christian theology announces, is precisely the marvel and mystery of Christianity. It proclaims a God who has crossed the chasm! A God who, already among the people of Israel, has chosen to enter history. And that choice and that entrance have come to their total and final fulfillment in Jesus of Nazareth, for in him God has become history by becoming human. The transcendence of God, for Christians, has become immanent and present within creation, for Christians believe in a God who not only acts in history but becomes incarnate and "takes flesh" in history.

Here we're touching the very heart of Christianity, and as I will try to explain in Chapter 5, this is why I remain a Christian. But problems still remain in bringing together in a coherent, engaging manner the abiding Christian insistence on the transcendent otherness of God and a convincing affirmation of God's action and incarnation in the world. To summarize in what I hope is a not too simplistic statement: given the chasm-like dividing line between God and the world, God's engagement in our history turns out to be one way, preferential, and, in its highest incarnational form, one time.

A one-way street

It's one way because given the Christian insistence on the perfection and unchangeability of God, God can certainly make a difference in the world. But the world can never make any difference for God. I remember my guarded perplexity when Father Van Roo, S.J., teaching us the "*De Deo Uno*" course ("On the One God") at the Gregorian University in Rome, carefully led us through the distinction that God's influence on the world is real, but the world's influence on God is "*rationis tantum*" – loosely translated, only figments of our mind's imagination. If the world *could* affect God, the professor clarified, it would tarnish his perfection and independence.

So God's action in history is a one-way street. But it also seems to be a street constructed rather preferentially, in some neighborhoods but not in others. What I'm getting at is something I've heard frequently from my undergraduate students: God seems to play favorites; he acts here, but not there; in Jewish history but not in Canaanite history. This pushes us back to the transcendent divide between God and the world. Since they're two totally different realms and since God is in total charge, his actions in history and the world have to cross a divide. God has, as it were, to build bridges.

And bridges, if I may extend the analogy, are built here and there. If they were everywhere, there would be no divide! This makes God's actions in the world interventions rather than natural or spontaneous happenings. And the interventions are "choices:" God freely chooses to act because, remember, he doesn't have to act. But then his choices seem to be selective, preferential, as if God loves some of his children more than others.

This last difficulty hangs heavily on what Christianity proclaims as the best of its good news: that this transcendent God has "come down" from his transcendent heaven and has identified, or become one with, his creation. The Divine was "made flesh" (John 1:14). Here the chasm no longer exists. Here we have the marvel of God's love – to "give up" the privileges of divinity, to cross the divide, and become like us in all things except sin. Miraculous, marvelous, incredible as it is, however, it still bears, for me and for many Christians, all the problems of a preferential intervention. This miracle of God becoming human happens not only at a particular time, within a particular people; it also happens, Christians insist, *only once.* Only in Jesus, nowhere else. We'll explore this issue more carefully in Chapter 5. For the moment I'll just state my struggle: while I'm perplexed by God having to "come down" in order to be part of this world, I'm even more puzzled over why he did so only once.

Dualism is the problem!

Even though many of my teachers at the Gregorian University in the 1960s may have been overly conscientious in their determination to guard God's transcendent untouchability, even though God's otherness may weigh more heavily on my generation's shoulders than on my children's, still, for many contemporary Christians I know that there is a deep-reaching, fundamental problem in the way Christians image and talk about God-the-Other. I'm going to give the problem a philosophical name, but it points to a personal malaise that many Christians feel at least once a week when listening to Sunday sermons or singing Sunday hymns.

Christianity, throughout most of its history (because of its historical conditioning, not because of its inherent nature), has been plagued with the problem of *dualism*. My dictionary defines dualism as: "a state in which something has two distinct parts or aspects, which are often opposites." My own simplistic definition would be: dualism results when we make necessary distinctions, and then take those distinctions too seriously. We turn those distinctions into dividing lines rather than connecting lines; we use them as no-trespassing signs. We not only distinguish, we separate. And the separation usually leads to ranking: one side is superior to and dominant over the other. Thus, we have the dualism of matter and spirit, East and West, nature and history, male and female, God and the world.

Here's our problem, I think. We Christians (we're not the only religion to do this) have *distinguished* God and the world, or the Infinite and the finite. Such distinctions are right and proper; indeed, necessary. But then we've made much too much of our neat distinctions. We've made these distinctions too clear, too defined. We have so insisted on the infinite distance between God and the world that we've ended up not with God and creatures on two ends of the same playing field but in two different stadiums! We have so stressed how different, how beyond, God is from creatures that our attempts to "connect" the two turn out to be contrived or artificial or partial or unequal.

That's the problem with dualism: it so stresses the difference between two realities, it so separates them, that it cannot then get them back together again and show how the two belong together, complement each other, need each other, form a genuine relationship with each other. That's it! That's the crux of the problem: Christian dualism has so exaggerated the difference between God and the world that it cannot really show how the two form a unity.

Of course, what I have summed up in these pages does not represent all of Christian tradition and experience, and even of Christian theology. But it does echo the dominant voices and reflect the prevailing images not only in popular Christian beliefs but in much of the "standard teaching" of Christian churches. So much of Christian belief and spirituality is burdened with what I have called the dualism between God and us. The "God all out there" (C.G. Jung), the God "above me" or "coming down to me" is a God I find hard to believe in. So do many of my Christian friends and students. If there is in Christian tradition and experience a God within, a God who lives, and moves, and has being within us and the world, we need help in finding such a God.

Buddhism, I believe, can provide some help.

PASSING OVER: NO GOD, JUST CONNECTIONS

I'll never forget the jolt I experienced as I made my first efforts to study Buddhism during my freshman year of college at Divine Word Seminary, Conesus, NY. (It was a private study, since the seminary curriculum then did not have space for "non-Christian" religions.) I was amazed. No – bewildered, stupefied. Buddhism didn't have a God! I had heard some talk about Dietrich Bonhoeffer's proposal for a "religionless religion." But Buddha's proposal for a "Godless religion?"

So in my first encounter with Buddhism I felt like I had hit a brick wall. Such a wall, I was later to realize, provides the safest way to begin the study of a religion not one's own. It keeps us from doing what we are all too inclined to do – to read our own perspectives and beliefs into the other religion and to declare that it's "really saying the same thing." Religions may have much in common, but they also have much, perhaps even more, that makes them different. And if there are any two religions between which the differences outweigh the similarities, I think it's Buddhism and Christianity. That's what makes the dialogue between the two so difficult, and so rewarding.

God gets in the way

So with my dialogical sails drooping, I slowed down and allowed Buddhism and Buddhists to speak to me. I was told, by books and by

Buddhist friends, that Buddha did not necessarily want to deny the existence of God. He just didn't want to talk about God or anything else that was formally religious. Why? I suspect it was because he wanted to talk about something else, and we can surmise that he was afraid that God-talk, like any other talk, would get in the way. He wanted to talk about what he discovered in meditation under the Bodhi Tree (Tree of Awakening) in the town now called Bodh Gaya in northern India, after he had left his princely home and family some six years earlier to begin his search for how to deal with suffering and figure out what life's all about. He wanted to share *that* experience. That was more important, for him, than talking about God or Brahman (the Absolute in Hinduism); in fact, it took the place of talking about God! For Buddha, experience was more important than talk.

But what was this experience he wanted to pass on? Before I try to answer that question, I have to bring up the Buddhist reminder that we can never find the right words to answer it. Still, the records tell us that under the Bodhi Tree, Buddha's eyes were opened (that's what the title "Buddha" means). He saw things as they really are. He experienced Enlightenment or Awakening. And the content or object of that Awakening later came to be called *Nirvana*. So this is what counts most for Buddhists – to be Enlightened and to come to the realization of *Nirvana*.

A short first sermon

In order to attain some, always-limited, grasp of what Awakening feels like and what *Nirvana* is trying to get at, we have to do a quick review of Buddha's first sermon. He preached it shortly after his Enlightenment to some of his old spiritual buddies and fellow searchers in Sarnath, or Deer Park, on the outskirts of the Hindu holy city of Varanasi. The contents of the sermon were "the Four Noble Truths," which made for one of the simplest and yet most effective sermons ever preached. Since that memorable day sometime around the end of the 500s BCE, Buddhists have been reminding themselves and trying to realize that:

1 Suffering (*dukkha*) comes up in everyone's life.
2 This suffering is caused by craving (*tanha*).
3 We can stop suffering by stopping craving.

4 To stop craving, follow Buddha's Eightfold Path (which consists
   essentially of taking Buddha's message seriously, living a moral life
   by avoiding harm to others, and following a spiritual practice
   based on meditation).

To understand why these Four Noble Truth make sense, and why they
work, we have to ask: just why does *tanha* cause *dukkha* – why does
selfish craving bring on suffering? Inherent in the answer to that question, Buddhists tell us, is something else that Buddha came to realize
under the Bodhi Tree: they call it *anicca*. Usually, this word is translated as *impermanence*: everything that exists (and if God exists, it
includes God as well) is in constant movement, constant flux.
Nothing, absolutely nothing, remains just what it is. For Buddhists,
the most basic fact or quality of the world is not *being*, as it is for most
Western philosophers and theologians: it's *becoming*. To be is to
become, one can "be" only if one is in motion. (We can note an immediate difference here from what we heard about the Christian God: for
Western, Christian theologians, to call God perfect means he doesn't
change; for Buddhists, if we call God perfect, it means that God is the
most changeable reality we could imagine!)

But just why is everything impermanent and in constant change?
The answer has to do with what might be called the flip-side of *anicca*:
pratityasamutpada, or, technically, "interdependent origination."
More simply: everything changes because everything is interrelated.
Everything comes into being and continues in being through and
with something else. Nothing, Buddha came to see, has its own
existence. In fact, when he wanted to describe the human self, or
the self/identity of anything, the term he used was *anatta*, which
means literally *no-self* (we'll look at this more carefully later). We are
not "selves" in the sense of individual, separate, independent
"things." Rather, we are constantly changing because we are constantly interrelating (or being interrelated). So, if for Buddha we
are not "beings" but "becomings," now he clarifies that we are
"becomings-with."

Now we can understand why selfishness causes suffering. When
we act selfishly, when we crave, when we try to possess and hold on to
something as our own, when we refuse to let go – we are acting contrary to the way things work. It's like swimming against the current, or
trying to catch and hold a bird in flight. Selfishness causes friction.
It makes harmful sparks fly because it rubs the wrong way against

reality. For Buddhists selfishness is not so much sinful as it is stupid. (But like Christian sin, it causes suffering, for self and others.) It's not that Buddhists are against enjoying other persons or things; they just warn us against trying to hold on to them and think we own them. As soon as we do, sparks will fly and people will get hurt.

What Buddhists are after

So this is the experience that the Buddha had and that Buddhists seek – they want to become Enlightened to the real truth of the Four Noble Truths, to the reality of the impermanence and interconnectedness of everything, and to the freedom and peace that result when they wake up to this reality of impermanence. This is what Buddhists are after, what counts most for them. As Christians seek God, Buddhists seek Awakening. You might say that for Buddhists, Awakening is their "Absolute." But does this mean that the Absolute for Buddhists is a personal experience? Well, yes and no. Yes, Enlightenment is, first of all, one's own experience. It has to be, for if one "doesn't get it," there's no "it" to talk about.

But there is an "it" – that is, Enlightenment is an experience of something. And that something is the way things are, the way they work. It's not a "thing" as we usually use that word; it can't be located here or there, like everything in the world, but even more so, it does not have its own existence. (I told you that Buddhists insist that what they're talking about is beyond words.)

Yet they do use words to get at the contents, or the reality, of Enlightenment. After *Nirvana*, one of the most common terms in Buddhism is *Sunyata*. Elaborated within the Mahayana tradition of Buddhism (the reform movement that set in a few centuries after Buddha's death), it meant, literally, *Emptiness* – but not emptiness in the purely negative sense of nothingness (like a room that is empty), but emptiness in the sense of being able to receive anything (a room that can be filled). The root "su" means empty/full – "swollen," not only the hollowness of a balloon, but the potentiality of a pregnant woman. *Sunyata* attests to the reality that everything does not find its own existence in itself; rather, it is open to, dependent on, and there-fore able to contribute to what is other.

In this sense, *Sunyata* reflects the literal meaning of *Nirvana*: to be blown out, that is, to have one's own existence blown away and so, blown into the existence of others. Other terms that Buddhists use to point to what they're after offer us slippery handles on what is really ungraspable.

That which became manifest in the historical Buddha is termed *Dharmakaya*, the "body of *Dharma*." "*Dharma*" here indicates both the infinite, unknowable truth of Buddha's message, and the power this truth has to transform.

More practically and personally, Zen Buddhists speak of Emptiness as the "Buddha-nature" that inheres in all sentient beings. Humans, through following the Noble Eightfold Path, can realize and express Buddha-nature in their lives. This mysterious, interrelated Buddha-nature is really our true nature, and we can experience it when we let go of our selfishness and allow ourselves to interact, in giving and receiving, with everything else in the interconnected fabric of reality.

Thich Nhat Hanh, a modern practitioner, scholar, and popularizer of Zen Buddhism, translates *Sunyata* more freely but more engagingly as *InterBeing*. It's the interconnected state of things that is constantly churning out new connections, new possibilities, new problems, new life. More teasingly and perhaps more challengingly, Pema Chödrön, the American teacher of a Tibetan style of Buddhism, likes to refer to *Sunyata* as *Groundlessness*. There is, happily, no solid, unchanging foundation to life, no place to stand permanently, since everything is moving in interdependence with everything else. When we realize this and swim with the Groundlessness rather than against it, both letting it carry us and moving with it, then swimming becomes not only possible but enjoyable.

A verb or an adverb?

At this point a Christian like myself, who is trying carefully and respectfully to pass over to Buddhist teaching and experience, will find him or herself asking: "But what *is Nirvana*?" Does it really exist in itself? Or is it just a universal description of how everything is and acts? Is it a "verb" (a real activity within it all) or is it just an "adverb" (a description of how everything acts)? (I know, grammarians will remind me that you can't have an adverb without a verb ... Maybe that's the point I want to make.)

These are typically Christian or Western questions, and yet Buddha is said to have faced such bewilderments in his own life. In general, he responded in a way that was meant, I suspect, to increase the bewilderment to the point of exploding it into a new insight. "Your question does not fit the case!" Or: "What you're asking doesn't make sense for what I'm talking about." He went on to "explain" that it is incorrect, or inappropriate, or misleading *both* to say that "*Nirvana/Sunyata* exists" *and* to say that "*Nirvana/Sunyata* does not exist."

In other words, you can't talk that way about what Buddha is trying to get people to experience and realize. *Nirvana/Sunyata* (or InterBeing/Groundlessness) is not something that "exists" the way we think everything else exists. It is not a "thing" as we experience other "things;" indeed it is a no-thing (another term some Mahayana Buddhists use). Whereas other "things" have their existence in and through interconnectedness, *Sunyata* or *Nirvana is* their connectedness. To use a term not found in the original Buddhist texts but adopted by contemporary Buddhists, *Sunyata* or Groundlessness might be imaged as a process, indeed, *the* process itself by which and in which and through which everything has its being. Whoops … I mean its becoming.

Another image that might be used for *Sunyata* is that of an energy field. It is the field in which and by which everything else is energized to interact and inter-become. Such an energy field "exists" with and through all the activities within it and could not exist without these activities. And yet, it cannot be reduced or boiled down to these activities. A well-known cliché might fit here: *Sunyata* or InterBeing is the sum of its parts and yet greater than all those parts put together. I'm struggling for words and symbols here as I try to pass over; I hope these are appropriate.

It's right here, now!

With this image of InterBeing as an energy field, we Christians can better appreciate what Buddhists, especially of the Mahayana traditions, are leading us to when they go on to insist that "*Nirvana is Samsara.*" This is a brain-teaser meant seriously to push us into a sense or feeling of the *non-duality* between what for Buddhists is Ultimate (what counts most for them) and what for all of us is this finite world. "*Samsara*" is our everyday, work-a-day, suffer-a-day life – our constantly changing, constantly relating worldly existence. This finite reality we call daily life is where we find *Nirvana* or Emptiness, for *Samsara* is *Nirvana*.

Or, expressed both a bit more concretely and abstractly in another Mahayana declaration: "Emptiness is Form, and Form is Emptiness" – that is, the transcendent, abstract reality of Emptiness is found in and gives expression to every concrete form in the world: people, animals, plants, events. You can't have all these individual forms without Emptiness; but you can't have Emptiness without these individual forms.

It seems to me that this is what we earlier called *non-duality* at its paradoxical best. A distinction is made and held between *Nirvana* and *Samsara*, or between Emptiness and Form; they are not two ingredients that can be boiled down to a common mush. Rather, in their distinctiveness, they are bonded in an essential interdependence that does not allow for a neat separation of one from the other. As Raimon Panikkar, a pioneer and sage of interreligious dialogue, has put it: in real non-duality – in this case, *Nirvana* and *Samsara* – the interrelating partners are *not two*. But neither are they *one*! Can Christians say something similar about the relationship between God and creation? It's time to pass back.

PASSING BACK: GOD THE CONNECTING SPIRIT

To remind myself of what I hope to do in these "passing back" segments: I want to try to describe as clearly as I can how my passing over to the way Buddhists experience and talk about *Nirvana/Sunyata*/InterBeing has served as a guide and a light in grappling with my "problem of God." In doing this, I want to be sure to show how this guiding light from Buddhism has, as it were, shone in two directions: backward and forward. It has helped me, I think, both to look back and rediscover or retrieve what has been part of Christian tradition all along, and it has enabled me to look forward in order to recreate my tradition and explore how "new treasures as well as old" can be drawn out of my Christian storehouse (Matt. 13:52).

Becoming mystics again for the first time

Marcus Borg has written a widely helpful book about the need for Christians to retrieve the correct understanding of Jesus, which, he claims, would be a much more appealing picture of Jesus. He titled the book *Meeting Jesus Again for the First Time*. I think the same can be said about the need many Christians feel to retrieve their mystical traditions: they need to become mystics again for the first time. Karl Rahner, one of the most respected Catholic theologians of the past century (and my teacher!), recognized this need in a statement that has been repeated broadly: "In the future Christians will be mystics, or they will not be anything."

Buddha has enabled me not only to understand and feel but to be kicked in the stomach by the truth of Rahner's words. Yes, it is a question of survival! Unless I retrieve my Christian mystical tradition, I'm not going to be able to hang in there with my imperfect, often frustrating church. Buddha has called me "to be a mystic again." But – and this will be hard to explain – the "again" is also a "first time." With what I've learned from Buddhism, I have been able to retrieve parts of the rich content of Christian mysticism as it is present both in the "professional mystics" of church history (Teresa of Avila, John of the Cross, Meister Eckhart, Julian of Norwich) and also in the New Testament writings of John's Gospel and Paul's epistles. But because of my passing over to Buddhism, it's been more than only a retrieval. It has been for me not just a matter of pulling out of my Christian closet the mystical mantles that were covered with dust but already there. I've also been able to *add to* the mystical wardrobe of Christianity. What I've added has "fit" what was already there, but it is also something really new. So, I've returned to Christianity's mystical closet again but also for the first time. Let me try to explain.

When Buddha refused to talk about God in order to make way for the experience of Enlightenment, he was making the same point, but even more forcefully, that Rahner was getting at in his insistence that Christians must be mystics: "God" must be an experience before "God" can be a word. Unless God is an experience, whatever words we might use for the Divine will be without content, like road signs pointing nowhere, like lightbulbs without electricity. Buddha would warn Christians, and I believe Rahner would second the warning: if you want to use words for God, make sure that these words are preceded by, or at least coming out of, an experience that is your own. And it will be the kind of experience that, in some way, will touch you deeply, perhaps stop you in your tracks, fill you with wonder and gratitude, and it will be an experience for which you realize there are no adequate words. Rahner listed all kinds of ways in which such experiences can take place in everyday life – falling in love, hoping when there is no hope, being overwhelmed by nature, deep moments of prayer or meditation. Often, or usually, such experiences happen before there is any talk or explicit consciousness of "God." They happen, and some such word as "God" or "Mystery" or "Presence" – or "Silence" – seems appropriate.

To put this more in our contemporary context, Buddha has reminded me and all of us Christians that any kind of religious life or church membership must be based on one's own personal experience. It is *not* enough to say "amen" to a creed, or obey carefully a law, or attend regularly a liturgy. The required personal experience may be mediated through a community or church, but it has to be one's own. Without such a personal, mystical happening, one cannot authentically and honestly call oneself religious.

But with it, one is free both to affirm and find meaning in the beliefs and practices of one's church, and at the same time one is free to criticize one's religion, which means to stand above, to confront, but at the same time to have patience with one's religion. Both Buddha and Jesus, because of their own extraordinary mystical experiences, were able to criticize bravely their own religions of Hinduism and Judaism respectfully (Jesus, to the point of getting into serious trouble) but also to affirm and preserve what they found to be true and good in those religions. Mystics are both loyal followers and uncomfortable critics – which, it seems to me, is exactly what Christian churches need today.

Using my Buddhist flashlight

I've used the word "experience" a lot in the preceding section, mainly in insisting that without some kind of a mystical experience, religion is merely empty sham or shell. I need to say more about just what I mean by "mystical experience." And that will require me, with the help of Buddhism, to say more about what my fellow Christians and I might mean by "God."

Perhaps the first or dominant adjective that scholars of comparative mysticism use to describe what they mean by mystical experience is *unitive.* There's no one way to unpack what they are getting at. To have a mystical or personal religious experience is to feel oneself connected with, part of, united with, aware of, one with, Something or Some-activity larger than oneself. One feels transported beyond one's usual sense of self as one grows aware of an expanded self, or a loss of self, in the discovery of something beyond words. Philosopher of religion John Hick describes mystical experience as the shift from self-centeredness to Other-centeredness or Reality-centeredness.

Certainly, our description of Buddhist Enlightenment squares with this unitive characteristic of mysticism, even though Buddhists, while strong on loss of self, use deliberately slippery terms for *what* they're connected with: Emptiness, Groundlessness, InterBeing. Christian mystics, on the other hand, are very clear about what they are united with. Christian mystical literature abounds with expressions such as "one with Christ," "temples of the Holy Spirit," "the Body of Christ," "Spouses of Christ," the "Divine indwelling," "participants in the divine nature."

The excitement, and the rigors, of my passing over and back from Buddhism to Christianity were launched when I began to explore connections between such Christian mystical exclamations and the Buddhist experience of *Sunyata*. I remember the zest but also the hesitation I felt when back in the early 1970s at Catholic Theological Union I started to ask my students and myself whether the Buddhist notion of dependent origination and InterBeing might open the doors to a deeper grasp of what Thomas Aquinas saw when he announced that God *participates* in creation, or that we participate in God's being.

Or even more eagerly, I asked whether the Buddhist claim that *Nirvana* is *Samsara* can help us make sense of Rahner's philosophical description of "the supernatural existential" – that is, his startling but perplexing claim that our human condition is not just "human" or purely natural because from the first moment of creation humanity is infused and animated by the grace of God's very presence. In other words, the "Natural" is really the "Supernatural!" Or could the Buddhist teachings on InterBeing throw dynamic light on Paul Tillich's elegant proposal (at the time quite revolutionary) that God can most coherently be understood as the Ground of Being?

On rereading my spiritual journals in preparation for writing this book, I've realized how much over the years I've struggled, delightfully but sometimes uneasily, with this kind of Christian–Buddhist interchange. But I've come to a point where I have to admit that as the result of those explorations, the God whom I profess every Sunday, the God whom I try to be aware of in my prayer and meditation, the God whom both my head and heart can relate to – this God or my God bears a much greater resemblance to *Sunyata* and InterBeing than to the prevalent Christian image of God as the transcendent Other.

Is God InterBeing?

So let me pose my question point-blankly and unsophisticatedly: is God InterBeing? Or, more carefully: is Emptiness or InterBeing an appropriate symbol for God, especially for men and women over thirty-five, in our so-called modern world? (We'll be talking more about symbols in Chapter 3.) I have come to believe – or better, feel – that it is. Certainly, as much of the contemporary literature on the Buddhist–Christian dialogue indicates, such a God of Emptiness and InterBeing is closer to what Christian mystics try to talk about when they describe their experiences of God. Pointing out similarities between Buddhism and mystics like Eckhart and John of the Cross is, you might say, easy, though always revealing and stimulating.

The theologian in me wants to push the case more broadly. I believe that on the shelves of the general store of Christian beliefs we can find images of God – perhaps a bit dusty – that indicate that Christians do have an awareness of the Divine as the mystery of InterBeing. For me, I needed a Buddhist flashlight to discover them.

As a first example, take the only "definition of God" found in the New Testament. The author of John's first letter announces that "God is love" (1 John 4:8). The author is not saying that God is a Father who loves but that God *is* love. I'm taking the passage literally and carefully when I let this language confirm what I sense and what Buddhists have helped make clear for me: to move beyond, or more deeply into, the common image of God as Father, we can and must speak of love. Why? Because the image of Father tells us (or is supposed to tell us, depending on what kind of father we had) that the very nature of God is love. To love is to move out of self, to empty self, and connect with others. Love is this emptying, connecting, energy that in its power originates new connections and new life. The God who, as Dante tells us, is "the love that moves the moon and the other stars" is the InterBeing of the stars and the universe.

All of this leads us into one of the most distinctive Christian ways of speaking about the Divine: the Christian God, I learned already in first grade, is both one and three, Trinitarian. (Remember? Three matches held together and burning with the same flame?) If all Christian beliefs, as theologians insist, have to be meaningful before they can be true, what is the *meaning* of the Trinity? How does it reflect the way the Christian community has come to experience the Divine? Without losing ourselves in the rich but often tangled landscape that is the history of Trinitarian theology, we can focus on what is one of the centerpieces of that landscape: to believe in a Trinitarian God is to believe in a *relational* God. The very nature of the Divine is nothing other than to exist *in and out of* relationships; for God, "to be" is nothing other than "to relate." That, among other things, is what the doctrine of the Trinity tells Christians.

For Christians God cannot be only one, simply because, as the cliché has it, it takes two to tango – and to relate. Therefore, although there is only one God, this one God must be more than one. This is what Christians experienced and learned about God from Jesus. True, he certainly didn't teach them the doctrine of the Trinity, but from reflecting on the impact he had on their lives, his followers eventually came to see God as three – three energies, movements, "persons" relating with each other; "Father, Son, and Holy Ghost;" or Parent, Child, Spirit.

All of this means that God's very being, or existing, or identity consists of relating, or inter-existing, or InterBeing. That's what theologians term the "internal Trinity" – God's inner nature. But what God is internally, God must be externally. What Christians have seen in Jesus of Nazareth is a God who creates and is present to the world through *relationships*, the same kind of relationships that we say exist in the very nature of God: relationships of knowing, of giving, of loving that bring forth ever more life and existence. Behind and within all the different images and symbols Christians may use for God – Creator, Father, Redeemer, Word, Spirit – the most fundamental, the deepest truth Christians can speak of God is that God is the source and power of relationships.

That sounds abstract. But it's not. It's the most basic, and the simplest, thing we can say about ourselves and about God: we exist through relationships of knowing and loving and giving because that's how God exists.

Here's where Buddhism has helped me feel or grasp what all this means. To experience and believe in a Trinitarian God is to experience and believe in a God who is not, as Tillich would say, the Ground of Being, but the Ground of *InterBeing*! God is the activity of giving and receiving, of knowing and loving, of losing and finding, of dying and living that embraces and infuses all of us, all of creation. Though every image or symbol limps, Christians can and *must* say what Buddhists *might* agree with – that if we're going to talk about God, God is neither a noun nor an adjective. God is a verb! With the word

"God" we're trying to get at an activity that is going on everywhere rather than a Being that exists somewhere. God is much more an environment than a thing.

And therefore, if we Christians really affirm that "God is love" and that Trinity means relationality, then I think the symbol Buddhists use for *Sunyata* is entirely fitting for our God. God is the field – the dynamic energy field of InterBeing – within which, as we read in the New Testament (but perhaps never really heard), "we live and move and have our being" (Acts 17:28). Or, from the divine perspective, there is "one God above all things, through all things, and in all things" (Eph. 4:6). This presence "above, through and in" can fittingly and engagingly be imaged as an energy field which pervades and influences us all, calling us to relationships of knowing and loving each other, energizing us when such relationships get rough, filling us with the deepest of happiness when we are emptying ourselves and finding ourselves in others.

Loving others, therefore, is not a question so much of "doing God's will" but, rather, of "living God's life." That's why Rahner used to tell us that there are a lot of people who live God's life in their actions even though they may deny God's existence in their words. (And vice versa, a lot of people who say they believe in God but who cancel out that belief in the way they live.)

The Connecting Spirit

Now I can try to make clear why I titled this passing-back section "God the Connecting Spirit." If there is any word in the Christian vocabulary for God that vibrates sympathetically with language Buddhists use for what they are seeking, it is *Spirit*. Interestingly, "*Pneuma*" or the Spirit of Wisdom was among the very first images that the infant Christian community used in trying to speak about Jesus' relationship to God; it soon lost out, however, to "Father" and "Son." My dialogue with Buddhism has enabled me not only to repossess but to be repossessed by the image of Spirit as a symbol for God. Passing back to Spirit after having passed over to *Sunyata*, I can understand and feel "again for the first time" that Spirit points more meaningfully to a pervasive energy rather than to a particular being, that Spirit energizes many things without being contained by any, and that Spirit merges with what it energizes in a manner that is much more a matter of interpenetration than indwelling. The relationship

between the "spirit" (or soul) and the body, Christian theology
teaches, is one of mutuality: without the spirit the body cannot live;
without the body the spirit cannot act. The same is true of Spirit and
creation.

Back in June of 2001, I put it, for myself, this way:

> In a very real sense, according to Christian experience and symbol-
> ism, the Spirit is given with creation, indeed is the instrument or the
> power of creation. She is with us from the beginning, grounding and
> connecting every living being, every being. I can rest in her, just as
> Cathy [my Buddhist wife] rests in Groundlessness. Utterly mysteri-
> ous, totally unpredictable, filled and directed by love/compassion,
> she is the womb in whom I rest and from which I issue moment by
> moment.

Earlier, in March of 2000, reflecting on Romans 8:9, I wrote:

> "The Spirit of God dwells within you." To believe that is to make life
> so very different from what it usually is. Here is the Reality out of
> which I can face all, deal with all, respond to love and hatred, carry on
> my work of writing and teaching. It is real. The Spirit is truly with me,
> in me, living as me. It is the "vast openness" that Pema Chödrön
> speaks of. It is the source of *Maitri* (loving kindness) with which I can
> be truthful and compassionate to myself and to all who are part of, or
> touch, my life.

Creation: the manifestation of non-duality

It is evident, I believe, that thinking about or imaging God as
InterBeing and relating to God as the connecting Spirit is a major
antidote to the dualism that has infected Christian theology and spirituality. It served me as a kind of new pair of glasses through which I
saw creation. This new vision was a clarification, a seeing more and
seeing more deeply, but it was also a correction for distortions caused
by my earlier pair of glasses. As I mentioned before, passing back to
one's own tradition after having passed over to another can lead to
repossessing, but also realigning, one's previous beliefs.

With God as the connecting Spirit, the Creator cannot be "totally
other" to creation. If the Divine is felt and imaged as InterBeing, and if
the world works and evolves through interbeing, then the act of creation by a Creator cannot be understood as a production of something
that stands outside the Creator. The dynamic of the divine life is precisely the dynamic of the finite world. Here I think I'm getting closer to

what Aquinas was trying to express when he described the relationship between God and the world as one of participation. Rahner, too, was trying to push us in the same direction when he mused that even if God created the world "out of nothing," this does not mean that creation simply sits there, as it were, on the divine workbench for God to admire or tinker with. What God creates, Rahner added, God includes. Therefore, a better image for creation might be a pouring forth of God, an extension of God, in which the Divine carries on the divine activity of interrelating *in* and *with* and *through* creation.

I can hear the objections: this smacks of – or simply is – pantheism. Everything becomes God. But it's not pantheism. It's what we called, for lack of a better word, non-duality: God and creation are not two, but neither are they one! Pantheism reduces God and creation to one element. Non-duality, if I remember my chemistry class correctly, is more like a compound substance (or, come to think about it, like a good marriage): two abidingly different actors inhering in, or being who they are through, each other. Christian mystics like Nicholas of Cusa speak of a "*coincidentia oppositorum*" – two "opposite" realities, Creator and created, coinciding, forming an integral unity, with each other. To put a twist on another Latin saying that happens to be the motto of the United States, non-duality is not "*E Pluribus Unum*" (Out of Many, One) but "*E Pluribus Unitas*" (Out of Many, Unity). Spirit and world do not lose their different identities, but neither can they exist without each other.

But here we come to something that *does* smell of heresy, something that seems to oppose traditional Christian doctrine: "Neither can they exist without each other." That means that the divine Spirit *needs* the world, that Spirit *had* to create the world. This seemingly flies in the face of the "defined dogma" that creation is a free act of God. Freedom, as we heard earlier, is when you do something you don't have to do. God didn't have to create because God didn't need the world.

This may make for a tight case of logic if you start with a Greek understanding of the Divine as "Being Itself." But if you begin with Jesus' experience of God-as-love and the subsequent Trinitarian understanding of Divinity as "Relationship-Itself," then to say that Spirit didn't have to create would lead to a contradiction. To say that Spirit doesn't have to create would be like saying we don't have to breathe. By our nature, we breathe. By her divine nature, Spirit loves. To love means to relate, to give of oneself, to bring forth Interbeing.

Spirit needs others to be Spirit. And if there are no others, Spirit will "create them" in order to include them in love. This, of course, doesn't mean that Spirit had to create this world but that she had to create some world.

As we heard in the section on my "problem of God," some Christians will respond that God's need to love is already satisfied within the Trinity. God is already totally happy by loving God's self within the relationships of Father, Son, and Spirit. Well, maybe. But what would we say to a person who declares that he or she is perfectly happy in loving just him or herself? We'd worry about his or her psychological health. What's wrong with needing others? If we humans can't be happy as rugged individualists, neither can God.

To understand this world and its multiple occupants as existing within the field of Spirit's interconnecting energy is also to move beyond the literal picture of Spirit intervening in the world. Spirit no longer has to "come down" in what seems like an arbitrary fashion, here but not there. The Spirit is already there, pervading it all, brooding, as the book of Genesis suggests, over the waters and all creation. So the Spirit doesn't step in but rather steps forth. What is already there emerges or takes shape or becomes fully active.

And just how this happens on the human level depends on how much individuals are aware of the connecting Spirit and/or how much they freely choose to respond. Non-duality, remember, can't be real without interdependency. Understanding the Divine as the pervasive Source of InterBeing means that God really depends on us. We'll look into this more carefully in the next chapter.

In my journal of fall 2004, I was wrestling with some of these different ways of feeling the non-dual God:

> There's a wonderful paradox here. God is always "God-with;" and humans are always "humans-with." When these two realities are really with each other – God with humanity, and humanity with God – that is when they are really their fullest, truest selves.
>
> The unity between what I call God and myself is one in which God genuinely acts as God insofar as I act in a truly human fashion.
>
> [Reflecting on Eph. 4:6: "God above all, through all, and in all …"] If God is indeed really acting through us, that means that God cannot be "in" unless God is "through." So, it is not just a case of God acting in me, but me being God as God acts in the world. Tritely, we're a team, though clearly and fortunately God is the main player. Still, God would not be a player if I'm not playing as well.

2

NIRVANA AND GOD THE PERSONAL OTHER

Chapter 1, on God as the Transcendent Other, provides the ground-work and many of the starting points for dealing with the two other aspects of Christian teachings about God that have befuddled me and, I know, many of my fellow Christians: God as a Person and God as Mystery. Such befuddlements, as I will try to show in this chapter and the next, can be dealt with more easily once we have shifted from an image of God as the Transcendent Other to God as Spirit of InterBeing. I begin with my difficulties in understanding and relating to God as a "you."

MY STRUGGLES: IS GOD A YOU?

To be distressfully honest about it: I have great difficulties in talking to God. It's distressful because from my first days in catechism class Sister Walter told me that that's what prayer is – talking with God. And prayer is on the list of essential ingredients for being a Christian. But since about middle-age – so right on schedule for the time in life when C.G. Jung said the problem usually pops up – I have found it more and more difficult to image God as a "you" and talk to "him."

Yes, part of the difficulty has to do with the particular images that clothe the Christian notion of God-as-you. Topping that list is, of course, "Father." For some Christians, this has led to pictures of the bearded white man in the sky who lovingly watches your every step, but who is also standing close and marking his notebook when you tease your sister or lose your temper. But I think most of us adult

Christians have grown out of such literal "he-knows-when-you've been-bad-or-good" pictures of God. The exclusive use of male faces for the Christian God is also a problem, and a big one. But with the help of feminist theologians, I've come to the firm conviction that symbols for the Divine cannot be limited to one gender. Still, to extend my honesty, I find it just as difficult to talk to God as Mother as I do to God as Father.

Anthropomorphisms

My problems with God-as-you lie deeper. I'm not sure I can get a clear hold on them. I think they have to do with the sense that although there is no other way to speak of God outside of symbols (more about that in the next chapter), when those symbols are drawn from what we humans experience ourselves to be as persons, such symbols become dangerous. They can be so easily misunderstood or misused. In picturing or approaching the Divine as a "you," I somehow feel I'm being inappropriate, or disrespectful, or offensive – something like talking loudly in the midst of the hushed beauty of a New Zealand forest. I think my problems gravitate around what the experts call "anthropomorphisms." Using human forms or putting a human face on the Divine may be something we humans can't avoid doing. But it's fundamentally inappropriate – something like a kitschy painting of the Grand Canyon!

Yes, when we picture God as a "you" in the form of a father or mother or friend or Savior we are giving the reality of the Divine a focus in our lives, but there is so much more in the Divine that we may lose, or maybe even distort. Father Hugo M. Enomiya-Lassalle, a German Jesuit who spent most of his life in Japan and became a Zen teacher, said somewhere that the precondition for addressing God as a "you" is the realization that we shouldn't. That rings so true in my own experience.

But the counter-consideration to all this, which I not only hear from others but affirm myself, is that the human being is the epitome of creation (or seems to be at the moment), and interpersonal relations are the most precious and necessary part of being human. Certainly it should be possible, or necessary, to have an *interpersonal* relationship with the Divine, which requires God to be a you. In attributing personhood to God we are, therefore, but recognizing that God contains what God has produced as the pinnacle of creation: personality.

Yes, yes. But I find myself responding to such tight logic with Father Enomiya-Lassalle: if we feel we can and must speak of God as a "you," we must also remind ourselves that there are good reasons why we should not do so. Without this reminder, we're in for the kind of discomfort I and many Christians, especially those over forty, are feeling.

And when I try to get at what sparks the problems that flare up when I bring together "God" and "you," I think it has to do with the tension, if not contradiction, between inherent qualities of "the Divine" and inherent qualities of a "you." The divine qualities I'm referring to are those that I described in the previous chapter with the help of my Buddhist friends – the non-dual, right-here God in whom we live and move and have our being, the God who acts *as* me and at the same time is more than me. When God becomes a "you" who stands opposite me or outside me, there's a danger, I sense, of losing these qualities of the God within, the God experienced as animating energy. For me, when God becomes part of an "I–Thou relationship," this God-as-Thou takes on a degree of otherness that just doesn't fit the intimacy that I feel, or hope to feel, with the Divine. I guess I'm saying that God-as-Thou so easily slips back into the dualism of God-as-Other.

A Super-you

This problem metastasizes when the God-as-Thou remains and is addressed (especially in liturgies) as the traditional *transcendent* Other that we talked about in Chapter 1. A simplistic formula expresses what I'm trying to get at: "Transcendent, almighty, all-perfect God" + "You" = a transcendent, almighty, all-perfect You. Or, a kind of Super-you. And, as many a failed-marriage partner knows, having a healthy relationship with a Super-you can present its problems. Now, I'm not saying that I'm looking for a relationship with the Divine that has the perfect balance of two equal partners. There are definite, and indeed needed, differences between the Infinite and finite, between Source and expression, between field and the elements in the field. But it has to be a relationship of authentic mutuality, one in which I exercise genuine responsibility, which means a relationship in which I make a difference for and can really affect the Divine. I feel it has to be not just God's show but *our* show.

Let me try to state my problem in an overly contrived but maybe helpful question. If your natural father were almighty and all-perfect

(I know, some dads already believe that!), how would you respond to him? I'm not asking about how he would behave toward you, but how you would behave toward him. If you knew he could control or determine everything that happened in your life and at the same time you knew that he deeply loved you, how would you feel? Would you tend to lean back and let him take care of things? Indeed, wouldn't you expect that since he *could* take care of things, he *would*, and that therefore you could relax?

Over the years, this question and this uneasiness have grown for me. As a youngster in my high-school seminary, and even into college, my relationship with God as an all-powerful and all-loving You led me to live my life a little like the way I dealt with the scary movies at the Argo Theater: no matter how many frightening scenes came up, I knew the hero was going to make it. So I could sit back and enjoy my popcorn.

As I grew older, I realized that life's threats and challenges were real, and I had to deal with them through my own intelligence and decisions. My problem was not how to depend on God in the midst of life, but how not to become overly dependent on a personal God who was in charge of everything. If God is my loving Father, a Father who controls everything, I really didn't have to worry. But a life without worry all too readily becomes a life without responsibility.

So I started to feel that relating to God understood as an almighty, loving You might be not only inappropriate and disrespectful toward God, but might also be inappropriate and harmful for me. In such a relationship, how much room was really left for *me* – that is, for my own freedom and for my own responsibility? If God is the captain of my ship, can I ever be more than a crew-member?

With such images, I don't mean to trivialize the problem. And I certainly don't want to imply that belief in a personal God necessarily prevented me, or prevents others, from making responsible, well-pondered decisions. But I know that others have struggled as I have with how to understand such decisions in a relationship with a personal divine Other who is also an all-powerful, all-knowing, all-perfect Other. If a personal God is always in the driver's seat, and if I let him drive, I really don't have to worry, do I?

Problems multiply when this personal almighty Other is presented in catechism classes and Sunday sermons as not only a God who loves tenderly but also who reacts angrily. The loving Father God is depicted in the Bible as a God who makes demands, and who can become mighty angry when those demands are not met – both the God of the Old Testament who could kill all the first-born baby boys of Egypt because Pharaoh refused to comply with God's orders (Ex. 11:5), and the God of Jesus, who struck a married couple dead when they lied about their contributions to the parish (Acts 5:1–11). Making God angry could be even worse than making Mom or Dad angry!

It's God's will

For many Christians, similar difficulties hover around the common understanding of "God's will." How often do we hear from the pulpit that this transcendent personal Other God, who is my loving Father, has a plan for each of us and for the entire world. From my early years I believed that my heavenly Father had a clear idea of what He wanted me to grow up to be. My job, as a good Catholic boy, was to figure that out and do it. If I didn't, there could be major problems, maybe even sinful problems. There were moral implications in not doing God's will. My good Catholic parents felt the same way. That's why, when I came to them in the last semester of eighth grade and told them I felt God was calling me to be a priest and to enroll at the Divine Word Minor Seminary in East Troy, Wisconsin, some 150 miles from our Chicago home, they were a bit nonplused. But how could their concerns that I was too young to leave home match up against "God's will?" (It didn't help that Father Dearworth, the vocational director, announced to my parents that God was calling me to be one of his chosen.)

I'm not saying that my decision to leave home for the seminary at thirteen years old was entirely a bad one. But I am questioning the propriety of making it under the rubric of "God's will." It's a rubric, I fear, that can be, and *is*, so easily misunderstood and then misused, and so it ends up a greater source of harm than of help in people's lives, usually without them realizing that this is the case. This can happen in a variety of ways.

Both in my youth and during my work as a priest, I experienced how often Christians become overly anxious, even scrupulous, about having to discover the one path or choice that God has predetermined for them. ("How can I be certain that this is the person God wants me to marry?") All too easily and perhaps subconsciously, God's will can be used as a cover to justify decisions that are really self-serving.

("God wants me to be rich.") Even more extensively and harmfully, we can see in history and in current reports on the daily news how easily "God's will" is used by some to take advantage of others. ("If you're poor on earth, you'll have a higher place in heaven." Or: "This war is God's cause against evil-doers, so if you die you'll die in God's service.")

My final example is more subtle and slippery. It's when a too-facile invoking of God's will lets us off the hook – when it keeps us from thinking more or asking further questions. I often feel a twinge of uneasiness when I hear people, in the face of sad or inexplicable events, declaring "It's God's will. What can we do?" Certainly, things happen in the life of each of us that just won't fit into the neat boxes of human logic and understanding. And an appeal to God and God's will may be an indirect or subconscious way of recognizing that "This is beyond us; only a higher intelligence can make sense of it." But when such an appeal is made too promptly or too conclusively, it can easily become not a way of bowing to reality but of running away from it. Immediately to dub a horrible airplane crash as God's will can prevent us from inquiring into the safety rules of an airline. To accept Uncle Lou's death from lung cancer as God's will may be distracting us from having to question and confront the tobacco industry.

I fear that what I did in my life, many Christians do: we sweep a lot of dirt under the rug of God's will when we should be cleaning up the dirt.

A mighty Father and a messy world

If *we* tend to sweep a lot of dirt under the carpet of God's will, it sure seems like God himself allows for a lot of dirt to accumulate on top of it. I'm talking about "the problem of evil." For many Christians (and for many religious people in the monotheistic religions of Judaism and Islam) it's discouragingly difficult, if not downright impossible, to understand how a personal God who loves us can put up with such a mess of suffering in his creation. Now, I know this is a conundrum that has broken the brains of both the scholarly and the ordinary through the ages. A whole subsection of theology, called theodicy, has developed over the centuries in an effort to squeeze some sense out of "the problem of evil."

Stripped down to its bare and unbreakable bones, this is the problem: if God is a person, a Father, who is really all-loving and all-powerful, then because he loves us he should *want* to prevent at least some of the apparently needless suffering his children endure, and because he is all-powerful he should be able to do so. But he doesn't. Something's wrong with this picture – either with God or with our understanding of God.

If I may generalize grossly, it seems to me that all our attempts to reconcile what looks like unnecessary suffering with a loving, power-ful God boil down to an appeal to *mystery*. In the final analysis, like Job in the Bible, we bow our heads and admit that "God's ways are not our ways" and that we'll never really understand the mystery of what God is up to. It goes something like this.

In the case of what is called human or moral evil, God mysteriously allows human beings to exercise their free will as they wish, even when it means sexually abusing an innocent five year old or murdering six million Jews. God *could* prevent such acts, but he respects and, for his own good reasons, allows human freedom.

In dealing with natural evil – the devastation and death caused by earthquakes, fires, floods, mountain slides – the problem, in a sense, thickens. Here there's no free will that has to be respected. A human father who could stop a mud-slide to save his family would certainly do so. God doesn't. For reasons beyond our comprehension, perhaps for some greater good that will be revealed in the future. Again, it's a mystery.

I certainly want to recognize and respect both the limits of my human intellect and the limitlessness of the Divine. We theologians need regular "humility-checks." But we also need "honesty-checks." And to be honest, it sure looks to me like the appeal to mystery in try-ing to reconcile the reality of evil and a personal God is all too often avoiding the problem rather than truly facing it. It's one thing to bow to mystery. It's a totally different thing to bow to contradiction. There are many aspects of our life and of this world that are beyond reason, beyond full comprehension. And before them, we bow in humility. But there are also many claims that are *contrary* to reason, contradic-tory in themselves. And before them, we have to declare honestly the contradiction and try to deal with it.

Let me bring all these abstractions down to a very concrete, strongly felt example. When people, including religious leaders, declared that the tsunami that took the lives of thousands in Indonesia, India, and Thailand in 2004 was God's will and that he had caused or allowed this devastation for his inscrutable good reasons, I found myself erupting emotionally and often verbally. It's one thing for a distraught parent to invoke God's will in the face of the loss of a child; it's a call for help more than a statement of fact. But when religious teachers make a case that this was, literally, "an act of God," I simply cannot believe it. Nor can I believe in such a God. According to the mind and intelligence that we claim God has given us, for any human being to bring about, or even permit, the death of thousands for a "higher good" would be immoral, a matter of the end justifying the means. If we have to exempt God from such morality, something's wrong.

The problem is Person, not personal

Reviewing and trying to get a handle on my difficulties with a personal God – the anthropomorphisms that make God into a Super-person, notions of God's will that dangerously imply that God is a puppeteer, and the reality of evil that doesn't square with a loving, powerful God – I suspect that the nub of my problems has to do with God-as-a-Person rather than with the Divine as personal. Most if not all of the struggles I've tried to describe stem from the common understanding of a God who is a Divine Somebody with whom I'm supposed to have a relationship that follows the model of any I–Thou relationship. My problem, I think, has been with a Divine Person who stands in front of me. But what if my image of the Divine shifts to an all-pervading Spirit that is not a person but a presence or energy with personal qualities? There's a real, though perhaps subtle, difference between these two ways of symbolizing God.

For me, Buddhism has been an almost indispensable help in grasping, and then living, this difference between God as Person and the Divine as personal. I hope I can now explain why.

PASSING OVER: COMPASSION WITHOUT A GOD OF COMPASSION

I can imagine that some of my Buddhist friends, having read the above description of my struggles with a God-as-You, might scratch their heads and ask: "What's the problem? For us, no God, therefore no person, therefore no problem." I admire their immunity and freedom from such difficulties. But I am, or I want to be, a Christian. And despite all my problems with the way Christians have taken their talk about God as Father or Savior so literally or facilely, I really do believe, because I really have experienced, that the personal symbols Christians (together with Jews and Muslims) have used for the Divine have enriched my life – and have something to contribute to inter-religious dialogue. But to deepen this enrichment and this contribution, I feel the need to approach these personal symbols more critically, carefully, seriously.

In explaining now how Buddhism has helped me to do just that, I have to repeat a little caveat I voiced in the Preface. It's especially needed for an issue that for Buddhists is rather foreign and therefore sensitive: whether there are personal aspects to the experience and nature of *Sunyata*/Emptiness. Although I have made every effort carefully to pass over to and accurately understand Buddhist teach-ings in their culturally diverse colors, what follows is one Christian's reading of Buddhism. As the postmodern philosophers would (and do!) remind me, I can never totally set aside my Christian glasses. As I step into the lush Buddhist garden, I see everything through my Christian lens, smell everything with my Christian nose, and under-stand everything through the filter of my Christian experience and problems.

Despite all that, I think, or I hope, that the following effort to explore Buddhism through the lens of my struggles with a God-as-You is a generally accurate reading of what at least some Buddhists have taught. Where that is not the case, I beg pardon, and await correction.

Two faces of Enlightenment: wisdom and compassion

As we have already heard, what the Buddhists are after – or in Western terms, what makes up their "Ultimate Concern" – is not the know-ledge or worship or love of God. It's Enlightenment. If Christians want to be saved, Buddhists want to be Enlightened. They want to experience *Nirvana*. And although the experience of Enlightenment or *Nirvana* is as much beyond the reach of human words as air is beyond the grasp of human hands, still, two of the words that come up most often when Buddhists do indulge in the unwarranted task of talking about Enlightenment are *wisdom* and *compassion*. Both words are the fruit of personal experience, not the products of rational thinking.

Wisdom, or *prajna*, is what one understands, or realizes, or senses when one wakes up to the felt reality that all is in flux and that all is interrelated. This is the dynamic truth of InterBeing that we looked at from various viewpoints in Chapter 1. In Enlightenment, one sees it and feels it. One's eyes are opened. And as a result one also sees and feels others differently, and begins to act toward them differently. This different way of acting is described as compassion, or *karuna*. As all Buddhists recognize, and especially the reforming Mahayanists emphasize, it is impossible to have wisdom without compassion. They are the two faces of Enlightenment. To see one is also to see the other. Therefore, if you think you are Enlightened but do not feel compassion for all "sentient beings" (not just humans, but all beings who are able to feel), then you'd better go back and check out your Enlightenment. Or, if you are trying to have compassion for all your neighbors but have not experienced your own "no-self" in the web of InterBeing, you'd better watch out, for your compassion will probably peter out or become contaminated by your own self-seeking ego.

These two faces of Enlightenment make sound, philosophical sense, if you do your philosophy based on Buddhist experience. To experience what is called the Emptiness of all individuality, or the reality of InterBeing, is to experience your constitutive connections with others. Whatever natural or biological concern you have for yourself, that same concern you will also feel toward others. If biology *naturally* leads you to be concerned about or love yourself, Enlightenment will *naturally* lead you to be concerned about and love others. You will, in Christian terms, love your neighbor as yourself. If Christians call this a "commandment," for Buddhists it's something that comes naturally, as part of the Enlightened experience of *Nirvana* or InterBeing.

To draw a conclusion from this somewhat more philosophical reflection, if *Nirvana*, as we said earlier, is not just a personal experience but a Reality in which or as which we exist, then this Reality – also referred to as Emptiness or *Dharmakaya* or InterBeing – contains, or consists of, or expresses itself through *compassion*. Compassion is therefore integral to what for Buddhists is Ultimate.

Now, we could leave it at that. But as a Christian, I can't. Even though Buddhists generally do not talk about, or want to talk about, a divine Other, they do talk a lot about "others." Even though there is no personal, supreme Other whom they love or by whom they are loved, they find themselves loving others. Although there is no Divine

Person that occupies the Buddhist center stage, their stage, as it were, is full of persons or others, each one making up the center. Each is at the center of the universe because each is a place where everything comes together.

Therefore, it seems to me, one should not speak about the goal of Buddhist life and practice as being *impersonal*. Buddhists do not feel called to an I–Thou relationship with a God, but rather with all sentient beings. Universal compassion toward others. Awakened beings feel compassion for all other beings because they have felt, in the very marrow of their InterBeing, that they are *no-selves*, that they are interconnected and part of all beings. One can't love oneself unless one is loving other selves.

But it also works the other way around: you can't love other selves unless you are loving yourself! This is a reminder that especially contemporary Buddhist teachers like Pema Chödrön, the Dalai Lama, and Thich Nhat Hanh hold up for their Western students who have grown up in a more individualistic culture and struggle with self-doubt and feelings of inadequacy. To enter into the experience of Awakening and grow in awareness of one's real interconnectedness with the whole picture is to value and care for not only all the other contributions to the picture but also one's own. The compassionate energy one feels toward others is like a boomerang that comes back to oneself. One's own being is swept along in the surge of compassion for other beings. Maybe Buddha's way of putting Jesus' commandment to "Love others as you love yourself" might have been "Love yourself as you love others!"

I suspect this is part of the reason why the experience of Enlightenment brings with it a sense of profound peace. Such peace has its deepest roots in the awareness of how everything is interconnected in the big, ever-changing picture of InterBeing; everything, including oneself, "fits" and has its place in the picture. This is peace that arises from wisdom, *prajna*. But such peace is also grounded in *karuna*, the compassion that one naturally feels toward all the "components" of the picture, including one's own transient "no-self." One becomes both the source and recipient of compassion. And one breathes peacefully.

What is perplexing, and challenging, for me as a Christian is that although *Nirvana*, as the Buddhist "ultimate concern," is in no way a loving Being or Lover, it oozes with love and peace. Or more personally and concretely: the same kind of peace that a Christian experiences through the awareness of being loved by God is felt by

Buddhists in their awareness of being within InterBeing. They are swept up by, or carried along by, compassion, but there is no compassionate Other. Is this something I can bring along when I "pass back?"

Other Power is self-power

I may have spoken a little too rashly when I said there is "no compassionate Other" for Buddhists. For some Buddhists, there is. Or, to a Christian, there appears to be. In many of the various schools of Mahayana Buddhism, Buddha has come to be understood as (because he is experienced as), if not a savior, then certainly a helper – an "other" who is there to boost people along toward their own ultimate experience of Emptiness or *Nirvana*. What I'm referring to is beautifully captured under the general image of a *Bodhisattva*. This is what all Mahayana Buddhists are called to be, because this is what Gautama was, or became, when he became a Buddha. Every Buddha must be a Bodhisattva. This is another reflection of what we called "the two faces of Enlightenment." A Buddha gains wisdom; a Bodhisattva adds compassion.

The role and example of a Bodhisattva is appealingly illustrated in the familiar story of the four men lost in the desert. After days of wandering on the sultry sands without water, they come upon a large area surrounded by a high wall. All of them scuttle up the wall and behold on the other side a lush oasis, abounding in water and fruit. Three of them jump over to immerse themselves in this desert *Nirvana*. One of them goes back to tell others about this oasis. That last fellow is the Bodhisattva. He doesn't keep *Nirvana* for himself but shares it with others. That is what we are to be for others, because that's what Buddha is for us.

As contemporary Buddhist scholars like David Loy point out, the relationship between being a Buddha and a Bodhisattva is not "first this, then that:" first practice compassion for others and then move on to Buddhahood. Rather, the relationship is "both-and." To be Enlightened is both to realize wisdom and to practice compassion. If you *know* (wisdom/*prajna*), you'll act accordingly. By acting (compassionately), you really know. To be a Buddha is to be a Bodhisattva, and vice versa.

Such a "both-and," rather than an "either-or," distinction also applies to another distinction that comes up in Mahayana Buddhism: between self-power and Other Power. The School of Pure Land, originating in China and today widely popular in Japan, sounds like flat-out heresy to traditional or Theravada Buddhists when it talks about "Other Power." As we saw in Chapter 1, there is no Transcendent Other for Buddhists.

To Christian theologians, Pure Land sounds a lot like the message that Martin Luther announced in his Reformation. The faithful of Pure Land Buddhism are called upon to give up all their own good works and to trust totally and solely in the Amida Buddha – a Buddha who has vowed to save all his devotees and bring them to what is called the Pure Land. Some Pure Land Buddhists do nothing but chant and invoke the name of Amida. Others don't even do that, for they don't want to turn chanting into an obligatory good work. For them, trust is all that really counts, all that is really necessary.

Similar expressions of finding help in an "Other Power" appear in Tibetan Buddhism. With their panoply of smells and bells, and images and candles, monasteries in Tibet have the feel of churches in Italy. There is a colorful and diverse assembly of Buddhas and Bodhisattvas, each resplendent in his or her particular personality and entourage, each to be honored and invoked through an elaborate script of chants, prayers, gestures, incense, ghee. I'll forever remember the inspiration and reverence I felt during a bumpy bus trip in 1999 from Kathmandu to Lhasa as my wife and I witnessed, in monastery after monastery, the long lines of Tibetans moving devoutly and intently from one image of a Buddha or Bodhisattva to another. They certainly seemed to be opening themselves to an "Other Power" in much the same way that I did back in St. Joseph's Parish when I knelt before the statue of the Sacred Heart, or the Immaculate Conception, or St. Joseph.

And yet, despite the external similarities, there are deep differences. The "Other Power" the Buddhists are talking about and encountering is essentially or ultimately not really as "other" as Christians might think. The power that Mahayana Buddhists refer to as "Other" turns out to be one's own "self-power." Again, we are touching that slippery, not-two-but-not-one reality that we called non-duality. We may *distinguish* Other Power and self-power, but we can never, ever *separate* them. They're interrelated. They inhere in each other. They "inter-are."

This ultimate non-duality in Pure Land Buddhism appears on the popular level in the ever-present reminder that as much as Amida might have to help his devotees to get to the Pure Land, that is not their final resting place. There's more to come. Once settled in the security of the Pure Land, they are to undergo the Enlightening passage to *Nirvana*, where what one thought was one's "self" will be integrated into the flow of InterBeing and where all neat distinctions between "self-power" and "Other Power" shift and blur in the much larger picture.

Mahayana Buddhist scholars point out that, psychologically speaking, this same blurring of distinctions takes place all along but unawares insofar as the devotees are called upon to give up all personal efforts and to have "trust alone" in Amida. This is a technique, or what Buddhists call a "skillful means" (*upaya*): forget the self and trustingly let "the Other" take over, to the point that the self is transcended and merges with the other. The language is dualistic: self and other. But the result is non-dualistic: no-self, no-other, just letting go and trusting. Self-power is given up in order to become Other Power; or, Other Power becomes self-power.

The Tibetan teachers, as they carefully and minutely explain and advocate the special roles of the various Buddhas and Bodhisattvas, are just as careful to describe the goal of devotion to these holy figures. Whether the devotees themselves are clearly aware, whether they would describe their experience in these words or not, the result of their devotions is to experience the "reality" of the Buddha or Bodhisattva as their own "reality." In envisioning and feeling the particular power or courage or wisdom that is contained in the face, in the many hands, in the actions of the individual Bodhisattva, the devotee comes to feel and perhaps to recognize this same power or courage or wisdom in him or herself!

This doesn't mean that the colorful, endearing, or frightening face of the particular figure is only a ploy, or that it has merely a provisional function, to be totally absorbed into the individual's own experience. The Other Power of the Buddha or Bodhisattva is not replaced by one's own self-power. Rather, the Other Power *becomes* or is *realized as* one's self-power. One's self-power becomes an expression of Other Power, as a wave is the expression of the ocean. Ultimately, one realizes that there is no individual self that can be neatly identified and that acts by itself. There is just interconnection, InterBeing, InterBeings.

Evil – it's really not what it looks like

If there is anything about Buddhism that can take the wind out of a Christian's sails even more than Buddha's reluctance to speak clearly about God, it is Buddha's reluctance to speak clearly about evil. The entire issue of "Buddhism and evil" bristles with complexity and controversy. So I want to step into this topic carefully and with the reminder that what follows is one person's careful but limited perspective. Ultimately, though, what I'm most interested in is not whether my understanding of the Buddhist view of evil is perfectly correct, but how I will use that understanding when I pass back and try to apply it to my Christian struggles.

Trying to get beyond overly simplistic declarations like "Buddhism denies evil," I can best begin with what impresses and perplexes me most when I talk about "evil" with my Buddhist colleagues and friends. They don't want to call any person, or even any thing or event, evil. It seems they are afraid that as soon as they identify or define any person or thing as evil, it will make a difficult situation or relationship even worse. As soon as one starts to "think evil," Buddhists fear, one will not be able really to understand a complex situation, and so one will not be able to deal with it in a beneficial way. To dub anything or anyone as evil, for Buddhists, is an example of the kind of ignorance that can get us into trouble, or more trouble.

This is all on the practical level – don't "think" evil because it causes problems. Just why this is so is explained by Buddhists in different, often complex ways. This is where things get slippery. The basic reason, it seems to me, why Buddhists are reluctant to define anything as evil has to do with the even more basic Buddhist claim that nothing has an enduring reality of its own. You can't define anything as inherently "evil," just as you can't define anything as inherently "good." Any person or act is, as Buddhists put it, a confluence of "causes and conditions." Some of these causes and conditions may produce suffering; others may not. So to stamp any body or any event as "evil" is to miss all that makes it what it is. There are other ingredients in the mix of its "identity" that perhaps are not so "evil" or that might give a pretty good explanation for what, at the moment, is producing suffering. In other words, if someone seems to us to be evil, or actually harms us, we have to be *mindful* (we'll hear more about that word in the chapter on prayer and meditation) that this is not all the person is. It's certainly not all the person can become.

Such a perspective on evil means that a Buddhist could never resort to the Christian response, often facetious but all too often serious: "The devil made me do it!" For Buddhists there is no original source of evil, no "dark force" either outside us (the devil) or inside us (a sinful nature). If they offer any kind of explanation for evil on the human level – that is, for the depressing frequency and efficiency with which human beings harm each other – Buddhists would say that such "evil" originates not from Satan nor from a sinful nature but from *ignorance*. More plainly put: we do awful things not because we're awful but because we're ignorant.

We'll be exploring this more carefully in a coming chapter on Jesus and Buddha, but for the moment I want to note the fundamentally *positive* Buddhist view of the "human condition." If we do bad things because we are fundamentally bad, we've got a problem that isn't going to go away, at least not in this world. If, however, we do bad things because we are fundamentally ignorant, we can roll up our sleeves and start educating (or in Buddhist terms "Enlightening") ourselves and others. Now we can better understand why Buddhists don't want to brand anyone as "evil."

But this doesn't make Buddhists into starry-eyed idealists who can't see the mud because they're always looking at the mountain. They clearly and explicitly acknowledge that when people do act self-ishly out of ignorance, as they so often do, such people can make a real mess of this world. Buddhists teach that when people act ignorantly and selfishly, such acts produce *more* ignorance and selfishness, and that means more suffering, for themselves and for others.

This is what is called the law of *karma*. Harmful acts always pro-duce harmful consequences. And if they were your acts, *you* have to deal with them. No excuses. That, we might say, is the "bad news" about *karma*. But there is also "good news" contained in the law of *karma*: you *can* deal with the mess you make. You're not stuck in your bad *karma*; you are capable of producing good *karma*. If, as Buddha told us, selfishness will *always* produce suffering, Enlightenment or wisdom can *always* remove suffering. It's up to us.

And if for Buddha that "us" was each of us individually, present-day Buddhist leaders are applying it to each nation internationally. It's up to us to deal with the "evil" or suffering we humans cause for ourselves and each other.

What we've been talking about so far is called "moral evil." But what do Buddhists say about "natural evil" – all the suffering brought about by quirks of nature like earthquakes and hurricanes? Here the Buddhist response may stun many Christians: such happenings, like the well-worn four-letter word, *just happen*. They're brought about by the "causes and conditions" in the movements of the winds or the

tectonic plates or shifts in temperature. The same would apply to defi-
ciencies in our genetic inheritance. It just is. At the most, we can
attribute them to pure chance, random happenstance, which is pretty
much like saying they just happen to happen. There's no particular
cause, no divine will determining such occurrences. They happen,
and we have to deal with them. But, Buddhism adds, we *can* deal with
them.

PASSING BACK: GOD AS PERSONAL PRESENCE

As I pass back to my Christian identity and struggles, I find myself
both attracted by and resistant to Buddhists' reluctance to use personal language for their Ultimate Concern. So much of their reluctance sets off sympathetic vibrations in my own religious feelings. It
makes sound sense to avoid what are really anthropomorphisms
pinned on to a Divine Mystery. But at the same time, my Christian
conditioning and my human reasoning tell me that the theists of the
world (as well as the polytheists!) – all those people who, like
Christians, address their Ultimate Concern as a "you" – are on to
something. They, too, have reasons, some of them very good reasons
I think, for calling the Ultimate "Heavenly Father," or "Divine
Mother," or "Holy Spirit." So although I am dismayed, and often
turned off, by the way Christians use that personal language, I don't
want simply to throw it all away. Although the bathwater may be
dirty, there's a baby in it!

Before I get into the particulars of how I think Buddhism has
helped me understand and use such personal language for God, let me
first state what is the general lesson – or better, reminder – that my
Buddhist friends offer me. All our talk about God as "you" and as "person" is *symbolic*. As theologians such as Karl Rahner and Paul Tillich
taught me, *all* of our language about the Divine can be nothing else but
symbolic, or, in the more technical language of Thomas Aquinas, *analogous*. We'll be looking more carefully at what this means in the next
chapter. For the moment, I only want to state how important and how
helpful it has been for me to remind myself, and reassure myself, that
every time I address God as "you" or pray to "our heavenly Father,"
especially in the liturgy, I am making use of symbols.

Symbolic language is both precious and dangerous. Therefore,
it must be used carefully. Symbols are words we utilize to open

ourselves to something that is essentially beyond words. Symbols are images that connect us with a reality that can never be contained in any one image. This means, as is often said but often forgotten, that while symbols should always be taken seriously, we need to be wary of taking them literally. If we take them literally, we run the risk of so inflating them that we turn them into idols.

So if all of our talk of God as a person is symbolic, we've got to be careful about the way we use it. If we forget that to call God a You or a Father is to make use of a symbol, if we take such symbols literally, they can prevent God from being something other than a "You" or a "Father." This brings us back to the admonition of Father Enomiya-Lassalle: we can use personal imagery for God only when we realize we shouldn't, only when we realize the dangers of doing so. That is, only if we take our personal symbol of God seriously and cautiously, and not literally.

Let me try to explain how Buddhism has helped me do that.

Not a Person, but personal

To draw a clear but I hope careful conclusion to the leads and lures that I've found in my passing over to Buddhism, for me God is no longer a Person, but God is definitely, and all the more engagingly, *personal.* That may be a fine-tuned distinction, but for me and I believe for many Christians, it is an important one. Buddhism has enabled me to identify and affirm what I have been sensing throughout the last few decades of my struggling spiritual life: that God is *not* an almighty, loving Somebody, a divine Personal Being with whom I have essentially the same kind of interpersonal relationship that I have with the other personal beings in my life. As I tried to lay out in Chapter 1, God is and has been for me, rather, the Mystery of InterBeing that surrounds me and animates me. But it is a Mystery that is also personally present to me. When I say "personally present," I mean that I have sensed that this Mystery touches me and affects me in ways that I can, and must, describe as personal. The kind of experiences that have stimulated my awareness of being part of the energy field of InterBeing have also made me aware that this energy is not blind, and its field is not inanimate. The energy, as it were, is up to something. There is something personal about it, even though I can't call it a person.

This is why, as I confessed in Chapter 1, the symbol of God that still speaks to me, and that speaks more powerfully after my passing over to Buddhism, is God as Spirit, as connecting Spirit. Buddhism has helped me identify as well as nurture the kinds of human experiences in which I find and feel this Spirit. The two principal fruits or characteristics that Buddhists discover in Enlightenment, wisdom and compassion, have enabled me to focus the two most fundamental experiences by which I know that the Spirit, while not a person, is a *personal presence* in my life: a sense of groundedness that produces peace within myself, and a sense of connectedness that produces caring for others.

Grounded in peace

By using the word groundedness, I'm trying to express the sense of being part of, or of belonging to, something bigger than myself; I feel that this something bigger includes me or even embraces me. In other words, it's *trustworthy*. Even though it remains evasively mysterious, even though it never offers a permanent place to stand (therefore Buddhists call it Groundlessness), I have the sense that in belonging to it, I can rely on it. Buddhists would name such an experience "wisdom" or understanding – waking up to the reality of the *Dharma* or of InterBeing – and though they usually do not speak of InterBeing as something that is trustworthy, they do clearly affirm that once one wakes up to it, one's life is changed. One finds a peace, a resting, an ability to live life that one did not have before. That's essentially the kind of experience in which I would identify the personal presence of the Spirit.

The kinds of human situations that can trigger such a sense of groundedness-that-produces-peace are as varied as they can be surprising. For Buddhists the primary setting or practice in which our eyes might be opened is the same as it was for Gautama: the silence of meditation. We'll be looking at that more carefully in the chapter on prayer and meditation. Christian spiritual teachers and theologians speak of other "signals of transcendence" that are, so it seems, more readily at hand, more a part of the daily fabric of life. Such signals are often picked up without our clear conscious awareness; or, we can identify them and name them only in looking back at them. They usually come either when we are soaring on the peaks of life, or trudging through the pits.

By peaks, I mean those positive situations that seem to pick us up and pull us out of our own confining skins into a bigger, beautiful world – when the power and magnificence of nature draws us into itself, when a particular piece of music so gets inside of us that, as T.S. Eliot put it, "we become the music," when the word or hug of a friend gives us a strength that neither we nor the friend had, when making love becomes so much more than having sex and leaves us both breathless and grateful. In all these very ordinary human experiences, something extraordinary can happen as we feel ourselves connected or grounded and held by a peace that can endure even after the hype of the experience is gone.

In pit experiences, instead of soaring beyond, we plunge through the bottom of life. When the ground gives way, when there's nothing there to support us, we can find ourselves somehow carrying on, sustained when there's nothing in ourselves or others to sustain us. In the Groundlessness, there is something that holds us or carries us. Paradoxically and mysteriously, there's a ground in the Groundlessness.

Such realizations usually do not come when we are in the pit but only afterwards when we have been able to crawl out. The senseless accidental death of a child, the devastation of divorce after twenty years of marriage, the failure to get into medical or law school, the crippling invasion of memories of sexual abuse – all experiences in which the very foundations of life give way and we fall into Groundlessness. And yet, through it all and perhaps only after it all, we see that we were able to carry on, that we kept getting up in the morning, entered another relationship, had another child. Yes, to get through it all, we had to make our own efforts; we needed the encouragement of friends. But in the actual moment of the pain and confusion and exhaustion, no effort and no friend, by themselves, seemed enough. In and through them, we can sense something else, something that sustained us and, a Christian would add, cared for us. Not a Father-God who steps in and rescues us, but a personal power, a Spirit who acts through, and yet is more than, our efforts and friends.

I can say, then, that there is that which grounds me, sustains me, and so gives me a peace. Not a definable Some Body but neither an inanimate Some Thing. I call it the personal presence of Spirit.

Connected in caring

The Buddhist insistence that Enlightenment brings not only wisdom but compassion has prompted me to identify and feel the Spirit in my life as not only that which grounds me in inner peace but also that which connects me in caring and love for others. It is especially in such experiences that the presence I feel shows itself to be personal. In my Christian experience – different but not entirely different from what I hear from Buddhist friends – it's not so much that I first feel the presence and then how it connects me with others, but that the way I feel my connections with others reveals a deeper presence or power.

My good friend and mentor Aloysius Pieris, S.J., from his study and practice of Buddhism in Sri Lanka, has helped me understand this. He points out that for Buddhists wisdom or *prajna* has a certain priority over compassion or *karuna*; for Christians, it's generally the other way around – compassion or *agape* precedes wisdom. I think that fits the way it's worked for me. It's in my relationships with others, in the way they touch and affect me, that I've become aware of the broader reality of the Spirit's presence, of the InterBeing that vibrates through my relationships.

There's a mystery and power in the way others can lay claims on our lives, the way they can enter our personal territory, uninvited, and call us out of ourselves. A clear example of such happy intrusions came for me and my wife in the faces of the *campesinos* of El Salvador, while we were working with a group called CRISPAZ (Christians for Peace in El Salvador) during the 1980s and 1990s. When we heard about the suffering these people were undergoing from a repressive government supported by our government, when we visited them and heard their stories and looked into their faces, filled with sorrow but also resistance, we had no choice but to respond in some way. "No choice" – there's the mystery and power I'm talking about. It's the way other people can elicit compassion and caring from us, even contrary to our own preferences.

This doesn't always happen, of course. But when it does, it's potent and mysterious and beautiful. Contrary to what some biologists have told us about our "selfish genes," there is also a part of us that is able to, and needs to, respond in care and compassion to other human beings. And when we do respond, we feel all the more human – all the happier, despite the burdens such caring can bring.

Some Buddhists would call this *bodhi citta* – the heart of loving kindness pulsing somewhere in every one of us. As a Christian, I would name it the personal power of the Spirit that touches me in the way others touch me. The Jewish philosopher Emmanuel Levinas has helped me understand and find words for what I'm trying to say and for what I experienced in El Salvador. He tells us that the most convincing, perhaps the primary, way in which we can encounter the reality of the Divine is *in the face of the other*. Looking into the eyes of another human being we feel, or can feel, both respect and responsibility; we feel obliged to cherish the identity of the other and never claim it as our own, but at the same time we feel the need to protect and foster that identity. The other elicits *action* from us, the action of caring and responsibility. And here, Levinas suggests, we can sense the presence of an Other in the other – which is no other than the Other that is present in ourselves. But it is a presence that is found in what the other calls us to do, in how we must act in the face of the other.

And so, Levinas tells us, when we attempt to speak about God, we should use not a "vocabulary of being" but a "vocabulary of action." It's what we said earlier – the deepest reality of the Divine is much more a verb than a noun. That would suggest that our first or fundamental access to the reality of God is not a matter of philosophy – of correct thinking – but a matter of ethics, of correct living. God is not primarily a being that we know but an activity that we feel when we allow that activity and energy to flow through us. We first have to act like God in caring for others before we can really think about God. That reminds me, again, of what my teacher Karl Rahner told us – that a person who has never really loved and cared for another person doesn't have a clue as to what the word "God" really means.

In a journal entry of December 2004, I tried to express this shift in my spirituality from a God who loves to a God who is Love:

> While I have difficulties with over-symbolizing or over-personalizing God, I do know that what makes my life valuable and fulfilling and exciting is to give and receive. That's what love is about – to give of oneself and to receive from that which is other than oneself. This is what I hope my life will be, especially in these later years: I give of myself in love and compassion for all sentient beings. And I receive from the Mystery that I feel within this movement of myself toward the other. I am nourished as I nourish. This is the Mystery of being, of living, of evolution. There is a Life within all life, a Spirit within all spirit. I give and I trust. The more I can give of myself – to Cathy primarily and to all who come into my life immediately or remotely – the more I can feel and be this Mystery.

Dancing together

Imaging and feeling God not as an almighty Person who looks down upon me but as a personal presence that surrounds and embraces me has enabled me to share the stage of my life with God rather than follow a divinely pre-authored script. The following reference to a passage from Pema Chödrön's book *Comfortable with Uncertainty* in my journal of February 2003 captures what I'm trying to say. Speaking about *maitri*, the loving kindness that suffuses us, Chödrön refers to the image used in her Shambhala tradition of "placing our fearful mind in the cradle of loving-kindness," and then goes on, with my own reflections following:

> "Another image for maitri is that of a mother bird who protects and cares for her young until they are strong enough to fly away … People sometime ask, 'Who am I in this image – the mother or the chick?' The answer is we're both …" We're both – the confident, loving mother and the fearful chick. This is precisely where Buddhism helps me the Christian overcome the dualism between God and self/world. The ability to accept myself, the ability to carry on is not something that comes from the outside. It is who I am, even though it is always much more than who or what I am. Not two, not one.

To these Buddhist images of mother bird and chick, of Other and self-power, I would add a traditional Christian distinction which is more technical, and which has been the cause of many a theological brawl through the centuries: divine grace and human free will. These are the Christian terms for Other and self-power. It's futile, Buddhists would say (and my own experience would confirm) to argue which is more important or which has the last word. While there's a difference between divine grace and my free will, grace becomes grace in my *free actions*, in my *decisions*. Buddhists would be happy with the way Karl Rahner put it: there is a relationship of direct proportionality between grace and freedom; the more I experience the power of grace in my life, the more I experience my own freedom. Though they are different, they exist in each other. Their relationship is *non-dual* – that is, interactive. More simply and a bit more boldly: Spirit needs me to be Spirit, and I need Spirit to be me!

We might compare this interactive, interdependent relationship between Spirit and spirit, between divine grace and human freedom, to a two-partner dance, with the Divine taking the lead. (This does not imply any masculine images of God!) God may be the source of the direction and innovation, but just what steps are taken, or when new steps need to be improvised, will depend on the responsiveness of the partner. In moving together, in responding to each other, dance partners, in their differences, and despite frequently stepping on each other's toes, create new movements together.

God's will in process

All of this helps me handle my problems, described earlier, with "God's will." If the God we feel in our lives is a personal presence rather than an almighty Person, if we take seriously the non-duality or interaction between God's grace and our freedom, then God's will becomes for us not something that *exists* but something that *happens*. It's not a prefabricated plan imposed on history, determining who wins which battle, or whether it will be sunny this weekend. Rather, God's will is being worked out through the interaction of the ever-present, ever-active Spirit on the one hand, and the free choices of humans and random happenings of nature on the other. But while the partners are different, their differences may be hard to determine in the one dance that carries them and relates them.

So in what we call God's will, there's a big space for "fill-in-the-blanks." Or as New Testament scholars describe Jesus' understanding of the Reign of God (or God's will for the world), it is both *already* and *not yet*. The "already" is the ever-present and trustworthy Spirit grounding us in peace and calling us to ever-greater compassion. As for the "not yet," the Buddhist image of Groundlessness has helped me grasp just how scary and just how trustworthy God's will really is. It's scary because it is still uncertain, still full of empty space in which we can't see any safety nets. It still has to be worked out, and that means there can be happy and unhappy endings. But at the same time, I can embrace the uncertainty, I can let myself fall into the groundless spaciousness because what is "not yet" and still to come will be the co-creation of my own wisdom and compassion and the Wisdom and Compassion of what as a Christian I call the Spirit and what some Buddhists might call the "cradle of loving kindness." "God's will" therefore is an interactive drama between the Spirit and finite creatures.

For me, and I hope for other Christians, all this can make sense intellectually, though always mysteriously. But for it to become real – that is, a felt reality in one's life – one often needs the perspective of the rear-view mirror. One instance of that for me took place unexpectedly when in 1991 I returned with my wife Cathy and our two children, John and Moira, to the German university town of Marburg, where about twenty years earlier I had received my doctorate in theology. For me, those had been wonderful, exciting years, but at the same time painfully and confusingly difficult years. Besides the to-be-expected struggles of adjusting to the unique rigors of a German Protestant doctoral program, I was caught in a not-so-expected emotional current of relationships and feelings that forced me to ask myself, after being in the seminary and religious life since I was thirteen, whether I really wanted to be part of a celibate priesthood. That was a question I never thought I would feel or have to answer. And during those years in Marburg, it seemed as if the question was as unanswerable as it was unavoidable.

But twenty years later, sitting silently with Cathy on the same bench, next to the castle above the city, where I had so often pondered and pained, I realized with a surge of clarity and gratitude that through all those years *something was going on in my life*. I don't know how else to put it. It's not that through all those struggles I had finally discovered a path that was already there but hidden to me. No, I had to forge the path. But in doing so, in all the good and bad decisions I made, in the supporting or complicating people who entered my life, in the joy and pain I caused others and myself, I was being held or inspired by something else. Something creative, something resourceful. Call it presence, call it Spirit. Twenty years later, it was clearer than it ever could have been earlier. And I was grateful.

Evil – it never has the last word

But what about our messy world – the debris of horrible suffering to be found in every corner of the world, caused either by what humans do to each other and to other sentient beings, or by what nature does to everyone? I'm talking about my struggles with "the problem of evil."

Certainly the amount, the intensity, and the senselessness of suffering that humans have to endure beggars comprehension. It bears an element of incomprehensibility that will never be removed. Still, Buddhism has helped me deal with, not run from, the mystery. It has aided me to retrieve resources in my Christian tradition with which I can approach "the problem of evil" more honestly, intelligently, and creatively.

First of all, if we understand God as the Spirit of InterBeing creatively interacting with the world, rather than as an almighty personal Being in charge of the world, we can no longer, happily, place the blame for "evil" on God. Like the wind in the sails of a skilled captain's boat, the Spirit interacts; she does not control. Or as the process theologians put it, if we want to describe God as "all-powerful," it is the power of persistent persuasion, not that of controlling coercion. I believe that this is a much more orthodox way of speaking about the Christian God's power than to declare that "God can do anything he wants." If God is Love, then God *cannot* do anything God wants. If lovers *force* each other, they are not really loving each other. Lovers refrain from coercion, even when it hurts.

But Buddhism also suggests that if we can't blame God for what we call human or moral evil, neither can we blame the devil or any pre-existing, self-standing source of evil. Here, I suggest, there is much for us Christians to learn. We can understand our traditional doctrines of original sin and our "fallen state" more coherently and deeply by bringing these beliefs into conversation with Buddha's second Noble Truth. That Truth tells us that we cause suffering for ourselves and others because we are selfish, and that we are selfish not because we are innately so, but because we are ignorant.

So from this perspective, we can say that evil does not exist in itself. It doesn't have its own reality or identity since it is always the product of something else – that is, ignorance. What we're saying here is not just an interesting philosophical insight. It has very practical consequences for how we understand and deal with our messy world. If "evil" is real – that is, a given element in the human condition – we have an incurable disease that can't really be fixed until we move on to the next life where it will either finally be removed or punished. If evil is not real in itself but the unhappy by-product of ignorance, call the doctor – there's hope.

Christian stress on our "sinful state," on our position of "sinners unworthy of God's love," can receive a healthy balance, I believe, from Buddhism's fundamentally hopeful assessment of human nature and the world. It's a realistic assessment, for it faces head on the depth and the breadth of the suffering caused by ignorance. *Karma*, as we heard, means that ignorance and suffering can snowball into a devastating avalanche. But Buddhists never abandon the Bodhisattva effort to remove the ignorance of all sentient beings; Enlightenment is possible for every human being because every single human being possesses

Buddha-nature. Therefore, there can be less suffering in the world tomorrow than there is today.

Such hopefulness is contained, but often missed or forgotten, in basic Christian beliefs: that no matter how much we might be mired in sin, we remain God's children; that we can't do anything that can't be forgiven; that, as St. Paul puts it, "if sin abounds, grace abounds even more so" (Rom. 5:20) – that is, no matter how much selfishness and suffering humans have heaped upon each other, there are even greater possibilities for compassion and collaboration. We Christians are supposed to believe this – and act on it.

I suspect that we would be much closer to Jesus' assessment of human nature if we understood "original sin" to be "original ignorance." If we're going to talk about what first got the snowball of selfishness and suffering going in humanity's history, we're closer to the truth if we locate the initial push not in some primordial corruption that now seeps into each of us in the very act of procreation, but, as the Adam and Eve story tells us, in a silly, indeed stupid, decision to believe the promises of someone dressed up as a snake. I don't mean to be disrespectful, but I'm convinced that if we understand the myth of Adam and Eve not as an act of evil rebellion but as a decision based on ignorant delusion, we are in a better position not to allow their "original sin" to overshadow or displace the "original grace" of God's creation. (Remember the part in the story about God stepping back and declaring it all to be "good, very good" in Genesis 1.)

Well, all this may help us handle the mess in the world caused by human decisions. But what about the mess, the horrible suffering, that the forces of nature can unleash? Again, if we understand God as the grounding, connecting Spirit that interacts with the world without controlling it, we can, and must, recognize that just as the Spirit respects and works with the way humans act, so the Spirit will respect and work with the way animals and the elements of nature act. Humans, ideally, act freely; they have control, or some control, over their instincts and natural dispositions. The rest of nature acts through pure instinct and/or random happenings. In given circumstances or in a particular confluence of events, sub-atomic particles will act as sub-atomic particles and volcanoes will act as volcanoes. And the Spirit, as interactive presence and not as commander-in-chief, lets it happen.

So, "when bad things happen to good people" (to borrow the title of Rabbi Harold S. Kushner's popular book), when we confront such things as earthquakes, tsunamis, volcanic eruptions, cancer, birth defects, we first have to examine diligently whether there were any human "causes and conditions" involved; if not, then, with Buddha and with Rabbi Kushner, we have to say "they just happened." They were not caused by God or any other good or bad supernatural agent. They came about through the random "causes and conditions" that make up the way nature works. Buddha would call it *tathata* – the suchness of things. And our first response should be *to accept them.* That doesn't mean to be happy about them; but it also doesn't mean to deny them or rebel against them or let them flatten us. As the Beatles' "Mother Mary" (whoever she might be!) wisely counsels: let it be.

But we don't stop there. Acceptance is only the first response. Buddhists, if I understand people like Thich Nhat Hanh and Pema Chödrön correctly, would first accept what is with as much mindfulness and compassion as possible, and then let whatever actions they take flow from this mindfulness and compassion. As a Christian I would try to do the same thing – accept the suffering contained in what happened as "what happened," but I would also be aware of the ever-present interactive Spirit of Wisdom and Compassion. And this Spirit, interacting with my spirit, can provide both the *strength* to accept what might feel utterly unacceptable, and the *creativity* to do something about it, or at least to take another step forward. This "creativity" is based on the trust that I have (and the trust that I think Buddhists have but don't need to identify) that in accepting what has happened I will find the ability to carry on and to make something out of the pain and loss that I have experienced.

Process theologians speak about the Spirit as the source of infinite possibilities for new life and new relationships that can be drawn out of anything that happens. My Christian faith tells me that even in the face of the loss of a child, the break-up of a marriage, the news that cancer has invaded my body, I have the inner resources, which are the Spirit's resources, to deal with such painful realities *and* to draw new possibilities from them. Buddhist teachings have helped me open myself to this Spirit and to feel her presence by counseling me first to accept honestly and bravely all the pain and horror of what has happened, and then to respond to it with as much patient wisdom and persistent compassion, toward myself and others, as possible. And I *will* be able to move forward. Perhaps I might also be able to draw "good" from the "evil" that happened. In the case of human-caused

3

NIRVANA AND GOD THE MYSTERIOUS OTHER

In this last of the three foundational chapters on God and *Nirvana*, we're dealing with an issue that has been bubbling under the surface of my problems with God as Transcendent Other and as Personal Other: how to find words for a Reality that, both in its very nature and in the way it touches our lives, is essentially beyond words. When Buddhists who have had something like an Enlightenment experience, or Christians who have stepped into realms of the mystical, try to talk about what's happening to them, they start stuttering. They discover that though their experience may have been prompted by words, it is always two steps ahead of, or it wiggles away from, any words they may use to describe it. That's why both Buddhism and Christianity, as well as all the religions of the world, recognize, in different ways, that what matters most for them is a *matter of Mystery*. In their heart of hearts, religions deal with a Reality they recognize to be indefinable, incomprehensible, unspeakable.

And yet, all religions speak. Some of them more than others. Christianity – together with, and I think even more than, the other two Semitic religions, Judaism and Islam – is one of the "big talkers." As we'll explore more carefully in this chapter, Christians throughout their history have used a lot of words to describe and even define what they believe, even when those beliefs touched on the very nature of God.

And therein lies my problem – how to hold together all the words about God that I have learned as a good Christian and then as a professional theologian with my growing awareness, especially over the last three decades of my life, of God as Mystery. Come to think of it, this problem of "words" may not only be bubbling under the other problems I've dealt with in the preceding two chapters: it may be one of the major causes of those problems.

So let me now try to find words to describe my problems with words.

MY STRUGGLES: WORDS THAT SHACKLE MYSTERY

Over the years, I have had mounting problems speaking the religious language I grew up with. Often, especially at Mass but also in conversations with fellow Christians or in reading Christian books, I've heard or read words or expressions that stop me in my mental or emotional tracks. My difficulties have to do with either comprehension or consternation. Either I've puzzled about "What does that really mean?" or I've gagged on "Can that really mean what it's supposed to mean?" I'm not talking only about the weird things that so easily find their way into conversations or books about religion. (As a friend of mine puts it: "Religion offers equal attraction to brilliant minds and to crackpots.") To be embarrassingly honest, I've had problems with words that form the fabric of Christian creed and dogma – like "only-begotten Son ... consubstantial with the Father ... coming to judge the living and the dead ... conceived without sin ... assumed bodily into heaven."

My problem with such language has been not so much that it doesn't make sense to me at all (although I must admit I still struggle with trying to get a mental grip on "consubstantial" or "assumed bodily into heaven"). What has tripped me up is that these words make too *much* sense; they have been understood and explained all too clearly or all too definitively. So the crux of my difficulties has been not in a *lack* of meaning but in an *excess* of meaning; not in the *possibility* of meaning but in the *determination* of meaning. The image that comes to mind is of a beautiful tropical bird – in a cage. Able to soar, it's not allowed to.

We kill religious language when we don't allow it to soar. If that can be a problem for any religion, for Christianity it's a major problem.

A delicate balance

By its very self-definition, Christianity bears the daunting task of having to maintain a delicate balance between human words and divine Mystery. On the one hand, we might say that words are what the Christian religion is all about. That's not just because it inherited from its Jewish mother a love of and respect for the *Dabar* or Word of God – a Word that brought forth the world ("And God said, 'Let there be …'") and then carried on the conversation through Moses and the prophets. Christianity went beyond its mother, and in a sense caused a good bit of grief for her, when theologians in the first centuries after Christ distinguished, as it were, a "Speaker God" from a "Creator God." The always-one God, Christians felt and then proclaimed, was not only Father (first Person of the Trinity) but also Word (second person). (The Spirit's job, then, was to elicit a response to the Word.)

And then, as if this was not enough to mark a difference of Christian offspring from Jewish parent, the author of John's Gospel made an announcement that has reverberated and amplified throughout Christian history, becoming the belief that, more than any other, has distinguished Christianity from other religions: this Word that created the world and spoke to Moses and the prophets has *become flesh* in the human being Jesus the Nazarean. "And the Word was made flesh and dwelt among us" (John 1:14). Jesus, Christians proclaim, *is* God's Word. The very God who is Word is the founder and the core of Christian belief and practice.

This respect for God as Word became, and remains, a central part of my own spirituality when I became, and for twenty-three years remained, a member of the Society of the Divine Word. As a Divine Word Missionary, the general job of all Christians became my partic-ular life's task – to listen to God's Word, to understand it in light of other cultures, and then to use other words to talk about it to the whole world. Thanks to the S.V.D.s (acronym from their Latin name), I'm still a lover of words.

Becoming a theologian both deepened that love and made me wary of it. During my years as a student of theology at the Gregorian University in Rome (1962–1966) – years which were providentially and wondrously co-extensive with the extent of the Second Vatican Council (1962–1965) – the emphasis, as expected, was on words, on the Word of God as given in the Bible *and* on the words of the church as contained in a book that we students simply referred to as "Denzinger" (the name of one of its Jesuit editors). On the dog-eared and underlined pages of my Denzinger, between two battered covers, I had all the official teachings of councils and popes through the cen-turies. These church-words, it was explained to us, were necessary and willed-by-God in order to interpret, protect, and sometimes infallibly define the true meaning of God's Word. So for our major examinations (always oral with three Jesuit examiners and always in Latin) we tremblingly entered the room with two books in hand – the Bible and Denzinger (the latter in my right hand since I usually used it more often). The truthfulness and the accuracy of our answers were to be measured, in the final analysis, by words – God's or the church's.

But amid the flow of words that was my theological education at the Gregorian, there were also reminders – only occasional but daunting – about the *limitations* of words and of the human reasoning behind them. We heard such reminders of Mystery in our courses on spiritual theology, when we studied the Christian mystics. For me, mystics like Dionysius the Areopagite, John of the Cross, Teresa of Avila, Meister Eckhart, Julian of Norwich became mental gadflies as I listened to professors expound profusely in other courses "On the Triune God," "On the Incarnate Word," "On the Last Things." Over the growing mass of my theological knowledge, there hovered the admonition of the mystics: all that can be known of God is by far surpassed, and must be held in check, by what is not and cannot be known of God.

Yet, as I also discovered during those years at the Greg, it was not just the mystics that leveled these caveats about our language. Even "Denzinger" explicitly recognized and knelt before the Mystery of what Christians call God. In the Fourth Lateran Council in 1215, and again in the First Vatican Council in 1875, the "Magisterium" (the official teaching body of the Catholic Church) formally defined the "incomprehensibility" of God (Denzinger #428 and 1782). In other words, it is a defined dogma that God can never be defined!

And herein lies the rub, which I felt already in those early years, but which later became an even greater spiritual and intellectual irritant: how do I hold together all the certain knowledge I have as a theologian and am supposed to affirm as a believer with what I have increasingly felt, and what the Magisterium has even defined, as the utter mystery and incomprehensibility of God?

A broken balance

The sad reality, and the source of my struggles, is that we haven't held them together. In theological classrooms, from Sunday morning pulpits, in catechism class, we Christians all too often do not respect the necessary balance between knowledge and incomprehensibility, between our human words and divine Mystery. We talk too much. Or, we're not careful of the way we talk. And so our words end up as shackles on the rich, unfathomable Mystery of God.

Let me try to list some of the ways this has happened for me. I'm going to try to speak as a person in the pews – which, since I left the priesthood in 1975, is exactly where I have been every Sunday (well, almost every Sunday). Perhaps the major source of my frequent discomfort with the language spoken in my church community has been that it is so concrete, or so precise – really, so *literal*. Now I know that many of us adult Christians have come a long way from the times when we took "the six days of creation" to be actual twenty-four-hour days. And I've come a long way since the early 1960s when I sat in Father Clemens Fuerst's class on "the last things" (*De Ultimis*) and conscientiously wrote down in my notes that we have to believe that the fire of hell is "material," and that although we don't know for sure what kind of musical instruments will be used to sound the call to the last judgment, "there will be sound."

Post-Second Vatican Council religious education has alerted many Catholics that they do not have to take all of the images and assertions in their creeds and catechism literally. Okay. That's a relief. But that's only half the solution. If not literally, how *should* we understand these beliefs? What are we asserting, what do we mean, when we say what we say or hear what we hear every Sunday? That there are "three Persons in God," that "Jesus sits on the right hand of the Father," that he "will come at the end of time," that Mary was a virgin "before, in, and after" the birth of Jesus, that some people go to purgatory while some will suffer in hell "for all eternity," that Mary was "assumed bodily into heaven?" I'm not asking for some kind of neat, well-defined meaning to take the place of the literal meaning of these beliefs. I, and many of my fellow Christians, are simply asking, "What *do* we believe if we don't believe in the literal sense of such statements?"

My problems with Christian language deepen precisely when we try actually to answer that question: "What do we believe if we don't believe literally?" So many of the interpretations of Christian doctrines have become barriers to exploring their deeper content, or to exploring *other* content. The primary reason for this seems to be the way the meanings given to Christian beliefs so often set up walls – walls that exclude. Either they wall off other, or different, interpretations by insisting that this is the only valid way of under-standing a particular doctrine (e.g. "transubstantiation" is the only way of understanding the real presence of Jesus in the Eucharist). Or they exclude, or denigrate, all truths on the other side of the Christian wall, in other religions. It seems that so often the way that we Christians affirm that "we hold these truths" leads us to deny or put down the truths that others hold.

What I'm getting at has to do with the "one and only" stamp that marks so much of Christian belief and teaching. If there is really only one God, then all other gods are false (that's why the other "gods" merit only a lower-case "g"). If Jesus is really the Son of God, he's the only Son of God; or if really the Savior, then the only Savior. If the Christian church is really the path to salvation, then it is the only path – or at least the best and final path. Or to pick up some of the issues of the previous chapters: if God is almighty, then "he" cannot be depen-dent. If God is really a Person, then religions that don't recognize a personal Supreme Being are atheistic.

"My truth" becomes opposed to, or destructive of, "your truth." To return to the image I already used: when we take the tropical bird of religious language and put it in a cage, it becomes a bird of prey.

I don't mean to overstate my uneasiness, but I'm afraid there are many such "birds of prey" flying around Christian communities. I've met them in Catholics who want to be united in a well-defined faith and who therefore call upon pastors to exclude certain members of the parish because they do not believe in the "true presence" of Jesus in the bread. I've met them in Catholic organizations that report bish-ops to Rome for allowing lay people to preach at Mass. I've met them in bishops who exclude Catholic politicians from Communion because of their views on how church law relates to state law on issues of abortion and reproductive rights. And yes, to be candid, I've also met them personally in Vatican officials who have forbidden theolo-gians from teaching or writing because of their efforts to explore new understandings of the role of Christ and the church in relation to other religions. I do not wish to pass judgment on the good intentions of such people, but I am venturing the judgment that they might be abusing religious language.

Such examples indicate that religious language is not only a neces-sary means by which a community gathers to articulate what holds it together and what it stands for. Religious language, like all language, can also so easily be used as an instrument of power by which some people seek to control other people. That's an abiding danger every time we open our mouth and speak, contemporary philosophers tell us, so we have to be aware of it and be on guard against it. Our guard goes down and the temptation to turn religious language into power language goes up when we take that language in a too literal, or too precise, or univocal sense.

Just that, it has been my experience, happens all too often in our Christian churches. In the way we understand and use our language, we not only shackle the Mystery of God: we shackle each other.

PASSING OVER: THE FINGER IS NOT THE MOON

As in all religions, words play a big role in Buddhism. But it's always a subordinate role. Experience comes first – the experience of Enlightenment, the Awakening to one's existence within InterBeing. Living comes first – living a life of compassion toward all sentient beings as a Bodhisattva. Words are important and have their meaning only insofar as they promote such experience and such living. For Buddhists, words are always *means to an end*, never an end in themselves. In fact, the traditional teaching of Buddha is that once the end is reached, you can toss away the words. You won't need them. Or you'll use them freely, easily, loosely – the way a bird uses the wind to soar and swoop.

Words for Buddhists are not only subordinate to a higher or deeper experiential end. They're also *inadequate* to that end. Of themselves or by themselves, they can never really get you there. Even though words may prime or prepare you for the experience and awareness of InterBeing, something else has to happen for that awareness to dawn – something else that is more than the evocative power of any words. And when that "something else" does happen, it also will be so much more than anything that can be captured by language. Words may have played a role in triggering the experience of losing one's own identity within the larger identity of InterBeing, but when the experience comes, it's an explosion in whose light the trigger can no longer be found. Stated more directly and in Western terms, in Buddhism "mystery" always holds priority over words, either coming or going – that is, either in preparing for or looking back at what one "sees" when one's eyes are truly opened.

To complete this generalizing and I hope not too improper overview of how Buddhists understand language, we need to add that because words are always subordinate and inadequate they are also *dangerous*. Because human beings are sentient beings privileged not only with the capacity to be Enlightened but also with the capacity to talk, their talk can all too easily, maybe unavoidably, get in the way of their Enlightenment. When words become more important than the experience of Emptiness, when we proclaim certain words to be "necessary" in order to come to Enlightenment, when, in our contemporary idiom, "talking" about compassion becomes more important than "walking" in compassion – then words show their ever-lurking danger. They become impediments to, or substitutes for, the experience to which Buddha called all human beings.

All these tags that Buddhists put on any packaging of words – "subordinate, inadequate, dangerous" – are rather abstract. Let me offer a few traditional Buddhist stories or images that can give them some substance and color.

Watch out for words

There's the oft-told parable of the man shot with a poisoned arrow. There he is, lying on the road with the arrow sticking out of him, when some friends come to his rescue. But before they can do anything, he starts plying them with all kinds of questions: "Who did this? Why did he do it? Where was he standing? What kind of arrow is it?" Gently but firmly they tell him to shut up. "Stop all that talking. We have to get this arrow out." That, Gautama the Buddha comments, is his job as an Enlightened being – to remove the arrow of suffering from our lives, not to answer all our speculative, dare I say theological, questions. Words so easily get in the way of that task.

A similar message is delivered in a phrase that the early Buddhist Scriptures frequently put on the lips of Gautama: "Your question does not fit the case." Whenever anyone would face him with a question like "Does the self exist or not exist? Do we live on after death? Where did the world come from?" that would be his retort. What you're asking doesn't have anything to do with the answers I'm offering. Your questions deal with matters what are either beyond words or beyond human intelligence. In any case, they're distractions from what we can do and need to do: figure out how to deal with suffering, how to live peacefully and compassionately. Do that first, and then there might be time to entertain questions – *if* that's needed.

Another well-known image suggests that words might not be needed. The Buddha compared his teachings, his words, to a raft whose sole purpose was to enable people to reach the shore of Enlightenment. But, he added, when you reach the shore, you can chuck the raft! Why hang on to it? You don't need it any more. To drag it around on land would be just that – a drag.

Zen Buddhists use an even more powerful, even disturbing, scenario to stress the danger of becoming too dependent on words, even the words of the Master. "If you meet the Buddha," they admonish, "kill him!" For otherwise non-violent Buddhists, the statement is evidently hyperbole. But the point it is making is not – don't let the words of even the Buddha interfere with the whole point of Buddha's message: to have your own experience of *Nirvana*, to experience the opening of your own eyes, to feel for yourself the exhilarating Emptiness of InterBeing. If any words, if any teacher, if any sacred book becomes more important than that, throw them overboard and sail on.

But the saying that for me (and for most of the Buddhist teachers I've had) best describes the way Buddhists use words and language is contained in the simple Zen sentence "The finger is not the moon." The moon represents what we are ultimately looking for (better, what we ultimately are): Enlightenment, *Nirvana*, Emptiness, Buddha-nature; or in more Christian/Western terms, we might say Mystery or the Ultimate. Fingers serve to point us in the direction of that Mystery, which can be as *real* in our experience as it is *beyond* our words and understanding. If we confuse the finger with the moon, we will miss the moon! The Buddhist view of language is as simple, yet as profound and challenging, as that.

Fingers have their purpose

Even though Buddhists are, to put it mildly, wary of words, even though their abiding intent is to get beyond words, I believe that as a Christian dialogue partner I am not entirely off base when I observe that Buddhism also recognizes the important role of words. As I like to tease my Buddhist friends: "But you never do throw away the raft! You never do kill the Buddha." The raft of the *Dharma* or of the teachings of the Buddha remains important; and the importance, it seems to me, is not just for the purpose of teaching others who are still plod-ding their way to Awakening. Even masters seem to need the contin-ued guidance or admonitions of the raft and the Buddha.

But in recognizing the importance, maybe even the necessity, of words, Buddhist teachers use them very differently than do Christians (especially if the Christian is a theologian, a bishop, or a pope!). The "Parable of the Burning House," found in the Mahayana Lotus Sutra, makes this clear. A wise and loving father realizes to his horror that the house in which his three children are happily playing with their toy carts is on fire. He's got to get them out as quickly as possible. But, engrossed with their toys, the children pay no attention to his gentle but urgent calls to come out. So he resorts to what we might call a "white lie" and tells them that he has some even prettier and bigger toy carts waiting for them outside – goat carts, deer carts, and oxen carts to be specific. The kids rush out eagerly and are saved. But are they disappointed? Not at all. Though the father told a fib, he ends up keeping his word even more fabulously. He gives his children a beau-tiful cart sparkling with precious stones and pulled by two beautiful white bullocks. That's a toy that surpasses all toys!

This quaint and time-conditioned story (nowadays the dad would have to use a new computer game to lure the kids out of the house) embodies the Buddhist teaching about *upaya* – "skill-in-means" or "skillful means." The Buddha or Buddhist teachers (the father in our parable), because of their overflowing and wise compassion, will use whatever "means" or whatever words they can – even if, as the para-ble indicates, that includes stretching the truth a bit – to rescue the children of humanity as they witlessly play in a house that is afire with suffering. The ultimate gift that is delivered through such skillful – we might say tricky – means is the bejeweled cart of Enlightenment, and the peace and compassion that it brings.

This skilled, adaptive, resourceful, even loose way of using words is based on the underlying Buddhist understanding of language as a means to an end. It almost sounds as if Buddhism, in this case, is urg-ing that "the end justifies the means" – use whatever means you like, as long as it reaches the end of Enlightenment. Not really. The moral teaching of the Eightfold Path that forbids harming others through speech or action would apply here as it applies throughout Buddhist living. But the notion of *upaya* does make abundantly clear that *the end is more important than the means* – or, experience is more important than words.

As a Buddhist friend of mine, David Loy, explained to me in an emailed commentary he made on this chapter: "For Buddhists, language is not something that saves us if we identify with it; rather, it is something that can transform us when we interact with it. Buddhist teachings, like all religious doctrines, have to be interpreted. But for Buddhists the interpretation is not a matter of beliefs but a way of life."

This does not mean that *any* beliefs or any words are therefore justified. But it does mean that many, varied, and adaptable words will be necessary. Clearly, there does not seem to be room in the Buddhist wardrobe for any "one and only," infallible, or one-size-fits-all doctrines or words. All words are servants of the Truth. And the Truth needs many servants.

Some of these servants can be sassy or sly. I'm talking about *koans* – the word-tools that some Zen teachers use to shepherd their students along the path to Enlightenment. These are the slippery, silly, utterly incongruous questions that sound to some Western scholars (Huston Smith) like a form of "transcendental horseplay." Some of the better-known koans are: "What's the sound of one hand clapping?" "Show me your original face before you were born." "Does a dog have Buddha-nature?" The students are supposed to spend long hours wrestling with these questions and then return to propose their answers to the teacher. The teacher keeps sending them back to do more homework until they "get it."

Far be it from me to state what "it" is. But I've been told it has to do with coming to the realization that the answer, or the way of answering, is not a matter of the "right words," or even of thinking – what we would call "rational thought." Koans, we might say, are words that are used to show the inadequacy of words, thoughts, or images, and their purpose is to propel students beyond all thoughts and images. To use an inappropriate image, koans are little sticks of mental dynamite, discreetly inserted by the teacher into the wall of rational thinking in order to blow it up. You might say that koans are intended to bring about a mental breakdown that will enable a breakthrough. This will free the student to find the answer by an entirely different path – by a more experiential, immediate, intuitive way of grasping, or being grasped by, the truth of what we really are. Koans, therefore, are a form of fighting fire with fire – words with words.

To summarize, I offer one of the clearest, simplest, and most challenging contemporary statements of the Buddhist view of language. It comprises the first two of the "Fourteen Principles of InterBeing" written by Thich Nhat Hanh:

> Do not be idolatrous about or bound to any doctrine, theory, or ide-ology, even Buddhist ones. All systems of thought are guiding means; they are not absolute truth. If you have a gun, you can shoot one, two, three, five people; but if you have an ideology and stick to it, thinking it is the absolute truth, you can kill millions.
>
> Do not think that the knowledge you presently possess is change-less, absolute truth. Avoid being narrow-minded and bound to present views. Learn and practice non-attachment from views in order to be open to receive others' viewpoints.

Nhat Hanh makes clear both the danger and the benefits of distin-guishing finger and moon. Fingers that are identified with the moon and so become the "only finger" also can so easily become fists by which we do violence to others who refuse to accept "our finger." On the other hand (pun intended!), fingers that are recognized to be "pointers" to the moon – the one moon we are all trying to see more clearly – leave us free, indeed they remind us, to learn from other fingers.

Can Christian language, even the language of the creeds and of dogma, be understood as fingers pointing to the moon? As I will now try to explain, such a question bristles with complexity and opportunity.

PASSING BACK: WORDS THAT CHERISH MYSTERY

One of the most evident, and perhaps most useful, fruits that we Christians can gather from a dialogue with Buddhists has to do with language. Buddhism can aid us in recognizing and then fixing the broken balance, described above, between the God whom we affirm to be Mystery and the words we use to speak about that Mystery. In my own spiritual life, I believe that in passing back from my dialogue with Buddhism, I am better able to use words in a way in which they *cherish* the Mystery of the Divine.

That word, "cherish," cuts two ways. Negatively, it expresses the limitations of all words when used to talk about the God whom we have called the Connecting Spirit; words must respect the Mystery and never idolatrously take its place. But positively, precisely when the limitations of words are affirmed and maintained, that's when they become all the more effective in revealing the Mystery. Words are like telescopes with which we gaze into the mysterious heavens: only when we bring them to a focus do we see anything; without a focus, by trying to see too much, we don't see anything at all. Or what we see is very misleading. Our words cherish the Mystery by seeing only part of it. Or in the Buddhist image: fingers identify the moon by not being identified with it.

All words are fingers

For myself and I believe for my fellow Christians, I need to press this point more forcefully. Another Buddhist friend, Rita Gross (a former Christian), has asked me pointedly: "Can you really say that all your Christian language – not only the musings of theologians but also the stories and teachings of Scripture and the precise wording of doctrine and dogma – are fingers pointing to the moon?" My earlier hesitant, but now firm, answer is: "Yes!" And I say that as a Christian. There are solid pieces in Christian tradition and teaching that not only allow but require us to agree with our Buddhist brothers and sisters. Christian language, like all religious language, is, in its entire vocabulary, made up of fingers pointing to the moon.

The bedrock reason for asserting this is the Christian doctrine, firm but often submerged, that God is a Mystery that no human mind or words can neatly and fully grasp. In the poetry of the Bible, we *always* "see through a glass darkly and only in part"(1 Cor. 13:12), or as we already have heard, in the precision of the Fourth Lateran Council, we must bow before the "incomprehensibility" of God. This means that for all that we can, and often must, say about the divine Mystery, there is so much more that is left unsaid. And this "unsaid" should be perched on our shoulders, like some angelic monkey, reminding us constantly that whatever we say or declare about God – whether we are the Pope giving an "official teaching" or good Christian parents admonishing our children – it can never ever be the only word, or the last word, about God. There's always more to say, more to know. And the "more" may not only enhance or clarify what we have already declared. It may also often correct it. I'm talking now not as a Buddhist, but as a Christian. This is sound Christian – I add, Catholic – doctrine.

What I just said is a theological statement. So allow me to use a bit of technical language to ground it. Buddhism has been an incentive for me, and might be for my Christian community in general, to dust off, polish, and retrieve what in the history of Christian thought has been called *negative* (or "*apophatic*") theology. Most of what we theologians and religious educators do is *positive* (or "*kataphatic*") theology, which speaks about who or what God is or what God has done in what we call "the history of salvation." Negative theology reminds us about what God is *not* – about why and how the Divine is not what we say because it is so much more than what we say. It's like the Hindu notion of "*neti, neti*" – "not this, not this" – which Hindus add, like a recurring footnote, to whatever they say about the Divine. Everything we affirm about God, therefore, must be negated, or qualified, or cut down to size in view of what we can't say and can't know. If we could write down (of course we can't) all that we *cannot* know of God, it would stand as an encyclopedia next to the pamphlet of what we can know.

One of the most brilliant and influential theological minds in all of Christian history, whose voluminous writings have been occupying and preoccupying theologians since the thirteenth century, recognized that he was just a pamphleteer before the utter Mystery of the Divine. "The divine substance surpasses every form that our intellect reaches," announced Thomas Aquinas in the philosophical argot of his time. And he drew the personal consequences: "He knows God best who acknowledges that whatever he thinks or says falls short of what God really is" (*Summa contra Gentiles*, 1:14:3; *De Causis*, 6). Maybe that's why, towards the end of his life, after a mystical experience in which he felt more of the Divine Mystery than he could ever know, Aquinas shockingly declared all the tomes he had written to be nothing but straw that could well be chucked into the fire!

The caveats contained in negative theology, or in the Buddhist reminder that our doctrinal fingers are not the moon, are particularly helpful, or downright necessary, when it comes to the Christian proclivity to use so much "one and only" language. We'll be taking up this issue at greater length when we explore "only Son of God" language in Chapter 5, on Christ. For the moment, I can state the simple but revolutionary conclusion that Buddhism has helped me recognize: if we really take our doctrine on the incomprehensibility of God seriously, if we really believe, as we say we do, that the Divine Mystery is always more than anything we can know or say, then we Christians have to be much more careful about the way we use the adjective "only" – if we dare use that adjective at all. To announce to the world that God can *only* be understood as Triune, that God "saves" through *only* one church, that there is *only* one way to organize the church, that *only* men can be priests – such statements run the risk of trying to stuff the divine Mystery into one container. And then we own the container. Or we use it to replace other containers. Idols, and idolaters, always end up fighting among themselves.

No way around symbols

If the Buddhists are right that all our words are fingers pointing to the moon and not the moon itself, then all our words about God are symbols. I suspect – no, I affirm – that if Christians who are struggling with what they are supposed to believe could grasp with their heads and embrace with their feelings that sentence – "All our words are symbols" – they would find that their struggles not only become easier but will actually bear fruit.

I'll never forget the astonishment I felt, followed by a sense of liberation and then exhilaration, when I first read Paul Tillich's exposé of why there is no way of talking about God except through symbols. (That was after my studies in Rome since, as a Protestant, Tillich was not on the list of required reading at the Gregorian University in the 1960s.) At first, Tillich thought that the only exception to this statement was the word "God," but he soon recognized that also "God" had to take his place among all the other symbols in all the other religions that were pointing to what Tillich called "the God beyond God."

So for Tillich – and I believe that most mainline Christian theologians would agree with him – symbols are indispensable for both the *experience* and the *expression* of the Divine Mystery. That means that for all of us there is no direct, unmediated (my students would say "eyeball-to-eyeball") experience of God. There's always a go-between, a vehicle – what we're calling a symbol. Perhaps some Zen Buddhists would argue with this, but even if they're right, even if there can be a symbol-less experience of the Absolute, they would admit that there's no way to talk about that experience outside of symbols.

But what are, then, these wonderful, though limiting, things called symbols? Trying to avoid all the philosophical verbiage that has piled up in answering that question, we might say that basically symbols are objects, words, pictures, stories, or pieces of ordinary experience that make present or give expression to realities that otherwise would be shapeless and indescribable. Symbols enable us to feel or talk about things that in themselves are difficult to feel or talk about. Some common, but also precious, examples: a ring that symbolizes love (at least in Western culture, for symbols are culturally conditioned), a dove that stirs the feeling of peace, a hero-story that elicits courage in us (Frodo in *The Lord of the Rings*). Such examples illustrate what Tillich also pointed out about symbols: they participate in, but are not the same as, what they symbolize. The meaning of a symbol cannot be willfully assigned, the way we assign red to mean stop and green to mean go. There's something "natural" about its meaning – the way the circularity of a golden ring communicates the precious eternity of love, or the gentle movement of a dove fills us with peace, or how the story of Frodo and his unrelenting, battered bravery appeals to our own reserves of courage.

I said that my reading of what Tillich had to say about symbols was liberating. It freed me from the burden, often too heavy to bear, of having to take all the language of my Christian beliefs literally. In fact, it happily warned me that if I take certain beliefs literally, I may be missing their point. What Tillich was saying became all the more imperative and therefore all the more liberating through my dialogue with Buddhism. I had already moved beyond a literal reading of the story of creation in six days and of so many other stories in "the Old Testament." But now what Tillich, and then the Buddhists, were telling me also applied to the New Testament, to the Nicene Creed, to "Denzinger!" *All* our words, all our talk, are fingers – symbols.

But if all this was a liberation, it was also a daunting challenge. This is what Tillich was getting at with his insistence that if we really understand what symbols are, we will never say "that's *only* a symbol." Taken as a symbol, an image or a word or a story explodes with meaning, and it can keep exploding with different meaning down through the centuries. If our religious language is primarily symbolic, not literal, that means that its content, its meaning, is deeper, more powerful, more personally engaging than it could ever be if taken "only" as literal. It's easy to take "Father God," or "sitting at the right hand," or "Son of God" literally. It's much more challenging and more rewarding to ask and then feel the symbolic meaning and power of these words and images.

How to do this? How, as is often said, do we take our symbols "not literally but seriously?" How, as we asked earlier, do we figure out what a symbol *does* mean if we don't take its meaning to be literal? There is, of course, no easy answer to those questions.

To begin with, what I have found helpful for myself and for my students is the reminder that to call something a symbol or a myth is *not* to deny its truth. Just because it "didn't happen," or it may not have happened in precisely the way that is reported, doesn't mean that it isn't packing a powerful truth. On the contrary, as we just said, its truth may be *more* wrenching and exciting.

To get at that deeper, more exciting meaning, we need to recognize that to take our religious language and stories as symbol and myth is to approach them in much the same way we approach poetry. We recognize that the truth they can deliver cannot be neatly pinned down. To get at it, we will have to let the symbols dance through our imagination before they can walk into our intellects. They are telling us something, but they first speak to the heart and feelings before they can be registered in the mind and thoughts. And of course, because we Christians are an inherently communitarian lot, this process of reading and feeling the poetry of our stories and beliefs needs to be done together. Each of us has to do it for her or himself, but we never do it *by* ourselves.

Another help in getting at the truth of symbols and myths is to recognize, and allow, their meaning to be more general than particular. I have to explain carefully what I mean since it can be easily misunderstood. Even though the contents of an image or story may be extremely concrete and particular, even though it may be based in a very particular historical event (e.g. the exodus from Egypt, the crucifixion of Jesus), what it's getting at in its particular imagery or content is true and illuminating about life, about human nature, about history in general. Symbols and myths and poetry are like the well-defined beam of a flashlight that illuminates something that we didn't realize existed, or only hoped was there, in the dark room of what we sometimes call "the human condition." The deeper power of a symbol is not determined by the size or shape of its own beam, but by the truth that it makes clear and alive. Now, this doesn't mean that the truths that symbols illuminate are always a wonderful, delightful discovery. The truth they deliver may also be a kick in the derrière that requires us to change the course of our lives.

But what about the historical or "factual" content of a symbol or myth? This is a question that Christians have to raise, for as we heard earlier they (together with their parent Judaism and their sibling

Islam) have experienced and believe in a *God of history.* Historical events, therefore, form the bedrock of Christianity. True. Yet if we recognize that all religious language is symbolic and that therefore historical events and figures are also "fingers pointing to the moon," then this bedrock of history must come alive as the poetry of symbol. By that I mean that unless the event – the exodus, the crucifixion – becomes a symbol that reverberates in our feelings and illuminates a *universal* truth of our lives, it is nothing else but a historical event or person that happened or lived in the past.

To make a real difference in our lives – in Christian language, to "save us" – history must become symbol. When theologians say that Christianity is based on the "Christ event," that means that our religion is grounded on a *historical symbol* or *historical myth* – history that speaks with the power of myth.

If this makes sense, as I believe it does or can, if even the foundational historical events of our faith are fingers pointing to the moon, then the really important thing to ask is not "Did it really happen?" or "Just what precisely happened?" but "What does it mean?" Even if we can't know for sure just what happened – or in some stories, whether it happened at all – the symbolic meaning of a symbol or myth can still enable it to be a finger that points to the moon; it can still deliver a meaning that illumines and revivifies our lives or turns them upside down and in a new direction.

A concrete example of what I'm trying to say: even if Jesus never did walk on water and bid Peter to do the same, the words he spoke (or is said to have spoken) to Peter, "O you of little faith. Why do you doubt" (Matt. 14:30–32), have had the power to shake and transform my life. (In the chapter on Christ and Buddha we'll explore how the resurrection, the cornerstone of Christianity, can be considered a "historical myth.")

Perform more than inform

In taking our language seriously rather than literally – or as I just put it, in focusing on "what does it mean?" rather than "what really happened?" – we might keep in mind some technical advice from professional theologians: all religious language, especially when it is recognized as symbolic language, is "performative more than informative." Translation: the primary purpose of all the language in the Bible and in the creeds and catechism is to tell us how to live rather than provide us with clear, final answers about the nature of God and the universe. Really, the theologians are announcing what the Buddha taught centuries before: as symbol and myth, our religious beliefs are there to get the arrow of suffering out of our body, not to answer all our questions about why the arrow is there in the first place. Whatever information our beliefs – our myths and symbols – provide us, what matters most is that we *feel* and *live* that information rather than that we label and define it. Symbols are meant to change our lives, not fill our heads.

And yet, they do offer something for our heads. In stressing performance over information, in no way do I wish to deny that our beliefs-as-symbols are telling us something real, something true. In the technical language of my theological trade, they have an "*ontological*" content, not just an ethical intent. In calling us to live and perform in a certain way, they are also giving us information about the "way things really are." I don't wish to play down what philosophers call "the truth claims" of our beliefs. But I do wish to play up two consequences of recognizing the symbolic packaging of all truth claims. 1) As the author of John's Gospel stresses throughout his story of Jesus, it's much more important to *do* the truth than to know it; in fact, we can know it only by doing it. Only in this way can "the truth set us free" (John 8:32). 2) Whatever we do know of the truth, that knowledge, as we heard from Thich Nhat Hanh, can never be made absolute. There will always be "other truth." Or there will always be the need and the opportunity to understand the truth that we do have more deeply, and that means differently.

Fingers are important – and different

After trying to explain how much I have learned from Buddhism about language and fingers, I find that I have to offer myself a Christian reminder. For all their inadequacy, words and fingers may be more important than Buddhists – and Christians – realize. If Christians have good reason in their experience and tradition to use the symbol of "Word" (*Logos, Verbum*) to describe the very nature of God (the second person of the Trinity is named "Word"), then words, despite all their limitations, are one of the ways in which the Divine *becomes present* in human lives and history. In Buddhist language perhaps we can say that words are one of the "forms" in which Emptiness manifests.

But let me take a further bold step in my Christian musings: if it is true that "the finger is not the moon," don't we have to be careful of making that statement too absolute? There are also reasons to say that "the finger *is* the moon" – not the moon entirely, but the moon really. Fingers – that is words, symbols, myths, doctrines – don't just *point*. In pointing, they really make the Connecting Spirit present. They *are* the Spirit – never fully but really. This was Tillich's point in stressing that although symbols can never be identified with what they symbolize, they do participate in what they symbolize.

Therefore, maybe Buddhists have to be careful about their insistence that words are only means to an end. They can also be embodiments – partial but real – of the end. Form *is* Emptiness – this "form" right here. Jesus *is* God's Word. Muhammad *is* God's prophet.

The practical implications of these rather abstract reflections are that, at least for me as a Christian, words are important in the *differences* that exist among them. The different words that we use for Mystery are not just different ways of saying the same thing; each word is saying something different about the same thing, the same Mystery. Therefore, the differences matter. Perhaps we might say that although all the different religious fingers are pointing to the same moon, each, as it were, points to a different part of the moon. Without the Buddhist fingers, there are parts of the moon that Christians would never see. But the same is true of what Christian fingers might mean for Buddhists.

Let me finish this section with a few entries from my journal. They will make these rather difficult issues more personal, and I hope more clear. In August 2005, while on retreat at Gethsemane Abbey, I was touched by the power of puny words:

> The Divine is utter mystery. It is so much more than our Christian language and experience; yes, also so much more than Jesus the Christ. And yet, the Divine is waiting, as it were, to be brought forth into finite reality through us humans and through our human words. When we humans – including the human Jesus – on the basis of our own experience speak about God and about salvation and about history – we enable the Divine Mystery to affect us and transform us precisely through such finite experiences and the finite, inadequate words and stories that result from them.
>
> Yes, to talk about God as coming at the end of times, or of Jesus as the only begotten Son of God, is to touch only a part of the Divine Mystery, the Creative Matrix that pulses in the world. But it is – it

IS – a very real and a very effective way of making the Mystery present. What we're getting at when we talk of "at the end of times" may be so very inadequate, and perhaps even misleading, when we place the meaning of these words in the limitless framework of the Divine. Still, these words, and this tradition, are inspiring, and have inspired, millions of people to love and to work for justice and to believe that this world can be different. When people do that, they are living the Divine life adequately, even though their comprehension through their symbols is so unsettlingly inadequate.

When we say God becomes incarnate in the flesh of history we are saying that our inadequate words, symbols, beliefs are as true as they are inadequate. They enable God to be God, they enable InterBeing to be InterBeing, all the more fully. How more true can they be, finite words as they are?

In July 2003 I tried to explain to myself how I can be fully committed to what I can know only partially:

In the words that I find in my tradition, the words that nourish me and so often insult me, I find what is absolutely necessary to nourish my spirit, especially my Christian spirit; but also, in those words, I feel what is utterly inadequate. I need words because they say something about what I'm feeling, what I hope for, what I am committed to. But if they say something, that something is meaningful for me only when I remind myself that they don't say everything. Something but not everything. That means enough for me to stake my life on, but also not enough to keep me from being open to more, and to the essential Mystery that is the reality I call God.

So all the words that I hear during Mass or read in the Bible or use in the classroom – words like salvation, end of time, second coming, Trinity, Mother of God – they are all pointers to realities that are as beyond us all as they are powerfully present. Powerfully present and yet at the same time only fragments of what we might know and of what we will never know fully. If I can stake my life on fragments, know that these fragments are powerful enough to reshape my life and the life of the world, but at the same time they are only pointers, never to be made absolute, or final, or unchangeable.

So the next time a word from the liturgy gets caught in my mouth, I must remind myself that it is only a fragment, try to make it a delicious fragment, and then swallow.

As much of a problem traditional Christian language presents for me, I need it. I live from it.

4

NIRVANA AND HEAVEN

My difficulties with the way so many of our words are disrespectful of the Mystery that is God, as described in the previous chapter, are basically the same as the problems I have had with the way we Christians talk about the mystery that lies beyond death. We talk too much. But in a certain sense, my problems with so much of Christian life-after-death talk are even greater, or more painful, than what I feel about Christian God-talk. At least in speaking about God, we Christians are generally more aware – or we can more easily be made aware – of the fact that we are dealing with Mystery. No one will deny that God is so much more than anything we can know or say. But when it comes to heaven and hell, it seems that we are much more certain about what we know and say. It seems we forget, or don't want to admit, that what applies to the Divine also applies to life with the Divine after death: all our language is inherently, stubbornly, delightfully symbolic.

The words "heaven," "hell," "purgatory," "last judgment" are symbols. They too are fingers pointing to the moon, not to be identified with the moon. Perhaps Christians fail to realize this because they believe that Jesus, or the Bible, has provided them with happily precise information or reliable reports on what is to come on the other side of death. They forget that even when "God talks to us" and reveals God's self to us, the only language God can use is symbolic. God, too, can only point.

When speaking about "the last things," maybe even more than in speaking about God, Christians do not take their language seriously enough because they take it too literally. At least that's my suspicion. And it's what I've felt even more acutely as I move into my seventies, aware that for me the "last things" aren't that far off.

Let me start by describing situations in which Christian talk about life after death has left me squirming with discomfort.

MY STRUGGLES: WE TALK TOO MUCH

Funerals. That's where I so often squirm. Whether it's the language of the liturgy itself, or the homilist during the Mass of Christian Burial, or eulogies at the funeral home, I've often found myself saying – and my wife can testify to this – "Gads, I don't want them talking like that about me at my funeral." Examples of language I wouldn't want to hear even if I could:

> "May the angels welcome you into the heavenly paradise."
> "Now he can sing God's praises with the choirs of angels for all eternity."
> "Now God will reward her for putting up with such ungrateful kids."
> "Finally, he's at peace after suffering through his cancer."
> "Well, Dad will now again be with Mom."
> "If he's going to have to spend time in purgatory, it won't be long."

I honestly do not want people someday to talk about me that way. Why?

I think the general reason why such language makes me uneasy – and I know from friends that they share this uneasiness – is that it's so neat and clear about things that cannot be known neatly and clearly this side of the grave. It's one thing to believe in "eternal life." It's quite another to spell out just how that life will be lived. I'm afraid that when we talk about "the next life," we forget that we really don't know what we're talking about. And so we talk too easily and too much. In talking too much, we fail to cherish, indeed we might even cheapen, the *mystery* of what lies beyond death.

Scared to hell

One of the areas where I feel that we Christians have talked way too much and so have not only cheapened but actually distorted both the mystery of "the last things" and the mystery of the Divine is in what we have to say about hell. Even when we do not take "the fire of hell" literally, even when, as Karl Rahner taught, we are required to believe that hell exists but we can't be sure that anyone is in hell – still, to be honest, I just can't do it. I can't believe even in the *possibility* of eternal punishment in hell. I would have to force myself to believe. And faith can't be forced.

I say that, first of all, out of personal, psychological reasons. As a child, because of what I heard at school (happily not from my parents), I had "the hell scared into me." It was I think in second grade when, having been duly instructed on the difference between a venial sin (two-way ticket to purgatory) and mortal sin (one-way ticket to hell), I was gripped by the fear that if I had committed a mortal sin and then if I hadn't confessed it properly to a priest, I could be punished for all eternity. For a young boy who took things too seriously, "eternity" – for ever and ever and ever – was a frighteningly long time, especially if it was to be spent cooking in hell. This fear of getting stuck in hell forever fermented into a case of scrupulosity (fear of sinning, even unawares) that pursued me through my seminary high-school years. So maybe my present aversion to the notion of hell is a compensatory over-reaction.

If it is, it sure seems to be a healthy over-reaction, both psychologically and theologically. To scare the hell into or out of children (or anyone!) by teaching them that God can do something that their parents, at their angriest, would never want to do – that is, punish them or allow them to be punished for ever and ever and ever – such a doctrine does not seem to promote mental health nor lay the foundations for a mature, adult morality. And as I was taught by Father Fringts, S.V.D., a wise spiritual director in Rome, if a belief makes for bad psychology, it probably makes for bad theology.

And in this case, the doctrine of eternal hell sure does seem to make for bad theology. Simply stated, there's a blatant contradiction between these two beliefs: "God is Love" and "God punishes eternally." If we use the symbol of loving Father for the Divine and take that symbol seriously, whether we interpret it as a Person or as a presence, then eternal hell cannot make sense. No parent would dish out, or allow their child to endure – no matter what she or he did – a punishment that was excruciating (fire!) and that would last their entire life (eternal!). If God does this, then, it seems clear to me, we can't call God Father or Mother.

Are we being selfish?

I have another, even deeper, discomfort with Christian words and images for the afterlife. This particular squirming results not from too much talking about heaven but from a particular piece of that talk which, many would argue, constitutes the keystone of Christian doctrine on "the last things." Over the past decades since I've been struggling with this issue, I've hesitated to bring it up in good Christian conversation. But the more I have talked about it, the more I've been surprised by eyebrows raised not in amazement but in agreement. "Yes, I've wondered about that, too."

I'm talking about personal immortality – about how or even whether we live on after death as individual beings. I find myself wondering not only whether I believe but, if I really understand Jesus' message, whether I *should* believe that after death I will live on as Paul Knitter, with, as I've been taught from grammar school through my seminary training, essentially the same soul or personality (though purified), and, after the last judgment, with the same body (though perfected, so I'll have my hair back!). To be honest, I am no longer consoled, but rather confused, by a vision of heaven in which I live forever as an individual, along with billions of other individuals. I fear that such a vision, taken literally, is another misuse of words in the face of mystery. Let me, briefly, try to explain why.

I found myself stammering some years back when an agnostic friend in Xavier University's biology department teased me with the question: "Nothing in the world perishes completely. Everything lives on after death – but in different forms, through a marvelous process of recycling. Why should humans want to hang on to their individual identities and miss out on this wonderful process?" I can't shake myself loose from my friend's words: "Everything lives on in different forms." Maybe the mystery of my life after my death will be so unexpectedly and wonderfully different that it will be beyond anything I can now describe as "my" or "me." Such questions make sense not just rationally but even, if we take the mystery and creativity of the Divine seriously, theologically. "No eye has seen, no ear has heard, no mind has conceived what God has prepared for those who love him," St. Paul reminds us (1 Cor. 2:9). That means we're really going to be surprised.

But more personally, and more discomfortingly, traditional images of a heaven in which individuals receive their eternal rewards seem to me ... well, rather selfish. Or egocentric. I'm not talking about the child's level of morality that such images can easily promote – being good in order to avoid the punishment of hell or gain the reward of heaven. Rather, I have the nagging concern that doctrines about heaven that insist that "I" will enjoy life with God with "my" loved ones are not only saying too much; they might also be obstacles to responding to, and realizing the joy of, what Jesus really meant when he said that we must lose ourselves in order to find ourselves. If we really "lose" ourselves, whatever we find will not be the same as what we lost. But what will we find? What will we be?

I think Buddhism has helped me peer a little more carefully into that mystery of life after death and into the Mystery that is beyond all words.

PASSING OVER: BE HERE NOW

I'll never forget the first time I brought a group of students to a Zen center. It was the early 1970s. I was teaching at Catholic Theological Union in Chicago, so the students were seminarians, and the Zen Center was on Halsted Street. In the conversation with the Zen Master that followed a half-hour of sitting meditation, the first question was: "What is the Buddhist view of life after death?" We were all nearly knocked off our meditation cushions when the Master calmly answered: "We don't have one."

Grinning at the stunned silence, he went on to offer an explanation that basically boiled down to Buddha's response to similar queries: "Your question does not fit the case." What we Christians were asking was not important – or better, it was not needed – in light of what Buddhists are trying to achieve. The focus of Buddhist energies and concerns is not on what comes after death. It's not even on tomorrow, or the moment that is to follow this one. Rather, it's on *this moment, now, right here.* You might say that Buddhists wish to be nowhere else but *now-here.* They wish to live their lives by being fully present. That means, as we shall see in the chapter on meditation, *mindfully* present and responsive – to what is going on, around them and in them, *at this moment.*

What is next is now

Based on the experience of Buddha that becomes their own experience, Buddhists are convinced that if they can be fully present and responsive to what is going on now, then what will happen next will take care of itself. In a sense, "what's next" is contained in "what's now." In order to get at "what's next" we need to be fully aware or mindful of "what's now" and respond to it as compassionately as we can. If we do this, Buddha tells us, if we can be fully present to, and responsive to, the "now," the difference between "now and next" won't make any difference! By being fully in the present moment, we will no longer have any worries about the next moment, and that includes the moment we die and the moments that come after our death.

But if Buddhist friends and scholars will allow me, I believe that Buddhists can say (and some of them do say) something about what is coming *next*, after death. The reason is, I think, simple. What they discover in this life will be true of whatever makes up the next life. What they experience themselves to be now, they will continue to be, perhaps even more fully, after death: no-selves. Remember in Chapter 1 I tried to explain how in the experience of Enlightenment Buddhists wake up to their true identity as *anatta*s – as no-selves. This doesn't mean that they don't exist, but that their true identity is to move beyond the individual self and to become part of, and con- tribute compassionately to, the larger reality of InterBeing. Happiness in this life consists of living selflessly. And Buddhists know that it will be the same in whatever happens after their present life. That's why, as the Zen Master told my students, they don't have to worry about what comes after death.

Just as in each moment of their lives Buddhists are able to over- come suffering and attain peace by letting go and not clinging selfishly to themselves or to anything, so in the moment of death they will also let go and not cling. And the results, they know, will be the same: there will be peace, there will be further InterBeing, there will be further life. Just as in each moment they found peace and overcame suffering by getting beyond their individual selves, so in death there will be, as it were, the final letting go of, and getting beyond, themselves. And it will be good to do so, in death as in life. A Zen saying tells us that "Every day is a fine day." That includes the day we die.

Rebirth – hang in there!

The previous paragraphs were a little too neat. They describe what is ideal more than what is actual. The smooth flow of passing at death from one level of selflessness to another, vaster level represents the ideal death, attained by the Enlightened ones, the saints and mystics.

For the rest of us, things may be a bit more complex. That, I suspect, is what the Buddhist belief in rebirth and *karma* tells us.

How to understand what "rebirth" (Buddhists prefer that word rather than "reincarnation") really means is itself notoriously and dangerously complex. The pivot of the problem is how to explain what it is that rebirths if there is no self (*anatta*!) to rebirth. There's a mishmash of theories, which I'll leave to the scholars to sort out. For my purposes, and I hope with the required caution and humility, I'd like to note what I think are the practical, spiritual fruits of a belief in rebirth, no matter how one explains it or how literally one takes it. The notion of rebirth, always combined as it is with the reality of *karma*, tells us two things. 1) Through what we choose to do, we can really mess things up for ourselves and for others. 2) But there's always the possibility and the hope that we can clean up the mess, though it may require a long haul with repeated efforts.

First, a quick review. *Karma* is the law of cause and effect: what you do is what you get. Rebirth, reduced to its basics, tells us that *karma* works even after death – that is, what a person does or is in one life is passed on, after death, to another life or lives. This means, first of all, that although Buddhists do not believe in an eternal hell, they do recognize that if we act ignorantly and selfishly, we can create a hell of a mess, for ourselves and for others, in the life we're living now *and* in lives that will come after us. In other words, how we use our intelligence and freedom really matters. There's always a payoff, which you might call a "reward or punishment." But it's not meted out by an almighty Judge at the end of your life. It just happens, according to the natural law of *karma*, both in this life and in other future lives. And whether you take the Buddhist imagery literally or try to get at its "deeper meaning," the image of being reborn as a slug sure seems to be, from a human perspective, a hell of a life.

That, you might say, is the bad news. The good news is that even if you're a slug, things can get better, though it may take more than one lifetime. *Karma*, contrary to popular Western opinion, does *not* mean "fate." *Karma* never gives a death sentence – or even a life sentence. Though there is no way out of having to deal with what we, or others, have done in the past, we *can* deal with it. Good deeds can clean up the muck of bad deeds, both our own and of others. But the Buddhist doctrine of rebirth tells us, realistically but never fatalistically, that given the choices some people have made or given the choices they may have "inherited" from being born where they were born, the process of waking up and of overcoming selfish *karma* through Enlightened *karma* may take more than one lifetime.

Or more broadly, in the grand scheme of InterBeing and in the way our lives are interwoven with each other, the meaning and the potential for "good" of a particular life can be worked out only *after* that particular life has run its course, as the grand scheme continues to unfold. What we said earlier about Buddhism in general applies to every human being in particular: no life, no matter how much of a mess it left, is entirely evil. Good can be drawn from it. But it may take a while.

Admittedly, my Christian concerns and conditionings shine through these comments on rebirth, as they do in this entire effort to "pass over." Trusting that what I've understood is not entirely off base for Buddhists, I'll try now to pass back with what I think I've learned.

PASSING BACK: WHAT AWAITS US WILL SURPRISE US

In trying to put into words how I think Buddhism has helped me deal with the mystery of what comes after we die, I really want to be as careful and respectful as I can, not only because I don't want to end up doing what I've complained about – talk too much. It's also because if there is any place in this book where what I'm proposing as a "reinterpretation" of doctrine may stand open to the accusation of being a "rejection" of doctrine, it's here. (I'm sure some people will find a few other places as well!)

Determining whether the "new" is "true"

Because this is so important, and because it touches on my identity as a theologian and a Christian, let me take a few paragraphs to summarize how I try to determine whether a new understanding of faith is a "reinterpretation" or a "rejection" of that faith. The particular "method of theology" that I follow holds that although fidelity to the Bible and (for Catholics) to the teachings of the church is always a matter of words, it is not *primarily* a matter of words. What we are called to be faithful to is not the words themselves, but the way those words are supposed to form or reform our lives. Christians believe certain things in order to act in a certain way. The purpose of doctrine is not primarily to fill our heads but to shape our lives. We express our beliefs in words in order to express our beliefs in actions. The words are meant to promote deeds.

Certainly, as I reminded the Buddhists at the end of the previous chapter, we need words; we need understanding and shared meaning in order to act, and to act together. But we can change the words without necessarily changing the action. In fact we often *have* to change the words if we are going to be able to figure out how to translate them into action when faced with the new questions, new problems, new discoveries that come up as history moves along.

So if a new interpretation of – that is, new words for – a traditional Christian belief enables people to live their lives according to the spirit of the Gospel, it's probably a faithful "reinterpretation" or a valid new understanding of that belief, no matter how different the words may be. In theological jargon, right acting (called "orthopraxis") is more important than, though it is dependent on, right believing ("orthodoxy"). Or in contemporary jargon, walking the talk is more important than talking the talk. So, if the new "talk" enables us to keep walking, it's probably okay. It's probably "orthodox."

I do believe that what I'm now going to lay out in this "passing back" section – that is, how Buddhism has enabled me to "reinterpret" my beliefs about life after death – can enable me and other Christians to understand our faith more meaningfully and therefore to *live* it more resolutely.

Karma can be hell!

As I've already candidly confessed, I simply don't believe in hell because I simply can't. The square peg of eternal punishment just doesn't fit into the round hole of God's love. If the "use of reason" means anything in Christian life, then we've got to make a choice between either a God who administers or allows eternal pain or a God who loves and never gives up on that love. I'm convinced, though I have no hard-nosed statistics to confirm it, that the majority of mainline Christians, at least in the U.S. and certainly in Europe (fundamentalists are a starkly different story), experience an unswallowable lump in their throats when they hear talk of "the eternal fires of hell." About a decade ago Andrew Greeley gathered statistics on what "traditional Catholics" believe and found that while seventy-five percent of them were sure there was a heaven, only forty-five percent were so sure about hell. Judging from what I hear from undergraduate and seminary students, I suspect that the hell-doubting percentage has grown over the past decade.

That's what theologians call "the sense of the faithful." It's one of the primary indicators of what the Christian community really believes. And it can serve as a flashing red light to warn church leaders and theologians that there is a discrepancy between what is officially being taught and what struggling Christian people really believe. An uncomfortably clear example in the Catholic Church of what I'm talking about is the bright red light of discrepancy between the official teaching of the Vatican on artificial birth control and what Catholics believe in their hearts and practice in their bedrooms. I suspect that the fires of hell also cast a bright red warning light (another bad pun intended) that official teaching doesn't reflect common belief. The talk is not keeping up with the walk.

Mainline Christian pastors are, I think, getting the message. In the liturgies that I have attended over recent decades (mainly Catholic but frequently Protestant), the preachers' repertoire no longer includes those good old "fire and brimstone" sermons that our pastor back in St. Joseph's, or especially the Passionist priests who preached the annual parish mission, would unleash on the congregation (and which would usually assure longer lines for confession next weekend). Nowadays, it seems to me, attempts to scare people back to church with threats of hellfire run the bigger risk of scaring them away from church. (Again I have to add: unless it's a fundamentalist church. But I'm writing this book for those struggling Christians caught in the middle ground between the black-and-white certainty of fundamentalists, for whom nothing is true unless it's literally in the Bible, and the black-and-white certainty of secular materialists, for whom nothing is true unless you can measure it or put it in your wallet.)

The theologians are getting the message, too. Here are some of the ways in which they are trying to put what you might call a "theological spin" on the traditional interpretation of hell.

Rather than consigning people to eternal punishment, some theologians suggest that eternal annihilation might be more appropriate. God's love, they reason, is more easily reconciled with God's creatures fading away forever rather than being tortured forever.

Others suggest that since humanity was created to be with God, it is reasonable to believe that those who are finally separated from God in hell are less than fully human; that would mean that since they are sort of semi-annihilated, they don't suffer as much.

Some Catholic theologians, as I already mentioned, take what looks like a more legalistic approach and point out that Catholics are *obliged* to believe that hell exists; however, they are *not* obliged to believe that there are any residents in hell. Hell is more of a menacing possibility than a certain reality. The hounds of hell, you might say, have a bark that is worse than their bite!

Finally, a few Christian thinkers go all the way and advocate what they call "universalism" and hold that, in the end, everyone is going to be "saved." They point out that in the Gospels, whereas the notion of "hell" appears some fifteen times, the adjective "eternal" is placed before it only twice, and only in Matthew's Gospel (Matt. 18:8, 25:41). This suggests that early church theologians may have built an airtight doctrine about eternal punishment from a few hyperbolic adjectives, which, they add, we can't be certain Jesus himself really pronounced. According to this view, therefore, heavy-duty sinners may have to pass through a type of punishment (which then very much resembles Catholic notions of purgatory), but it won't last forever. Eventually everyone makes it home.

I suppose I would be most comfortable with that last category, but I would like to tailor it, as it were, with some Buddhist scissors and patches. In attempting this, I believe I'm in pretty reputable company: Karl Rahner, in one of his occasional suggestive asides, commented that perhaps Christian efforts to make sense out of traditional teachings about such last things as purgatory could find some valuable help from the Asian notion of reincarnation. I'm trying to follow up on Rahner's advice.

I believe that the underlying, practical meaning of the Buddhist teachings on *karma* and rebirth are fundamentally the same as the underlying, practical meaning of traditional Christian teachings on heaven and hell: the heart of both these teachings is that our free will is no joke. It's not to be taken lightly. There are grave, lasting consequences for the choices we make. And the Buddhist image of being reborn as a slug or other apparently lower forms of life, as well as the Christian image of hellfire, inform us that when those choices are selfish and harmful to others the consequences are so serious that they can extend into the reality of what comes after our individual death.

What Christians call "the wages of sin" or what Buddhists term "bad *karma*" will usually have to be paid back in our present life; the consequences of selfishly hurting others bounce back to haunt or harm us pretty quickly. But even if that is not the case, even if some form of "gated community" manages for the most part to keep the results of our greed out of our sight, the message of "hell" or "rebirth" is that what may not have haunted us in this life will do so in the next. The results of our free choices are so serious that they will extend beyond the grave and affect, for better or worse, what comes next.

So even when we do not take "rebirth" or "eternal hell" literally, even when we take them as fingers pointing to a larger moon, the meaning or the moon they are pointing to looks something like this: the mess that our sinful or selfish choices create extends even beyond our own lifetimes; in fact, the mess that we make can be even greater after we pass on than it was when we were still around. That mess lives on, for ourselves but also for others. The "evil that men do" during the few years they strut upon this earth can be such that it carries on even after their footprints have long disappeared. That, I believe, is the central message of the Christian doctrine of hell.

And this message, even though it does not take "eternal" literally, can still affect and guide our lives the way traditional belief in hell was supposed to. It can still warn us of how serious and long-term the results of our free choices can be. Even though those results may not last for ever and ever, they still can lead to consequences, as the Buddhist vision of multiple rebirths tells us, that last a "hell of a long time" and produce a mess that may take "lifetimes" to clean up. Just how these messy consequences will play out, just how they will affect us individually and socially, we cannot say, for these beliefs are "fingers" and not the moon itself. But what we do know is that our selfishness or bad *karma*, when not addressed in our lifetime, will extend beyond our lifetime. To believe this, even without the adjective "eternal," is sufficient, it seems to me, to foster the "right acting" in this life that is the criterion of all "right believing."

Hope *can* spring eternal

So the Buddhist understanding of *karma* and rebirth, blended with the Christian view of hell, does not soft-sell what can be the genuinely awful results of our self-centered decisions and actions. But where Buddhist views happily nudge Christians toward a needed reinterpretation of their traditional beliefs about the afterlife is in what you might call the positive flip-side of *karma*; no matter how awful and hellish the bad *karma* of our selfish acts might be, it never has the last and lasting word! This is where Rahner's suspicions that Asian views of rebirth can help us Christians were right on target. He realized that with the symbol of purgatory, Christian believers and theologians recognized that it often takes more than a lifetime to clean up one's act in order to move on into the ongoing mystery of eternal life. The purpose of purgatory, expressed in Buddhist symbols, was to allow time to "burn off" bad *karma.*

But Christians limited the cleansing potency of purgatory only to what Buddhists might call "light-weight bad *karma*" – in Catholic terms, venial sins. These are low-range, occasional acts of selfishness that color everyone's life, not the big-time, life-pervading egocentricity of "mortal sin" that turns everyone and everything into instruments for one's own profit. According to traditional Catholic belief, the effects or bad *karma* of venial sins are washable in purgatory. Mortal sins are permanent stains.

My conversation with Buddhism has helped me see more clearly what the theologians mentioned above were groping for: if we really believe our symbols that call God Father or tell us that the Divine is Love, then there can be no permanent stains. No permanent or eternal hell. As Rahner perhaps suspected, Buddhists are nudging Christians to expand the meaning of their symbol of purgatory: we can be "purified" not only of our blemishes but also of our stains. And that will usually take more than one lifetime. The process goes on. And it goes on because, in Buddhist terms, "bad *karma*" never has the last word; there is always the possibility of it providing an opportunity for "good *karma.*" In Christian language, human decisions, no matter how mean-spirited and death-dealing to others they may be, never have the last word over Divine Love. What the poet calls "the Hound of Heaven" never gives up.

So, even though Dante's *Inferno* may have been accurate in depicting the horror that is the bad *karma* of our sinful acts, he was wrong when he posted his sign: "Abandon all hope, ye who enter here." If Christians are right in calling God Love, if Buddhists are right in affirming compassion as a quality of the ongoing process of InterBeing, then there is always hope. Buddhists have reminded me, as I believe they can remind my fellow Christians, that what we Christians say we believe is really the case. Love is stronger than hatred. Good is stronger than evil. The good that we do, or can do, will outlive, or offset, the evil that we have done. But it may take more than what we define as one, single lifetime!

That this is true, I trust firmly. *How* it works, I cannot say clearly. The moon is so far away from the finger. The glass through which we view the other side is always dark. Our symbols are much better at pointing than describing. But if, as I trust, the Divine Life is real, if the interconnected Spirit continues to act, if the process of InterBeing carries on, then after my death, what I did and who I was will be taken up, for better and for worse, into that Life and Spirit and interconnectedness. I trust that the good as well as the harm that I have done will "make a difference" in the way the process unfolds or in how what we Christians call the Reign of God takes shape. Just how especially the harm and the selfishness in my life will make a difference after my life, I can't say exactly. But again, I trust that whatever bad *karma* I have produced, however much hurt I may have caused to others, it will somehow – eventually, slowly, painfully – become the occasion for, or be absorbed into, greater life and greater good.

In such a vision of how who we are and what we do lives on and makes a difference after our present life, the neat distinction between "who" and "what" is bound to blur. That returns us to the question of "who" or "what" lives on.

What we find is not what we lost

The Buddhist teachings on rebirth, especially as they have been understood by contemporary Buddhists, have helped me come to what I believe is a picture of immortality that is closer to the spirit of Jesus' message than what I have been taught through much of my Christian education. "There is that which is reborn," the Buddha tells us. But the reborn "that" is very different from the "that" of who I was in my lifetime. Or, as the Christian liturgy puts it: "life [after death] will be transformed, not taken away." "Transformed" means the "form" of who we are will be different; there will be continuity but also real discontinuity. We Christians have been good at talking about the "continuity," not so good in accepting and trying to deal with the "discontinuity." I suspect that the "who and what" we are now will not be able to recognize itself in the "who and what" we will be after death.

I say that not just because I've learned a lot from Buddhism but because Buddhism has helped me take another and deeper look at what I believe as a Christian. We say that eternal life is "life in God." But, as was suggested in Chapters 1 and 2, if we offend the Mystery of the Divine by limiting that Mystery to the confines of a "person," if God is more accurately "pointed to" as a personal presence, or as the Spirit-energy that grounds and connects everything, then just as God is not literally a person, so our eternal life in God will not be literally as the persons we think we are here in this life. If the deepest identity of what we call God cannot, and should not, be captured in the notion of an individual self, then surely our own ongoing life in the Divine cannot and should not be symbolized as an extension of the individual self called Paul or Cathy. Indeed, this life, this identity of ours, will be *transformed.*

The occasional experiences (or, for the saints and mystics and poets among us, the frequent experiences) of transcending our own limited personal consciousness in spiritual or mystical moments will be, we can expect, intensified in what follows after death in our eternal living in God. The poetic outburst of T.S. Eliot that I quoted earlier, "I become the music," might well serve as a metaphor for life after death in which "I become the Divine." The "I" is not totally annihilated. But neither does it exist as it was. It endures as something much more, much greater than what we have experienced it to be at this stage of our existence.

As I passed back from my dialogue with Buddhism to my Christian identity and tradition, I found that many of the words that I had repeated or read throughout my life started to glow with new meaning, especially in their significance for how we Christians might envision the "eternal life" we call heaven.

The statement of St. Paul that makes multiple appearances in this book (especially in the coming Chapter 6 on prayer and meditation) gives us a general indication of what we can expect our "life after death" to be. To the Galatians Paul exclaimed: "Since I've been crucified with Christ, I'm not the one who is now living. It is Christ who is doing the living in me" (my free translation of the Greek in Gal. 2:19–20). The ideal of Christian life is to lose one's own self-centered identity in the wider activity of the risen Christ-Spirit. It is to step back and let this Spirit live in and as us. Surely, this will be the further, unimaginably deeper, reality of life after death. The "I" that lives on is the Christ-Spirit that lives on in all. (St. Paul saw no difference between the "risen Christ" and the "Spirit.")

Buddhism also throws new, and I believe fuller, light on an oft-quoted passage from John's Gospel: "Unless a grain of wheat falls into the earth and dies, it remains just a single grain; but if it dies, it bears much fruit" (John 12:24). In this passage, Jesus, in looking ahead to his own death, speaks about death for all of us. Death means that as "single grains" we really die. The "singleness" of our identities is no longer to be found. The "fruit" that comes forth is very, very different from the single, little seed. Again, we're dealing here with symbols, with pointing fingers. But they seem to point to a life after death that is no longer life lived as individuals.

The same message, when seen in the beam of my Buddhist flash-light, comes through in the five different passages in the Synoptic Gospels (Matthew, Mark, and Luke) in which Jesus tells us that if we really want to "find" or "save" our life, we first really have to "lose" it. In my past readings of these texts, I generally placed the emphasis on the finding or saving. Buddhism has urged me to take the *losing* part more seriously. The Greek word, *apoluein*, to lose, means that what you once had, you no longer have. Your life as you understood it is, after death, gone. The "you" you thought you were is no longer around. *What you find is not what you lost.* That's the "good news" about heaven! (If you care to check out these texts: Matt. 10:39, 16:25; Mark 8:35; Luke 9:24, 17:33.)

To ask what it is that we will find is to ask too much. That's the mystery of the moon. But I think we can say, simply and profoundly, that life after death will no longer be life lived as individuals. That's really what Karl Rahner was guardedly (because it sounded like heresy!) suggesting back in the 1960s when I first read his little book on *The Theology of Death.* The terminology he used then to speak about life after death nowadays would sound a bit new-agey. He rea-soned that in the "next life," since we would no longer be tied down by the limitations of our material bodies, we would have a "pancosmic" existence in which our consciousness or awareness would no longer be just our own. Rather, we would all have a kind of shared con-sciousness, a deeper mutuality, that allows us, as it were, to live a shared life in God.

"Weird stuff!" I thought then. But my conversations with Buddhism and with the Buddhist central claim that our true exis-tence, in this life and whatever comes after it, is to be "no-selves" has enabled me, I trust, to come to a deeper understanding of, and a deeper respect for, what my brilliant but simple teacher was explor-ing. "Pancosmic" might be a suggestive symbol (or new-age finger!) to point to what we find after we lose our life.

Back in June 2002, during a retreat at Gethsemane Abbey, I think

I got carried away with some flowery imagery in trying to express what I believe about my own afterlife:

> The Buddhist notion of impermanence has helped me feel my way into the question of what comes after death. Will I live on? Yes and no. The nature of reality and of the Divine is impermanence. That means change. Which means – especially in light of what science seems to be telling us about evolution – real change. The purpose of existence, all existence, human and all living beings, is to be conduits, or incarnations, of the Spirit's efforts to bring forth ever-greater beauty and unity in this wonderful drama of existence. The primary way in which such beauty is brought forth is through the interconnections of ever more diverse beings … Another word for such life-giving interconnections is compassion – loving kindness, love.
>
> The image of a garden came up in my readings of yesterday. The beauty of the garden is in its ever-changing diversity. Its beauty takes form in the divergent cast of flowers, and their ever-changing expressions, living and dying. I am to be a flower in this Divine garden. What I am will make it what it is, and what it will be. Will I be part of it in the future? Yes, definitely. But not as the little flower that I splendidly was, but rather as the flowers that splendidly continue to be.
>
> Isn't this a deeper, both more demanding and more satisfying, part of the Christian call to love, to give of self, to die in order that the planet may flower? An overly personalized notion of life after death can be very selfish, bordering on the petty. I give of myself and in the process discover myself. But what I discover can be very different from the self I thought I was – tantalizingly different.

Darkness, my old friend

But I've talked too much. I've not followed my own – or, the Buddha's – admonitions not to ask too many questions, or give too many answers. I guess I can't help it. I'm a Christian, and on top of that, a theologian. I need words. I keep asking questions and exploring possible answers. That's okay, as long as I remember that all my words are symbols, all my answers are but pointing fingers. In the end, after offering words that might be helpful for me and others, after trying to point to the moon, I have to fold my hands and close my mouth and *cherish the Mystery* of life and death.

In the end, all I am really left with is trust. Whatever the value or accuracy of the words and fingers I have used to express the content of my trust, in the end, I just trust. I trust that after my death, our death, the death of this planet, there will be life. Or in the words of Julian of Norwich, all manner of things will be well.

During a retreat in March 2004, my wife Cathy and I, following the advice and example of some close friends, tried to write down our wishes for our final moments with family and friends and for our funeral services. It turned out to be an exercise that not only will be very practical in the future but was very revealing for the present. The following are my own journal entries in preparing for that exercise. I think they offer fitting final words for this chapter.

"Cherish the Mystery" is the way I'd like to formulate the motif of my funeral Mass. Honor the Mystery, don't violate it; let it be. To say too much is to dilute it. All that I want to say is that it will be a darkness that is rich. Also, that it will be something much bigger than little 'ole me. Real and bigger than anything I can now imagine.

So it will be good to die. As Pope John XXIII put it, any day is a good day to be born and any day is a good day to die. What has been the basic, yes the ontological, pattern of life will also apply at death: as it has been good throughout life to breathe in and to breathe out, to take in and then to let go, so it will be good to be mindful and fully present to what looks like the final breathing out, the final letting go. Throughout life, I could never be sure just what that letting go was going to lead to; so also in the final letting go. Just as throughout life I trusted that "something is going on" in my life as I let go, so something will be going on in that last minute. What it is is part of the lovely Mystery, or in Buddha's terms, the lovely Dharma.

In my funeral liturgy, I want the language of the texts and prayers, and all the comments that will be made, to respect the Mystery of death and what it leads to. I want to die trusting in this Mystery, trusting that as it was good to live, so it is good to die, that the values that I wanted to nourish and direct all my decisions during life are also the values that will guide me into death. So, please respect the Mystery. Don't take from me the reasons I have to trust, to hope.

I'd like the opening hymn for my funeral liturgy to be Paul Simon's 'The Sounds of Silence'.

5

JESUS THE CHRIST AND
GAUTAMA THE BUDDHA

If Jesus Christ is rightly considered the heart of Christianity, then this chapter is going to require all the delicacy and boldness of heart surgery. I say "surgery" not because there is anything at all wrong with Christianity's heart itself. The problem, if I may somewhat inelegantly extend the analogy, is found in the doctrinal arteries and veins that are supposed to connect Jesus-the-heart-of-Christianity with the members that make up the body of Christ called the church. For many of us Christians, those arteries and veins are clogged.

I call them doctrinal arteries and veins. Once again, the problem has to do with what we Christians, starting in grammar school or catechism class, have been taught about Jesus. I know I'm not alone when I confess that I often am not able to make the kind of connections with these beliefs that will engage my brain and stimulate my feelings. The clogging is caused not by what Jesus himself has said – that is, his vision of the Kindom* of God as recorded in the Gospels – but by what *others have said about him.* By this, I mean the titles and rankings that were heaped upon Jesus after his death by the authors of the New Testament books and especially by church leaders and theologians in the councils of the third to sixth centuries.

Just what do I mean, or what am I telling myself and my friends (especially those in other religions), when I announce that Jesus is the Son of God and the *only* Son of God, that he came down from heaven to become man, that his "nature" is both divine and human but his

---

* To avoid the patriarchal tones of "Kingdom," I'm following the advice of feminist scholars who suggest this neologism as being closer to the familial society of love and justice that Jesus intended with what the New Testament calls the *Basileia.*

"person" is only divine, that his blood has saved us from our sins and opened the gates of heaven, that he physically stepped out of his burial place three days after he died, that he is physically going to come on the clouds at the end of the world, and that if a Hindu or Muslim knows God and is "saved" it is really because of Jesus?

So often, when I hear the way these foundation-stone beliefs are talked about and preached about in Christian churches, I find myself returning to the privacy of my home or the quiet of my conscience to ask myself: do I really believe? And over the decades I have had to confess honestly to myself – and to other Christian friends who I discovered were making similar confessions – that I don't. I don't because I can't. To say that honestly is as painful as it is unavoidable. When I try to grasp and affirm these foundational beliefs about Jesus in the immediate or literal sense with which they are usually talked about by both laity and clergy, I find that they get clogged up in my mental and emotional arteries.

They don't make sense. They fly in the face of so much of what I know about the world and how it works, and of so much of what I believe about how the Connecting Spirit works in the world and my life. I'm not saying simply that these beliefs are false. I'm saying that, whatever their inherent truth, they're not working for me and, I know, for many of my friends and students. They did work, and therefore were true for the early Jesus-followers insofar as these beliefs "spoke their language" and used the thought patterns and scientific knowledge and symbols of their culture (Jewish and Greco-Roman).

But today they don't seem to speak our language, or they clash with so much of what our scientific and cultural experience tells us. Certainly, I'm not suggesting that there always has to be a snug, comfortable fit between what the Bible tells us and what our culture tells us. Indeed, much of what the Jewish prophets and Jesus himself proclaimed was counter-cultural enough to get them executed! But if there is an ongoing, nagging disconnect between, on the one hand, what I can and must affirm to be true and good on the basis of my present "culturally conditioned" experience and, on the other hand, what "the Bible tells me is so," something has to give. Sometimes something has to give on both sides. Sometimes that "something" is more on one side than the other.

When something has to give on the side of the Bible or traditional beliefs, that something will generally be a matter of finding new language for old truths. That sounds much simpler than it really is. Because the bond between "language" and "truth" is so tight, when we change the language, the truth can look and feel very, very different. It's like the relation between our personalities and our bodies. The person I am with a seventy-year-old body (and all its accumulated experience) will not only look but will truly *be* different from the person I was with an eighteen-year-old body. Same person but – thank God – so different!

Once again, we're back to the topic of Chapter 3 – language. The reason why so much of the traditional way of talking about Jesus gets clogged in the minds or feelings of many Christians is because that language is taken – or delivered – too literally! We again forget that all our talk, including our talk of Jesus as Son of God and Savior, is symbolic, fingers pointing to a moon that is always beyond. The solution for this predicament is the one theologians usually prescribe in such situations: take this language seriously or imaginatively rather than literally. The meaning of these symbols and images of Jesus, like all symbols, does not lie primarily in how people originally understood them in the past (as important as that definitely is) but in how people can understand them in the present.

But here, once again, is the rub we've felt in earlier chapters. How do we understand all this traditional language about Jesus for our times? How can we take these symbols seriously but not literally? Or simply: if the meaning of these words and images is not in their literal sense, then where is it? What is it? What do we really mean when we proclaim – from the rooftops to the world or in the quiet corners of our home to ourselves – that Jesus is God's Son and Savior of the world? Buddhism has been a decisive help for me in struggling with those questions.

MY STRUGGLES: THE JESUS WHO EXCLUDES

Son of God?

Sometimes it's only the questions of a friend that enable you really to feel your own questions. That happened to me the first time I taught at the Center for Religious and Crosscultural Studies in Yogyakarta, Indonesia. That was in 2003; the class was ninety-five percent Muslim. I was explaining why I believed that just as Muslims recognize Jesus as a genuine prophet, Christians can do the same for

Muhammad. That brought one of those "gotcha" gleams to the eyes of Iqbal, one of my brightest students.

"But you Christians also say that Jesus is the Son of God," he retorted. "That makes Jesus very different from Muhammad. We would never say that about Muhammad because we believe that he was a real human being, just like us. Besides, we can't understand how Allah can engender a son. How is that possible?"

Stammering somewhat, I trotted out my standard response: "Of course, literally, God cannot have a son. Many of us Christians would view 'Son of God' as a symbol."

The gleam in Iqbal's eyes grew brighter. "Well, why use it? What does it mean?"

I won't go into the exercise in friendly frustration that was the rest of the class. But I did walk home realizing that the questions of my Muslim students were still really my own. I had been, and still am, feeling the effects of so many intellectual, and even spiritual, complications that had congealed around my Christian belief in Jesus the Son of God, God himself.

If we take it for granted – as all Christians would or should – that God, according to Christian doctrine, is *pure spirit*, non-material, without a body, then what do we really mean when we say that this Pure Spirit can engender offspring and produce a son (or a daughter!), and in fact did so in the person of Jesus the Nazarean? If we insist, as I did with my Muslim students, that this does not mean that God procreates, then what does it mean?

Such questions were "procreated" for me, and then grew stronger, when I first stepped into – and then never really left – the theology classroom. What my Jesuit professors of New Testament at the Gregorian University only suggested in the guarded atmosphere of Rome and the Vatican, my German professors in Marburg laid out with lavish textual analysis of the Gospels: as far as we can tell, Jesus never really called himself the Son of God or claimed divinity. That came later, after his death, when his followers were trying to find words for the way Jesus had touched and transformed their lives. And I learned that one of the stories they told in this effort – the one about Mary being impregnated by the Holy Spirit – was told by only one of the Gospel writers, Luke. St. Paul, who dictated his epistles some twenty years before Luke, didn't seem to know about this virginal and divine conception; in fact he evidently assumed that Jesus was born like the rest of us! The meaning behind my belief in Jesus the Son of

God became for me both more murky, but also more engaging. I felt I was free to explore.

God in a man-suit

While my New Testament courses explored the origins of Christian belief in Jesus' divinity, the courses in "systematic theology" tried to unpack the meaning of this belief. But the venerable professors in these courses (Bernard Lonergan, S.J. was among the most venerable!) did so mainly by working with the language of the early councils of the church. In these meetings throughout the first five centuries of church history, bishops and theologians struggled to achieve a clearer, deeper understanding of how Jesus the man could also be Jesus the Son of God. But the answers they provided in one council always seemed to create even more questions and disagreements for another council. Every answer was a new log for the fire of controversy.

If I may simplify to clarify: one reason why their answers never really worked, either for the scholars or for the ordinary faithful, was that they were trying to explain how, in the case of Jesus' divinity, one plus one equals one! For them, the challenge was to lay out, philosophically and coherently, how the Father-as-God plus Jesus-as-God still equals one God. Or, how the divine person in Jesus and the human person in Jesus still equals one person. As the Council of Chalcedon put it in 451, in Jesus we have a truly divine being/nature and a truly human being/nature but only one individual/person. Despite the efforts of my venerable professors, this official, dogmatic declaration of how to understand the divinity of Jesus still gets stuck in my mental and emotional arteries.

Karl Rahner, in what seemed like a cute, throwaway remark in the midst of his ponderous analysis, helped me identify just where the problem lies. He used to say that for most Christians, Jesus is God walking around in a man-suit. The first time I heard that, I was stopped cold in my mental tracks. "That's precisely true, not only of 'most Christians,' but of me!" I told myself. In my mental picture of Jesus, in the way I had been taught to image him, he looks like a man, talks and walks like a man – but inside, he's God. (Which, when I thought further, looked a bit like Superman dressed up as Clark Kent.) God (or the second person of the Trinity) came down from heaven and when Mary said "Okay" became the inner person of the newly conceived Jesus.

This means that as he moved through Galilee and Judea he knew everything, could foresee the future, could do miracles, and anything else he wanted. He was God among us. God walking around as a man.

Such a widespread view of Jesus is not only, as Rahner pointed out, quite silly or off-putting for many Christians, it is also heresy. It's heresy because Christians are supposed to believe that Jesus was "truly divine and truly human" – and a human being whose human person has been replaced by a divine person is no longer a human person like the rest of us. That's what makes it silly and off-putting – it de-humanizes Jesus. It does not allow him to be "truly human." As Rahner very delicately suggested, it makes Jesus a bit of a freak: a human being without a human "insides." And this puts Jesus in such a totally different class from the rest of us that when he tells us to "go and do likewise" we really can't take him seriously. He was divine, so he knew and could do all and could never really make a mistake. We're just struggling, blundering humans.

The only Son of God

This unsettling sense that Jesus is "out of reach" and therefore superior over all other humans is underlined in red by the traditional insistence not only that Jesus is Son of God but the *absolutely only* Son of God. "Only-begotten," in the language of the Creed. But doesn't the Bible also say that we are all sons and daughters of God? The answer to this natural question creates, for many Christians, even more problems than the original question! Jesus is the *natural* Son of God; we are God's *adopted* children. So, in the family that God seeks to have with humanity, all the kids except one are adopted? I guess the experts would say that at this point the analogy breaks down.

It breaks even further when we compare Jesus not to all other human beings generally but to central figures and founders of other religions particularly. To say that only Jesus is the Son of God means not only that he is different from other religious leaders or teachers but also that he is in a totally different league. It's a difference that makes for a superiority that no one else can claim. If Muhammad is God's prophet, Jesus is God's Son. If Buddha is Enlightened, Jesus is divine. If Confucius is an eminently wise man, Jesus is the very source of all wisdom. This means that for all the wonderful things these other religious figures may have taught their disciples, if these Muslim and Buddhist and Confucian disciples really want to embrace God's

genuine and full truth, they would need to switch their primary allegiance to Jesus and his religion. Their original religion would have to
be either replaced by (according to fundamentalist Christians) or
absorbed into (according to mainline Christians) Christianity. The
"one and only" language that is applied to Jesus spills over to the
Christian church: "only Son" leads to "only authentic religion." All
the others, as Cardinal Ratzinger, now Pope Benedict XVI, told us, are
"gravely deficient."

To respect my own faith as well as that of my Christian brothers
and sisters, I feel the need to move with extreme caution on this point.
On the one hand, the affirmation of Jesus as the only Son of God has
held a pivotal place in the Christian creed through the centuries; to
simply detach it and toss it away is to collapse the entire structure. On
the other hand, to remove "only" from Jesus in a way that would make
all the religious figures just differently colored versions of the same
model car would be to do injustice not only to Jesus but to
Muhammad, Buddha, and Confucius. There are *real differences*
between the religions. To deny or dilute differences is to distort the
religions.

And yet, and yet, if my belief in Jesus as the only Son of God
requires me, explicitly or implicitly, to denigrate or subordinate other
religious figures and religions, then such a belief becomes a clot in the
free and life-giving flow of my faith's circulatory system. I'm sorry. It
just does. And I know I'm not alone.

Jesus Savior of all humankind

Such clots become bigger when we come to another pivotal Christian
belief: "Jesus saves." As God's only Son, Jesus is God's only Savior.
Here, again, we're dealing with an absolutely central building block in
the Christian house of belief. But for me and many of the Christians I
teach or go to Mass with, it has become one of the major stumbling
blocks in trying to connect our faith with our daily lives. When we
find ourselves asking questions like "Just what are we saved from?" or
"How does Jesus save?" traditional answers seem to contradict our
experience of life or our common sense.

We're saved from sin. That's the standard answer. And this sin is
generally explained as a state of affairs that affects both us and God.
There was an "original" blunder that so changed the human condition that we all have one, maybe two, strikes against us before we even

step into the batter's box. Because of both internal and external pressures, we're inclined toward selfishness, and that means sinfulness. Further, because of this sinfulness – both originally given and individually appropriated – we are disconnected from God. According to standard Christian teaching, because of our sinfulness there's a gap between humanity and God. God's love is alive and well, but unless this gap is bridged it can't reach us, and we can't reach it and get to heaven. Original sin means original, and enduring, mess.

I may be painting this picture of sin in overly harsh tones. But I think it would be hard for any pastor or counselor to deny that Christianity's stress on sinfulness or fallenness or separation from God weighs heavily and often harmfully on many Christians' sense of self. Yes, selfishness is a recurring infection, yes, we so often hurt the people we love, yes, it seems impossible really to get our act together. But to define ourselves by these weaknesses and blunders, to see ourselves as "sinners" before we can be "lovers" or "children of God," seems both inaccurate and thoroughly unhealthy. As some theologians have commented, if we're convinced that the starting point for our individual lives, or for the human project in general, is marked "original sin" rather than "original blessing," it's going to be all the more difficult to move on.

If our problem is a condition of sinful estrangement from God, then the role of Jesus as Savior appears to be essentially that of a repairman. I don't mean to be disrespectful, but that's how it honestly looks. There's a rift between God and humanity. God didn't make it that way, the doctrine of original sin informs us, but our ancestral Adam and Eve messed up in the beginning, broke their relationship with God, and we've all been caught in that mess and that distance from the Divine ever since. Jesus comes to fix that mess and to bridge that distance. And until he comes, the mess is irreparable and the distance is insurmountable. As I've grown older, I've painfully felt that such a picture doesn't reflect the reality of what we human beings are, or feel we are. It's as if we first have to convince ourselves that we're thoroughly messed up and lost before we can be picked up and saved.

My discomfort takes on a sharper edge when I try to make sense, for myself and for my students, of the way Christian doctrine has explained *how* Jesus fixes things – how he saves us. From the earliest years of the fledgling community of Jesus-followers, efforts to explain how Jesus saves have been focused on his death by execution on the cross. Associated with the spilled blood of animal sacrifices in the

Jewish Temple (and in Greek–Roman rituals), Jesus was seen as the Lamb of God, sacrificed for our sake, once and for all, to make amends for our sins. His was a sacrificial death. This understanding developed over the years into what is called the "satisfaction theory." His death is certainly an expression of God's love for us, but it is also, and perhaps more fundamentally, the *necessary price* to be paid to make amends for the infinite offence that our sins had leveled against God. God may love us, but God was also offended – some texts even say "angered" – by our disobedience (Rom. 2:8; Heb. 4:3). A price had to be paid. Amends had to be made.

This image of an offended, even angry, divine Parent who then "lovingly" calls for the death of his own Son, or this picture of our sins having to be washed away in the blood of Jesus, may have spoken to the cultural context of the early Christian community. And from what I see and hear on radio and television Sunday mornings, it may still speak to many evangelical Christians. But, for me, if this is what the divine Mystery we call God really is, it's a mystery that repulses rather than embraces. When I first heard that some feminist theologians deem such a God to be an abusive parent, I thought they were going a bit too far. But the more I think about it, I'm not so sure. New Testament scholars tell us that there were many different ways besides this symbol of Jesus as sacrificial victim by which the early community tried to understand how Jesus saves (many different "soteriologies," they're called). Among these other ways, there's got to be a better way.

Only Savior

If we take literally this general symbolism of Jesus as he who fixes the disconnect between God and humanity, then it's clear that not only does Jesus do the job, but he is the *only* one who does the job. If the problem is the need of repair, once the repair work is done, it doesn't need to, or it can't, be done again. And this is why even though the Second Vatican Council took the revolutionary step of recognizing the spiritual values in other religions, and even though in subsequent years Pope John Paul II and mainline Christian theologians in general have affirmed that other religions are also "ways of salvation" by which people genuinely experience the Divine Mystery, still the official teaching of the Catholic and most Christian churches is that if there's any "salvation" to be found in other religions, it has to bear the label "made in Christianity!"

If Jesus is the "price" that was paid to satisfy divine justice, he is the *one* conduit through which God's saving grace pours back into the history of humanity. This conduit, of course, is extended throughout history through the church of Jesus. So if there's any divine, transforming presence of God in the other religions, it has trickled down, as it were, from Jesus and the church. And more so, its purpose is to trickle back to the Christian community where it can really be recognized for what it is – the saving action of God brought about by Jesus. As the Second Vatican Council itself phrases it, all the truth and value of other religions is there as a *praeparatio evangelica* – as a way of preparing people to embrace the Gospel and become Christians.

That's why the "revolutionary" and positive view of other religions launched at Vatican II is called *inclusivism*. It certainly moves away from the exclusivism that prevailed through most of the history of Christianity and that saw no value whatsoever in other religions. But while this new view does not exclude other religions from God's love, it does intend to include them, ultimately, in the Christian church, which is the one really true religion because it has the only real Savior.

As I pursued my theological studies in Germany in the late 1960s I subscribed to this image of Jesus as the one funnel through which all of God's saving action flows into the world and into other religions and then draws them all back into the church. After all, for me this was a liberating break away from my previous Christian exclusivism. I even wrote my doctoral dissertation at the University of Marburg in defense of Vatican II's inclusivism and used it to critique Protestant approaches to other religions. But as the years passed, as I actually studied other traditions, and especially as I made friends with people from other religions, this defense crumbled and my critique boomeranged.

My Muslim Pakistani friend Rahim is an example of what I mean. He was a graduate student in chemistry at the University of Münster and a very devout Muslim. We became good friends when I was in Münster to begin my doctoral research with Father Rahner. Always smiling, unable to speak a mean word to or about anyone, devoted to his family back home, and gifted with a wry sense of humor, he was a welcome member in our circle of fellow student friends. Though he didn't talk a lot about his faith, he prayed five times a day, and always ordered apple juice when we called for our round of beer. I realized, slowly and uncomfortably that, according to my theology, Rahim, although definitely a "good person" and eligible for heaven, would be better off – that means closer to God and a happier human being – if he would embrace Jesus and join the church. That should be my hope for him. Well, I couldn't hope that, because I couldn't believe that. Given what I saw in Rahim, my suspicion began to grow that "God's will" would not want Rahim to be anything but the devout, loving, happy Muslim that he was.

The more friends from other religions I made and the more I studied other religious traditions, the more I felt, often painfully, that my understanding of Jesus the Savior needed revamping and expansion.

Risen from the dead

As if I didn't have enough struggles with many of the catechism images of Jesus, there was one more. For a number of years, it sort of simmered below my consciousness; only as I moved into my forties did I allow it to boil up into words. The resurrection of Jesus. The cornerstone of Christian faith.

What really happened? Did Jesus literally and physically step out of his tomb, walk among his followers for forty days, and then disappear up into the clouds? It all seemed so enchanting, so storybook-ish. If, as I was coming to realize, all our talk of the Divine is symbolic, if the New Testament like all religious literature is filled with symbols and symbolic stories that, though often based on historical events, need not be taken literally, might the resurrection itself be a symbol or a myth whose real truth lies not in its historical facticity but in its empowering meaning?

Part of my problems had to do with the way Christians use the resurrection to prove the truth and the superiority of Christianity over all other religions. "No one else has ever come back from the dead!" It seemed to flat out contradict Jesus' admonition that one's faith should not be based on stunning miracles. In fact, he generally refused even to make an appearance among people who were hankering for miracles (Mark 8:12; Matt. 16:4). And in the story about doubting Thomas, who refused to believe unless he could see and touch Jesus' resurrected body, what was Jesus' punchline to Thomas's insistence on a hands-on miracle? "Thomas, blessed are those who have *not* seen and still believe" (John 20:29). That seems to imply that the resurrection is not a matter of seeing and touching.

My queasiness about the resurrection of Jesus was both deepened and, as it were, blessed when in my undergraduate courses at Xavier University I explored with my students what New Testament scholars were saying about the early stories of Jesus' coming back to life. The experts made clear that in these final chapters of the Gospels (although the earliest manuscripts of Mark's Gospel didn't even include the resurrection!) there is an even more lavish use of symbols and storytelling than in other parts of the Gospels. And there are uncomfortable discrepancies between the stories. Some have Jesus appearing in Galilee, others in Jerusalem. Some imply that he stayed around for a week, while Luke is clear that it was forty days. There is not even agreement about who was the first witness of the risen Jesus, Peter or Mary Magdalene. Some accounts stressed that he had the same physical body he had before his death; others give Jesus a body that could disappear at will, pass through walls, and not be recognized by disciples who had long known him.

Added to that, the very earliest account of the resurrection, in Paul's first letter to the Corinthians, doesn't even mention an empty tomb and insists that the body that Jesus rose with was not "physical" but "spiritual" (1 Cor. 15)! But the really stunning discovery of historians of first-generation Christians is that in some of the earliest communities of Jesus-followers in Palestine, they didn't even talk about the resurrection. Their faith was focused on Jesus being exalted with God after his death and about to come in glory to bring things to a triumphant end.

So the question that has both disturbed and prodded my Christian faith in the resurrection of Jesus over these past couple of decades has been: might the past reality, and present meaning and power, of the "resurrection" be something much bigger than what we have been taught about Jesus stepping out of the tomb and talking with his followers? Might the resurrection be a symbol of something that is much different from and deeper than the miracle of a dead person brought back to life? Might the resurrection be a finger pointing to a moon that is much more than the finger?

In struggling to answer such questions, in trying to review and revivify my belief in Jesus the risen one, Son of God and Savior, Buddhism has proven to be for me, as it were, a different pair of glasses by which I could see things I had never before seen and felt in my Christian heritage.

PASSING OVER: BUDDHA THE ENLIGHTENED AND
ENLIGHTENER

The differences between Jesus of Nazareth and Siddhartha Gautama
are perhaps even greater than the oft-noted differences between
apples and oranges. They lived in very different historical periods
(Gautama some 400 to 500 years before Jesus) and in a very different
cultural context (Jesus at a time when Israel was occupied by a foreign
power, Gautama at a time when India was undergoing great economic and political development). Jesus and Gautama were as different as a modern-day Israeli and Sri Lankan. That's why some would
say that, like apples and oranges, they shouldn't be compared.

But I'm going to do so anyway, mainly because I've discovered that
it is precisely the stark differences between Jesus and Gautama that
have formed for me the lines of communication and comparison
between them. For Buddhists, notions or symbols such as "Son of
God," "Savior," "resurrection" offer few sympathetic vibrations for
their own experience of who Gautama was and how he has affected
their lives. And yet for me, the Christian, it is precisely what Buddhists
say about Buddha that has resonated with my own questions and
thrown new, revealing light on my inherited beliefs about Jesus.
(Whether it might work the other way around for Buddhists is for
them to say.)

What follows in this section is a very selective, and comparative,
review of "Buddhology" – what Buddhists believe about Buddha. The
stress is on religious belief, not historical fact. The Buddhist sources
on the life of Gautama the Buddha, like the New Testament sources
on Jesus the Christ, tell us what the early community believed about
their founder, not precisely what happened in their founder's life.
These are religious texts, not history books.

Siddhartha Gautama: the searcher

While we know very little about what has come to be called "the hidden life" of Jesus, Buddhist sources tell us a good bit about the early
years of Siddhartha (Buddha's personal name). The differences
between the two are immediately evident and exceed, as we noted,
even those between apples and oranges. Had Jesus been born at the
same time and place as Siddhartha (around 563 BCE in what is today
Nepal) they would have grown up in very different parts of town.

Siddhartha's father was king or lord of the tribe of the Shakyas. Unlike Jesus the carpenter's son, Siddhartha led a very privileged, even pampered, life. He married (it was arranged) the beautiful Yashodara, who bore him a son, Rahula. But when it came time for both Jesus and Siddhartha to leave home and step into the world (both of them around the age of thirty), perhaps the most noteworthy difference between them was that while Jesus, according to the reports, had his act together and knew what he was about, Siddhartha was a confused searcher.

One of the few reports of the hidden life of Jesus that we do have shows him in the Temple of Jerusalem with answers that stunned the official teachers of Judaism. Buddha, as he grew into maturity, had more questions than answers. His father, having been warned by a sage that his son would become either a spiritual leader or a mighty warrior, tried to squelch the spiritual questions and nourish the warrior by keeping his son at home and lavishing him with all he might want. But as legend has it, Siddhartha, already a bit of a rebel, ventured out on his own into the surrounding town of Kapilavastu and encountered "the four sights:" a sick person, an old person, a dead body, and a wandering monk. The questions stirring within him came to a focus: how to deal with the inevitable sufferings of human existence embodied in sickness, aging, and death? Might answers lie in a religious search?

So, at the age of twenty-nine, knowing that his wife and son would be well provided for (though none of the accounts give us Yasodhara's viewpoint), Siddhartha left his life of luxury and power, shaved his head and beard, donned the robes of a monk, and began his search. He spent the next six years learning and testing the then-current road maps for the spiritual journey. First he studied with two teachers who led him into the theory and practice of yoga. Results: helpful, but not enough. Then, with five ascetic monks, he vigorously followed the practices of fasting and total self-denial, to the point, we are told, that when he touched his stomach he could feel his backbone. Results: deadening!

Thus it was that Siddhartha met a poor cowherd woman named Sujata who, seeing him emaciated and exhausted, responded with humanity and common sense and offered him something to eat – some milk-rice. Her message, though silent, rang home for Siddhartha. Whatever you're doing to attain whatever you're after sure isn't working! Having eaten the delicious milk-rice, and taken a good bath, Siddhartha at that point realized that if he was going to carry on his search he would have to do it by hewing to what he called "the Middle Way." He would avoid the extremes of "too much" and "too little," of self-indulgence and self-mortification.

Launched on the Middle Way, Siddhartha felt that a breakthrough was imminent. So he sat himself down under what has since been called the Bodhi Tree (the Wisdom Tree), assumed a cross-legged position, and following the basic guidelines of the yogic meditation he had learned, he waited for something to happen.

And it did. By the time the morning sun came over the eastern horizon, Siddhartha Gautama had become the Buddha, the Enlightened One, the Awakened One, he whose eyes had been opened. He saw, not only with his mind but with his whole being, just how the world and human existence in it worked, how everything was in a constant process of interconnected movement, how suffering is caused when humans greedily try to break the interconnections and hold on to things just for themselves, how suffering can be stopped through letting go not just of selfishness but of the very self in compassion for all sentient beings, and finally, how all human beings can realize such Awakening especially through the regular practice of meditation. (All this is a thumbnail summary of his first sermon on the Four Noble Truths.)

Happily weighed down by the bliss of his Awakening, Buddha remained sitting under the Bodhi Tree, we are told, for forty-nine days. When he made ready to re-enter the world and begin the task of sharing with others what he had discovered, there was an encounter uncannily similar to what Jesus experienced right before he began his public ministry. Buddha was tempted by "Mara," the devilish Lord of Death, who tried to persuade him that since no one would understand the depth of his experience he should not waste his time. Better to abandon the world and slip into the full bliss of *Nirvana*. Mara's arguments stunned and sobered Buddha, but they could not overwhelm the great compassion he felt for all sentient beings. Rejecting Mara, he resolved to begin his mission of sharing the good news of the *Dharma*, the empowering truth of what he had seen and become under the Bodhi Tree. The Enlightened or Awakened One became the Enlightener or Awakener. He carried on this mission of preaching and of forming the *sangha*, or community of followers, for some forty-five years.

This *Dharma*, and the Awakening that it inspires, has been

preached and practiced by Buddha's followers for some two-and-a-half millennia.

Gautama Buddha: the Enlightened One

Because of what Siddhartha did, for himself and for others, people were bound to ask *who* he was. There developed what we might call a "Buddhology" – an effort to understand who or what this individual must have been in order to explain the effect he had on so many people. Similar to what Christians have attempted in "Christology," they looked at the work of this man and tried to draw conclusions about his person. As Christians did with Jesus, they began to drape a wardrobe of different titles around Siddhartha. For both Siddhartha and Jesus, among the earliest of their titles, there was one in particular that stuck: just as Jesus of Nazareth became Jesus the Christ, the Anointed One or Messiah, so Siddhartha Gautama of the Shakya was recognized as Gautama the Buddha, the Enlightened One.

If we step back for an overview of the historical terrain of Buddhism, we see clearly two very differently colored streams of interpretation of "the person" of Siddhartha. Both begin in a common source – the affirmation of him as Buddha, the Enlightened One – but they then move in diverse directions. The earlier stream flows through the lands that would call themselves Theravada Buddhist: Sri Lanka, Thailand, Burma, Laos, Vietnam, and Cambodia. The other stream, which started to take shape about 200 years after Buddha's death, moves through the countries that are predominantly Mahayana Buddhist: China, Korea, Japan, and some would include Tibet. The question we will take up after exploring both streams is whether they flow in totally diverse directions, or whether they can crisscross and so enrich each other.

(Some further background in parentheses rather than a footnote: these two major traditions of Buddhism might be roughly compared to the two major forms of Christianity. The Theravadins, like Roman Catholics, boast of being the earlier and therefore more faithful form of Buddhism and tend to be more clerical or monastic. The Mahayanists, like Protestants, claim to have brought necessary reforms which, in particular, made for a more user-friendly Buddhism available to the laity. Some observers stretch the comparison a bit further and note the similarities between Orthodox

Christianity and Tibetan Buddhism, both of them replete with "smells and bells," ritual and images.)

Buddha the teacher

For Theravadin Buddhists, Buddha is primarily a teacher. Or perhaps it would be more accurate to say *the* teacher. This earlier tradition of Buddhism lays great stress on Buddha's humanity. Like us, he was freighted with the limitations, uncertainties, fallibilities of every person's life's journey. Conditioned by what Buddhists believe were the karmic conditions of his previous lives, he had no unique revelations, no divinely instilled light or powers as he walked his path. Like all of us, he had to do it for himself. Certainly, he drew on the guidance and wisdom of his Hindu tradition, and he opened himself to learning as much as he could from others, whoever they were, whether his wise yoga-masters or the practical cowherd woman Sujata. But his bottom line was a thoroughly human line. Awakening would not be gift but gain.

And herein lies the meaning, the drawing power – Christians might say the saving significance – that Buddha has exercised over millions of people for hundreds of years: human though he was, he *did* gain Awakening. He made it. He attained his goal. One of his earliest titles was *Tathagata*, "he who has arrived." His was a long, arduous journey toward the truth of Awakening; in fact, early tradition tells us that Buddha's path to the transforming moment under the Bodhi Tree extends back over multiple lifetimes. But he *did* arrive. And this constitutes his attractive power – he shows, he embodies what all of us can achieve. What he did, we can do; we just have to wake up to it. And this is what Buddha helps us to do – by being our teacher. But a very special, indeed a necessary, teacher. He delivers his lessons not only by speaking but also, and especially, by being. What he teaches he is. And what he is we are, or can be.

But we will realize this and attain it only through our own efforts. Buddha, for the Theravadins, will not, because he cannot, do it for us. As he lay on his deathbed, having eaten some contaminated pork innocently offered to him by a humble blacksmith, he told his disciples: "Be lamps unto yourselves. Be your own refuge. Hold firm to the truth as a lamp and a refuge." If you are to attain what I attained, Buddha was making clear, you, like me, will have to do it for yourselves. And yet he was also making clear that they could not do it by themselves, for the "refuge" they must resort to was both themselves and the truth he had taught them. We need a teacher. But a good teacher, as Buddha makes clear, does not do the work that the students must do for themselves. Rather, he makes that work possible.

So Buddha for the Theravadins is only human, only a teacher. But an extraordinary, even archetypal human being. And an extraordinary, even necessary teacher.

Buddha the savior?

For Mahayana Buddhists, Buddha is also a teacher – but much more. Because of what they understood Buddha to have been during his years on earth, but especially because of what they continued to experience Buddha to be in their own lives, Mahayanists, in an assorted and creative variety of ways, recognized in Buddha qualities that were more than human. They gave him a kind of glorified status by which they could identify the multiple ways he continued to be a transformative presence in their lives. (Some Mahayanists so stressed Buddha's glorified or transcendent aspects that they ended up doing to Gautama the same thing that some early Christians did to Jesus: they distorted his humanity.)

As a Christian, as I've studied these ways and witnessed them in the lives of Buddhist friends, I have to confess that Buddha sure looks like what I would call a savior. His message and life were very different from Jesus', but in the end, he transforms the lives of his followers. To be transformed in a way in which one gains peace for oneself and shares it with others is to be saved.

That Buddha's role was not just to teach but actually to step into human lives and provide assistance for the difficult job of achieving Awakening is clear in the central Mahayana image and ideal of the *Bodhisattva*. We've talked about this image in Chapter 2. The dominant ideal for many Theravadins is the *arhat* – the monk or practitioner who zealously works daily at his or her Awakening, with the steadfastness and strength, as the texts tell us, of a rhinoceros that has plowed its way through the thick jungle of ignorance. For the Mahayanists, the goal is to become, like Buddha, a Bodhisattva, one who having caught a glimpse of the oasis of Awakening (remember the tale in Chapter 2 of the four men lost in the desert) runs back into the desert to lead others to this discovery. That's what Buddha does. He illustrates that one cannot experience the personal transformation of *Nirvana* without automatically devoting oneself to doing all in one's powers to enable others to be transformed also. Buddha the supremely Enlightened One is also Buddha the supremely Compassionate One.

Just how consuming is the Bodhisattva's compassion and how versatile in responding to human needs is captured beautifully in a well-known eighth-century description of "the path of the Bodhisattva:"

> I am the protector of the unprotected and the caravan-leader for travelers. I have become the boat, the causeway, and the bridge for those who long to reach the further shore. May I be a light for those in need of light. May I be a bed for those in need of rest. May I be a servant for those in need of service, for all embodied beings.

In the literature of Mahayana, the difference between a Buddha, a fully Awakened being, and a Bodhisattva, a being who postpones Awakening in order to save others, blurs and blends into two outlets for the same overwhelming experience: what one sees one must share, what one receives one must give, the peace in one's heart calls for the service of others. Simply, to be a Buddha *is* to be a Bodhisattva.

Many Buddhas

As Mahayana Buddhism seeped into Asia and took on myriad cultural forms, the saving role of Buddha exploded into an exuberant lineup of Buddhas and Bodhisattvas. Mahayana Buddhists recognized, we can say, that there could not be just one Buddha. There had to be many, in order to meet the different needs of human beings as they struggled to follow the path of the Enlightened One. While the members of this growing choir of Buddhas and Bodhisattvas were clearly different from their lead singer, Gautama, all of them, each in his or her different voice, harmonized on the same theme of calling and aiding all sentient beings to Awakening. So, although there was only one Gautama, there were many Buddhas and Bodhisattvas.

To identify some of the better-known voices in this choir: there was the most popular of the Bodhisattvas, the *Avalokiteshvara*, the supremely compassionate one, who from his male origins in India became the female *Kuan-yin* ("She Who Hears of the Cries of the World") in China and *Kannon* in Japan. There is also *Manjushri*, the

Bodhisattva of wisdom, who cuts through confusion; *Tara*, the popular female Bodhisattva who takes on different colors corresponding to the different needs of her devotees; *Jizo*, a Bodhisattva who liberates living beings from hell and protects travelers and children; and the *Maitreya* Buddha who is yet to come to save humanity when it faces future dangers.

But after Gautama, the most broadly known and deeply trusted Buddha, throughout East Asia and especially still in modern-day Japan, is the *Amida* Buddha. This is the Buddha who vowed to come to the aid of all those ordinary people who found the list of "required practices" for achieving Awakening to be too much for their busy, work-a-day lives. Sounding very much like St. Paul or Luther, Amida assured his followers that "good works" were not at all necessary: all they had to do was confidently chant his name, or merely entrust themselves to his compassion, and he would bring them to a place after death (called the Pure Land) where Awakening would be assured. Clearly, Amida Buddha fits the job description of a savior.

These, and a multitudinous cast of other Buddhas and Bodhisattvas, will likely appear to the Western Christian like an uncontrolled profusion of the religious imagination. But for these Mahayana Buddhists, perhaps more at ease in the world of myth and symbol, these figures are as real as they may be imaginative. They are all different, and very real, ways in which Buddhist devotees and practitioners experience themselves to be helped along the one path toward Awakening. And as especially the Tibetan Buddhists remind us, all of the Bodhisattvas and Buddhas, in their external reality, are reflections of, and means to identify, realities within our very selves. Remember what we said in Chapter 2 about "self-power" and "Other Power:" for Buddhists these two powers are really two sides of the same coin, two really different forms of the same reality. Whatever outside help a devotee may receive from a Buddha or Bodhisattva turns out, always, to elicit and merge with what one already possesses in oneself.

This understanding of the Buddha's "saving" role as one who shows us who we really are, rather than changing us into something different, is especially clear in another popular and widespread form of Mahayana Buddhism: Zen. Although Zen Buddhist meditation halls are full of statues of Buddha encircled devoutly by the smoke of incense, Zen Buddhists do not speak of Buddha as a savior.

But they do talk a lot about *Buddha-nature*. This is what Gautama, under the Bodhi Tree, discovered within himself. This is what lies hidden, or forgotten, within all of us. Buddha-nature is one of those fingers pointing to a moon that can never be clearly photographed. It points to our true identity as no-selves, as ever-changing participants in the InterBeing of the universe. Buddha's role was to discover it, embody it, show that it is real in everyone, and then teach people the practical steps by which they can discover it for themselves, *within* themselves. Again, that sure looks like another way of being a "savior."

Buddha's three bodies

For Christians, one of the most interesting, and engaging, doctrines of Mahayana Buddhism is contained in the symbolism of "the three bodies" of Buddha. This teaching developed, we can say, as Mahayanists tried to explain to themselves how Gautama achieved and then continues his role of helping others to Awakening. Although this Three-Body Doctrine (called *Trikaya*) took on different forms and functions within the history of Mahayana, its underlying intent was to comprehend what Christians would call the "person and the work" of Gautama Buddha – who he must have been and how he affected and continues to affect people's lives.

Gautama is said to have, or to have acquired, three different but thoroughly complementary bodies or *kaya*. Here, the word body tries to point to and express different ways in which Gautama the Buddha (or any other Buddha) acts or is present. Historically speaking, there was his physical body (*Nirmanakaya*) in which he was present to, or "appeared" among, his contemporaries. But to get at what is most significant about Gautama, what he achieved and became, Mahayanists recognized his "essence body" (*Dharmakaya*). The word "*Dharma*," as we heard in earlier chapters, points to the highest reality that Buddha discovered and became under the Bodhi Tree, the goal of all Buddhists: Awakening, also called "*Nirvana*" or "Emptiness" or "Inter-Being." Gautama became one with this ultimate reality of *Dharma*. This is why an oft-quoted text has him saying something to one of his disciples that echoes what Jesus said to his followers: "Who sees me, sees the *Dharma*." (For Jesus the last word in that sentence was "Father" [John 12:44–46].) To meet Buddha was to meet, and be drawn into the reality and power, of the *Dharma*.

But this ability to embody and communicate the *Dharma* continued, for Mahayanists, even after Buddha's death. And so they came to
speak of his "enjoyment body" (*Sambhogakaya*) – the body by which he
can still, as it were, be "enjoyed" by his followers, the body, we may say,
by which he was still truly and effectively present among them. The
remains or relics of Buddha's physical body could still be found in the
stupas or huge mounded reliquaries that soon marked the lands that he
had walked during life; but his followers came to be convinced that he
was still very much present and active among them in what they called
his enjoyment body. Different from his flesh-and-blood body, it was a
kind of spiritual body by which, even after death, he was still with them.

Teacher or savior?

So, which one is it? Is Buddha's role primarily that of a teacher or of a
savior? Are the Theravadins or the Mahayanists closer to the real
Buddha? For me, such questions have the same teasing feel as the
quandary that in the past pitted Catholics and Protestants against
each other: are we saved by grace or by good works? Is it God's doing
or our doing? Many a theological (and even physical) battle has been
waged over that question. Today, however, over the past three or four
decades, through the calm of conversation rather than the heat of
battle, Protestant and Catholic theologians have come to recognize
that to ask whether "salvation" is a matter of either grace or good
works is pretty much like asking whether a coin is to be identified by
either heads or tails.

It's the same case with the issue of whether Buddha is primarily a
teacher or a savior. To understand how he saves is to realize how he
teaches. To comprehend how he teaches is to recognize how it can
transform and save us. So, to call Buddha *only* a teacher is to run the
risk of picturing him standing before a class of students imparting
knowledge that they duly write down and memorize. The kind of
"knowledge" that Buddha offered was not imparted, it was instilled or
imbibed. It didn't remain in the head but rather vibrated through and
empowered all of one's being. Buddha did not teach only by speaking
but by being. And one "got" what he taught not just by comprehend-
ing in one's mind but by "getting it" in one's whole being.

Also, to call Buddha only a savior incurs the danger of forgetting
how Buddha saves. For Buddhists, salvation or Awakening is never an
entirely external transaction, something that takes place outside the

person. The "Other Power" or help that a Buddha or Bodhisattva may provide, as necessary as it may be, always, at some point, involves or becomes "self-power." Even for the devotees of Amida Buddha, after they arrive at the Pure Land having done nothing else but trust Amida, the experience of full Awakening will have to become their own. The bottom line, therefore, appears to be that there is no contradiction between Buddha the teacher and Buddha the savior. Buddha is such a powerful savior *because* he is such a good teacher.

This general understanding of who Buddha was and how he saves (his person and his work) has been immensely helpful to me in struggling to understand what it means for us Christians to call Jesus Son of God and Savior, as I will now try to explain.

PASSING BACK: JESUS – THE WAY OPEN TO OTHER WAYS

Divinity and Awakening

If we admit that the title "Son of God" was one of the *many* different ways in which the early Jesus-followers tried to articulate who this man was for them, if we also recognize that "Son of God" is not a statement of a literal fact (like the procreating Greek gods) but a symbolic finger pointing to a moon that is always beyond our full view, if we try to continue the ongoing task that Jesus himself gave us when he teasingly asked "Who do you say I am?," might we then understand "Son of God" to mean something like "the Awakened One?" I have grown convinced that we can. And I have discovered in the classroom that this is a much more engaging and challenging way of understanding the divinity of Jesus than talk of God coming down from heaven to produce a being who has "two natures in one person."

But in suggesting "Awakened" as a means of translating "divine," please understand that I am not simply equating the two, as if to imply that Jesus underwent the same experience that Buddha did under the Bodhi Tree. As I'll try to make clear, there are very real and telling differences between the two men and what they experienced. But I am suggesting that Jesus' divinity was not something that "came down" and landed in him; rather, it was something he *became.* And what he became was something within him that he realized, became aware of, responded to. Jesus grew into divinity. He "woke up" to it, much like Gautama woke up to Awakening. And I suspect that much of this waking up and this searching took place during what we call his "hidden life." After all, the Gospels do say explicitly that during those early years "he *grew* in wisdom and grace" (Luke 2:40). And it suggests he left home to study under a teacher, who happened to be his crazy cousin John living out in the desert.

So in trying to understand Jesus' divinity through the lens of Buddha's Awakening, I'm not amputating a traditional Christian belief and replacing it with a Buddhist transplant. Rather, the notion of Awakening has become for me a flashlight by which I've discovered and retrieved symbols and teachings that were on the dusty back shelves of Christian tradition or simply not noticed and appreciated by many of us Christians.

One of the most significant, and I must add oldest, of Christian images of Jesus that Buddha has helped me retrieve is contained in what theologians call "Spirit" or "Wisdom" Christology. Here Jesus was seen and felt to be the embodiment, and therefore the supreme Teacher, of God's Wisdom – or in Hebrew, God's "*Hokma*," which was translated into the Greek "*Sophia*" (both, by the way, female!). And the reason why he was so filled with God's Wisdom was because he was so filled with God's *Spirit*. This was a way of speaking about God that was part of the current Jewish theological vocabulary.

And so the Gospels are full of references to how Jesus was led by the Spirit, filled with the Spirit, empowered by the Spirit. Such Spirit-filled images of Jesus preceded the later symbol, used by John, of Jesus as the incarnation of God's "Word" or *Logos*. Jesus was divine, according to this early Christology, because he was so responsive to the Divine Spirit, because he became aware of this Spirit within him and was fully in tune with it and therefore a perfect expression of it. His spirit and the Divine Spirit, though different, were indistinguishable. To meet Jesus was to meet and feel God's Spirit.

This, mainly this, is what Christians were trying to say when they later called Jesus the Son of God. They called him God's Son not because they were told to do so. They used this way of talking about him because of what they saw and felt in him, because of what happened to them when they were in his presence. To be with this Jesus was, somehow, to be with God, to feel the presence of the Divine. Here was a human being so filled with and tuned to what they called the Spirit of God that they realized that to know him was to know God. So imbued was he with God's Spirit, so identified was he with God's purpose that they would naturally apply to him a symbol or image that was readily available both in their Jewish heritage and in the Greek culture that they soon moved into: he was, par excellence, God's Son.

To understand Jesus' divinity as the result of his waking up to the presence and action of the Spirit within his spirit is to make him a very special human being, but it is also to keep him a very real human being. He remains one of us, though he "arrived" way ahead of most of us. As I "passed back" to what I had been taught about Jesus, having passed over to Buddhist teachings about Gautama, I came to realize the amazing resonance between Jesus' divinity-as-Awakening and my teacher Karl Rahner's "transcendental Christology." Rahner insisted that when Christians say that Jesus is divine, they are not making him into some kind of a wonderful "freak," some kind of a divine Superman who descends from Krypton to save us.

Rather, when we say that Jesus is divine, Rahner insisted, we are saying that he realized the *full potential of human nature*; he attained what all of us, whether we realize it or not, are striving for. We are all imbued with this openness to the Infinite; we are all "finite beings capable of the Infinite." Buddhists might say we are all endowed with and therefore called to realize our Buddha-nature, or in Christian terms, our divine nature. Rahner reminded us that to say that Jesus was truly divine was another way of saying that he was fully human.

With this understanding of Jesus' divinity, his admonition to all of us to "go and do likewise" is a mighty challenging task, but it's not an impossible task. We can't make excuses for ourselves by putting Jesus in a totally different league. What Jesus was, we are called to be. What he attained is what we are all called to strive for. And we can feel and respond to this call even though we can't imagine that we will ever attain what Jesus did, or that we will "arrive" at where he (or Buddha) arrived. He has already crossed the goal while we, so it seems, are still struggling to make a first down. But what is unimaginable is still attainable. If we can't imagine finally getting there and realizing our divinity as fully as Jesus realized his, still, we can come a little closer tomorrow than we are today. We know, or trust, that the effort is worthwhile. Such trust is grounded in what we see, and continue to feel, in this Jesus who became Christ.

"Salvation" = "Awakening"

If my passing over to Buddhism enables me to understand Jesus' divinity as something that he woke up to and grew into through a process of Awakening, it has also brought me to understand what we Christians call "salvation" as our own Awakening – or our own discovery of our divine nature as "children of God." And this, in turn, has moved me to realize that the reason we Christians call Jesus "Savior" is because we have experienced him to be such a powerful "Teacher," or in more Christian terms, "Revealer." To understand salvation as Awakening and Savior as Revealer is, once again, to rediscover and deepen our own Christian tradition.

As regards salvation, Buddhism has become for me another inspiring reminder that when we Christians talk about "being saved" we're not simply talking about "getting to heaven." Yes, we have firm hopes for continued life after death (as we explored in Chapter 4). But that life begins already in this life. In this life, salvation is not just a matter of "previews of coming attractions" – the attractions begin now. And Buddhism has helped me see and feel in my own self that Christian salvation, like Buddhist Awakening, is a matter of waking up to our own unity with God, or oneness with the Spirit. To be saved is to realize that we are indeed children of God; as divine children we can feel the very life and energy of God – that means love and compassion – coursing through our being. To feel truly what Rahner called "our immediacy with God" is to feel the peace and groundedness that enables us to deal with whatever there is to deal with; and it is, also and just as much, to feel a spontaneous and enduring interest in and compassion for all the other of God's children (which, as the Buddha reminds us, includes all sentient beings).

Salvation, therefore, is not a transaction that takes place outside us, but rather an empowering awareness that explodes within and then pervades our entire being. It is, basically, to realize what in our early chapters we called the non-dual relationship that already exists between the connecting Spirit and our very selves.

When Buddhists try to describe how this experience plays out in daily life, they speak, as we have heard, about being a no-self. For Christians, to be Enlightened or saved is described in the mysterious and powerful phrase that occurs throughout the letters of St. Paul: "to be in Christ" (*en Christo einei*). *To be saved is to be in Christ.* What this means can never be adequately put into words. But for me some of the most helpful words are in a passage from Paul's letter to the Galatians that I refer to a number of times in these pages. It's a text that for me has taken on not just deeper but I dare say new meaning when I read it with my Buddhist glasses: "It is no longer I who live, but it is Christ who lives in me" (Gal. 2:20).

In a journal entry from October 2003 titled "No-Self/ *en Christo einei*" I tried to compare these Buddhist and Christian ways of speaking:

> There is a complementarity here. One might say that Buddhism describes our true being in a negative way – call it, perhaps, the *via negativa*. Christianity takes a more positive path, the *via unitiva*.
>
> Our true being, according to Buddhism, is beyond our individual selfhood. We are not selves. What we are, Buddhism does not spell out. Rather, it hints at a way of being that is totally devoid of self, of self-concern, of selfishness – a way of being in which we simply and totally open ourselves to the larger picture and take our place within it.
>
> For Christianity, that place is described as the way of life and being that is embodied in Jesus of Nazareth. Getting beyond the self is living like Christ, with his total trust in the Power that animates the whole, and especially with his central concern for justice and for the marginalized.

In September 2004, during a conference in Padang, Indonesia, together with my good friend and mentor from India Sebastian Painadath, S.J., I might have been a bit carried away:

> It felt powerfully clear to me that I am Christ, that Christ lives in me, that my life is nothing else but giving Christ the opportunity to continue his Spirit and his way of life in and as me. This is what existence is all about. Whether there will be individual immortality, whether there will be a world that is one with the Reign of God, whether we will be able some day to resolve our conflicts nonviolently – it really does not matter. Just let the love and compassion and concern for justice that was Christ Jesus live in me.
>
> "I don't live" – what Paul meant by that, I think, is that if I can feel the living Christ living in me, then I will not be concerned about "me" … As Sebastian put it during our long walk yesterday, let Christ be subject in me.

But Paul's way of speaking about "being in Christ" adds something to or makes clear what is only implicit in the Buddhist talk about Awakening. Salvation understood as a revelation of our being in Christ or of our Buddha-nature is not just a wonderful revealing of what we are; it can also be a jolting kick in the pants, a transforming corrective to what we thought we were. This jolting ingredient is contained in the Christian notion of grace. I was reminded of this by a group of Protestant ministers to whom I was speaking back in April 2004. From my journal:

> A Lutheran friend told me how she had given up on the pluralistic, Jesus from below, [the human Jesus, one of many saviors] frightened here in America as she witnessed how easily Christians flow along with the American way of life. "We have to preserve the paradox," she said, "the tension, between the human and the divine. We can't explain how they come together too easily or neatly or satisfyingly. Otherwise, we lose the power of God."
>
> To be fully human is to be fully divine, I have often said. But by becoming fully divine, the human is changed, lifted up, put in touch with what is more than what it thought it was ... Be ready for the "plus." Be ready for grace.

"Savior" = "Revealer"

To understand salvation as Awakening is to understand Jesus the Savior as Jesus the Revealer. This realization has come into focus for me as I wrestled with the way Theravada and Mahayana Buddhists, in saying two very different things about Buddha as teacher and Buddha as savior, are really saying the same thing. Buddha saves precisely by the way he teaches. Jesus transforms our lives through what his words and his deeds *make known* to us.

The frequent objection to such a picture of Jesus the Savior/ Teacher is that it belittles his role as Savior, making him "just" a teacher, or "just" a model. With my Buddhist friends, I would gently suggest that such an objection perhaps belittles what it means to call Jesus or Buddha a teacher. In Jesus' preaching of the gospel, as in Buddha's announcing of the *Dharma*, they were not just teaching truth that engaged and filled the mind; it was truth that, as it passed through the mind, became energy that filled and then reorganized and animated the entire lives of their pupils – that is, their way of being and living in this world. And this power in their teaching had to do, first of all, with the content of what they taught – that is, with the way "what they said" made clear "what really is." When someone enables us to understand and feel the way things really are and the way things really work, we are experiencing the power of truth; we are experiencing the way "truth sets us free."

But people felt this power of truth in Jesus not just because of what he said but also because of the way he embodied it in his own life. Jesus was such a powerful, "saving" Teacher because he *was* what he taught. He embodied it, he lived it, he incarnated and enfleshed it. The title of a book by Lama Surya Das captures what I'm trying to say: *Buddha Is What Buddha Does.* Similarly, Jesus is what Jesus does. Or, he is what he teaches. That's what so empowers his teaching. That's why what he teaches transforms and saves us.

Philosophers would say that Jesus was a powerful symbol of what he was communicating. Christian theologians (especially Catholics) would use a different term to say the same thing: Jesus was for them the perfect, or the original, *sacrament* of God's truth and presence.

And when we say that Jesus saves by being a symbol or a sacrament we are saying much, much more than that he simply provides us with an image or a picture. Symbols and sacraments don't just give us a picture of truth, they *are* the truth, and they deliver it in a much more powerful, transforming way than mere words or ideas ever could. As the medieval theologians put it, "*symbolisando causant*" – by symbolizing, sacraments are causes of grace or God's transforming power. That's why, as I stated earlier, if we really know what we're talking about when we call Jesus a Revealer or Teacher or Symbol, we would never even be tempted to say "just" a Teacher or "just" a Symbol. A symbol, a teacher, delivers the real thing.

Such an understanding of Jesus–Savior as Jesus–Revealer/Teacher is nothing new. It dusts off and re-polishes one of the earliest soteriologies of the New Testament – that is, one of the earliest attempts of the community of Jesus-followers to try to understand and proclaim how he had saved and transformed their lives. There were many such attempts, each geared to the mindset and culture of the different communities. As I pointed out in the first part of this chapter, one of these soteriologies or ways of expressing how Jesus saves came to dominate in later church history – the one that imaged Jesus, and especially his death, as a sacrifice, as an act of atonement to a God offended by humanity's sinfulness. This is the figure of Jesus as a kind of repairman who "fixes" the problem between God and humanity and bridges the gap caused by sin.

But there were other ways by which the New Testament communities sought to express the power and mystery of what Jesus had done. These are found especially in the writings attributed to John. They see Jesus primarily as the "Word" of God, or the very Wisdom of God, who teaches and embodies the truth of God in such a way that it, indeed, "sets us free" (John 8:32). In this understanding of how Jesus saves the stress is not on fixing what is broken and can't otherwise be fixed, but on revealing what is true, so profoundly and amazingly true that we either miss it or are afraid to believe it. The early followers of Jesus, I think we can say, looked upon Jesus in much the same way as the early disciples of Buddha looked on him – the disciples knew that without this Teacher, they could never really grasp or trust the truth that Jesus and Buddha were making known and embodying. Without Buddha they could not imagine being Enlightened. Without Jesus they could not imagine being saved. Such teachers are saviors.

A passage from my journal of March 2000 was trying to express more personally what it means to experience Jesus as a Teacher-become-Symbol:

> In a way that transcends discursive thinking or hard-hitting proof, Jesus the Christ embodies for me the reality of the Spirit/Divine in my life. He is sacrament, symbol, myth that makes Reality clear and present and gripping. In my mind, as a being swimming in the current of our modern world, I am tossed back and forth on questions of whether there really is a Something More, whether it is truly worthwhile to struggle for love and justice, whether there is anything beyond the portals of death. The results of these struggles are always inconclusive. So, I trust. So I let go. So I believe. It is Jesus, in his story, in his life and death, and especially in the way in which he is present in the community and in my life through the resurrection, that I know in trust what I cannot know in reason.
>
> Simply, because of the way he lived and lives in people like [Archbishop] Romero and [Jon] Sobrino and the Dalai Lama and [Pope] John XXIII – I know that such a life is worthwhile because it is grounded in what is true and real. Not I, but Christ lives in me – that statement takes on more life and meaning than I ever can imagine. *Vivat et regnet in me Christus vivens.* [May the living Christ live and reign in me.]

The uniqueness of Christ – and the uniqueness of Buddha

Understanding the saving role of Jesus, with the help of Buddhism, as that of a Teacher rather than a repairman has enabled me to deal with one of the most worrisome clots in the circulatory system of Christian faith: how to get around all the "only," "best," "final," "no other" language about Jesus in the New Testament and tradition.

As I tried to describe in the first part of this chapter, it seems that for us Christians to affirm what we believe about Jesus, we so often have to deny it about others. To be positive about Jesus we have to be negative about others. In affirming that Jesus is "Savior" or "Son of God," we have immediately to add "and there is no other." Or more directly and uncomfortably, it feels like we Christians have to claim that "my Savior is bigger or stronger than yours." That leads to "my church/religion is bigger than your church/religion" (which is precisely what the architects of St. Peter's Basilica in Rome tried to prove when they clearly marked the spots in the main aisle where all the other major churches of the world would fit!) Such claims that "mine is bigger than yours" may be important for patriarchs and teenage boys. But for many Christians today they sure seem to run counter to what Jesus was all about.

This is where a retrieval of the New Testament perspectives that saw Jesus' divinity in terms of his total responsiveness and transparency to the Spirit of God, as well as the traditions that view his role of Savior as one who reveals rather than as one who fixes, can make a liberating difference in the way we Christians understand Jesus' uniqueness. It enables us to continue to affirm and proclaim who Jesus was and is for us and for the world without having to deny similar roles to other religious figures or founders. It enables us to continue to say that Jesus is "truly" divine and "truly" Savior without having to insist on "only."

This is the difference between "fixer" and "revealer." If salvation is essentially a matter of fixing a problem, or paying a price, then once the problem is fixed or the price is paid, it need not, and cannot, be done again. "Only one fixer" and "only once" make sense. But if salvation is a matter of revealing or embodying the deepest and already existing truth about ourselves and the world – in Christian vocabulary, that we are already children of the Divine called to wake up to and live our oneness with the Spirit – then it is indeed possible that there be other teachers and revealers who have seen and taught other aspects of the Mystery of who we are. In fact, given the diversity of human cultures and the movement of history, it will be probable, maybe even necessary, that there be many teachers, revealers, saviors, each speaking to different cultural or historical contexts, each making known different and deeper depths of what Christians call the Divine and Buddhists call Awakening.

To understand Jesus' divinity along the lines of Awakening and to feel his ability to save as his ability to reveal does not mean that we will no longer speak of Jesus' uniqueness. Christians will continue to say and to feel what people naturally say and feel about their spouses or lovers – "there is no other like him/her." The reason why people are or remain Christian is (or should be) the experience that no one else has so touched them, spoken to them, enabled them to discover who they really are as has Jesus. Certainly we Christians will recognize that there are others, in other religious traditions, who have transformed and filled the lives of other people in similar ways. And perhaps we will have a friendly relationship with those other religious figures like Buddha or Krishna or Lao Tzu, and we will learn much from them. But if you're a Christian, the relationship with Jesus is different, special, unique; there's a closeness or intimacy experienced with Jesus that, just naturally, is reserved for Jesus – perhaps analogous to the sexual intimacy that spouses or lovers feel.

But I also have to add that what makes Jesus unique for me is not simply something only "for me," something that only I or my fellow Christians can appreciate. There's a universal quality about it. I want others to see what I see in him; I want Jesus to make a difference in their lives as he has made in my life – perhaps not as deep or sweeping, but still, a real difference. Here the analogy with marriage again helps me express what I'm trying to get at: I want other people to appreciate and value the goodness and beauty of my spouse, even though I know they are committed, as am I, to their own spouses. I believe that meeting and understanding Jesus can add something, maybe something very important, to their primary relationship. Each of us has his or her central, unique relationship. But that doesn't prevent us from valuing and learning from other relationships.

Understood in this way, the uniqueness of Jesus becomes an energy that does not exclude others; indeed, it includes and is open to others. Again, as in marriage or a deeply committed relationship, the happier, the more satisfied, the more secure I am in my relationship with my partner the freer I am, the more enabled I feel, to appreciate and be enriched by other friends. Philosophically we can say that the uniqueness of Jesus, far from being exclusive, is a complementary or relational uniqueness. By its very nature, it is able to, and it needs to, relate with others, engage them, learn from them, challenge them. As I have truly experienced over the past years, being a "disciple of Christ" has enabled me, I can even say "called" me, to become a friend of Buddha. This is the meaning of the profound and encouraging statement of my good friend John B. Cobb, Jr.: "Jesus is the Way that is open to other Ways."

But, still, what do we do with all the "one and only" language that so lavishly populates our Bible and our liturgies? Let me offer a suggestion. Such language, as scholars of the New Testament point out, is "confessional" language – the way of speaking the early communities of Jesus-followers used in order to put into words what they felt about this man who had so affected their lives. Or, in more ordinary terms, it was "love language." And like all love language, it made spontaneous and abundant use of superlatives and exclusives: "You're the most beautiful person in the world." "You're the only one for me." But – and here's my point – such language is meant to be used in situations of intimacy, not in the presence of other people who have their own spouses or lovers.

Now, "situations of intimacy" for the Christian communities are their liturgies or services where they share their commitments and sing their faith. I'm suggesting that our traditional love language that speaks about Jesus as "the one and only" be reserved for "internal consumption only" – for use *within* the Christian communities, or within one's own personal prayer. It should not be used in our relations with others. It's the way we Christians speak among ourselves to share our faith and commitment to Jesus and the gospel; it's not the way we speak with others, for that would possibly belittle their faith and commitments. This corresponds to the original purpose of such confessional, one-and-only language about Jesus in the New Testament: it was meant to extol Jesus, not to put down others.

Just what makes Jesus unique?

In my efforts to understand the uniqueness of Jesus in a relational rather than an exclusive way I've had to remind myself of something that, as far as I can see, Jesus reveals much more clearly than does Buddha. You might say it is much more unique or distinctive of Jesus than it is of Buddha. I'm talking about the importance of history, or of the particulars of history. As we touched on in Chapter 3, for Christians, history, and all the clutter that makes up history, matters, and it matters for them, I suspect, more than it does for Buddhists. This has to do with the centrality of the incarnation in Christian belief and experience. Even though Christians have traditionally limited incarnation to Jesus, they take its meaning very seriously. The Divine is identified and utterly oned-with the human, with what John's Gospel calls *flesh*: that means with the historical.

So if we extend, as I am suggesting, "incarnation" beyond Jesus of Nazareth and recognize that Buddha and Muhammad and others may be "enfleshments" of Ultimate Reality or Ultimate Truth, then because these enfleshments take place in very, very different historical contexts, the truths that they reveal will be very, very different, one from the other. Or, in Buddhist imagery, if we call Jesus and Buddha different fingers pointing to the moon, we can't simply say they are pointing to the very same thing. They are pointing to really different parts of the moon – or maybe it's better to say they are pointing to different moons, both of which are orbiting around a Mystery that is beyond them both.

In other words, in saying that Jesus and Buddha are both unique manifestations of Holy Mystery or the Spirit, we are saying that although the Mystery may be "one," Jesus and Buddha remain really different. Or perhaps it is more accurate to recognize that there are real differences within the one Mystery. Only by preserving the differences, and then letting them speak to each other, can we preserve and better understand the Mystery.

I started to become aware of this in a journal entry of July 1998:

> I believe in history, in what happens within the course of human–divine events. What happened in the "Christ event" was not just another manifestation of Mystery; it was a historical, particular, never-to-be-repeated revelation of that Mystery – not all of what Mystery is, but something tremendously important about Mystery that cannot be found, in this same form or with this same power or in this same story, anywhere else. Something happened in him that makes a difference in the way the world can now work and become aware of itself.
>
> And the same can be said of Buddha or Muhammad or Moses. They are all particular, unrepeatable, unique revelations of Mystery.

But if we Christians insist that history matters, what is it in the history of Jesus that matters most? Again, we are asking the question: what makes Jesus unique? When we pose that question, we are *not* asking, I want to remind myself and my fellow Christians, what makes Jesus *better* than the other religious figures of human history. Rather, we are asking what is so distinctive about Jesus' preaching and being that, taken away, we don't have Jesus anymore. What makes him who he was – or is?

That's a question that cannot have a "once-and-for-all" answer. It asks about the core identity of Jesus. And the core identity of anyone evolves and adapts as he or she grows through life's changing contexts and demands. Since Jesus, as Christians claim, continues to live in them, his core identity will be expressed differently in different historical or cultural circumstances. So we have continually to answer and re-answer Jesus' question: "Who do you say I am?"

For me (and as I have found for my students) one of the clearest, most convincing, and most challenging ways of grasping and proclaiming the uniqueness of Jesus in our present world has come from my dear friend Aloysius Pieris, S.J., a Sri Lankan scholar and missionary. In Aloy's poetic way of putting it: "Jesus is God's defense pact with the poor." Like other religious leaders and founders, Jesus experienced God or the Ultimate as the power of love. But what was distinctive of Jesus' experience was that this God who loves everyone has a particular, perhaps we can say "preferential" or more pressing, love for those people in every society who have been stepped on, pushed aside, neglected, or exploited. Jesus embodied this preferential, pressing love for the poor and hungry and cast-aside even to the point of dying like one of them – that is, like any one of them would have been disposed of had they woken up and spoken up against the ruling powers. The God embodied in Jesus suffers not only for the victims of the world; this God suffers *like* them and *with* them.

This, I think we can say, is the distinctive or unique contribution that Christians can make to the dialogue with other religions. As I put it for myself in a journal entry for June 1, 2003:

> Christianity is a religion that reminds its followers and all other religions that to know God is to be concerned about the victims of our world and about how we are to reconcile victims and victimizers.

Or as it became clear to me after a trip to El Salvador in 2004, Christians claim that the victims – those who cannot feed and provide medicines for their children – can even take precedence over God:

> The suffering of others must call us, claim us, with a priority that ranks above even the Divine priority. If we are not responding to the suffering of others and think we are responding to the reality of the Divine, we most likely are following a misleading path. The Divine, at least as it has made itself known in Jesus, calls us precisely in and

through the suffering of others. Here is where the Divine becomes real for us. If we are not experiencing the claim that the suffering ones make on us, we are not experiencing the reality – or at least, not the full reality – of the Divine.

So while what the Salvadorans say is true – "*primero Dios*" [God comes first], it is also true to say "*primero las victimas*" [the victims come first] … God is Ultimate but the Suffering Others are Immediate.

Pieris has told me that when he talks to his Buddhist, Hindu, and Muslim friends about the uniqueness of Jesus in this way – as God's defense pact with the poor – they hear it as "good news," not as something that belittles them but as something that enriches them.

The resurrection: the Christ-Spirit alive and well

Back in the first part of this chapter, I concluded my nagging problems about the resurrection of Jesus with this question: "Might the resurrection be a finger pointing to a moon that is much more than the finger?" Buddhism has enabled me to answer that question with a solid, engaging "Yes!" It has added strength and clarity to the other "yeses" I had already found in the New Testament and in the work of Christian scholars.

More particularly, the teachings of the "three bodies of Buddha," especially what the Buddhists say about the enjoyment body by which Buddha continues to be a presence and power in their lives, has helped me, I believe, grasp and feel more deeply the mystery of the resurrection. It has enabled me to unpack and apply what Paul might have been getting at with his insistence that when Christians talk about resurrection they're talking about a spiritual body (*soma pneumatikon*) rather than a physical body. And this is why, I suspect, Paul almost makes synonyms out of "the risen Christ" and "the Spirit of Christ" – because Jesus' risen body was a Spirit-ual body! It was through the Spirit that the early Christians could (as the Buddhists might put it) "enjoy" Jesus after his death – that is, continue to feel his presence and power. As one New Testament scholar (Luke Timothy Johnson) puts it with forthright clarity: "The Holy Spirit is the mode of Jesus' resurrection presence to the world: 'Now the Lord is the Spirit' (2 Cor. 3:17)."

I know there are Christians who would shift uneasily in their pews

– or their pulpits – when considering such a Spirit-based understanding of the resurrection. It looks to them like a spiritualizing of the
risen Christ that loses all concern for the physical body; or, it appears
to be a subjectivizing shift that reduces the "fact" of the resurrection
to a "feeling" in the hearts of his followers. I agree: to "dematerialize"
or to "over-personalize" what Christians believe about Jesus' resurrection is to lose touch with Christianity's distinctive claim that the
Divine becomes real in the flesh and blood of history.

But such concerns, understandable as they are, miss the point.
When Paul tells us that the risen Lord is the Spirit, and when we say
that the resurrected Christ is the Spirit-Christ, in no way are we saying
that this Christ-Spirit is now disembodied. On the contrary, this resurrected Christ-Spirit is now real *in our bodies.* As Paul announces, *we*
are now the Body of Christ (1 Cor. 12:27). Even though Paul does not
speak about the empty tomb, even though he doesn't tell us just what
happened to Jesus' own physical body, he is very clear and insistent
that Jesus-become-the-Christ is no longer limited by his own physical
body. He is alive in the flesh-and-blood lives, in the daily decisions
and actions, of those who have experienced him and chosen to
follow him.

Also, when Jesus' disciples experienced the risen Christ-Spirit,
they were experiencing something *real,* something that could not be
reduced to "just a feeling." The conviction that he was alive for
them and in them was not the result of subjective auto-suggestion
or hallucination or stubborn "let's-believe-anyway." Faith in the
resurrected Jesus was brought about by something other than, or
more than, the disciples' willpower or emotions. They *encountered*
this Christ-Spirit; they felt its presence and power in the midst of
their gatherings and in their individual lives. These encounters,
as some theologians suggest, most likely took place in essentially
the same ways that they continue to take place today: when the disciples did what Jesus told them to do and gathered together to retell his
story and break bread. There was a "real presence" – that means a real,
spiritually tangible presence in their physical lives – of Jesus in their
midst.

With such an understanding, based on such an experience, of the
risen Christ as the Spirit-Christ in the body and bodies of the
Christian community, questions such as "Was the stone rolled back?"
"Was the tomb empty?" "Are the Easter appearances to be taken literally?" become secondary. Whatever *really* happened, what is most

important, is that the Christ-Spirit is *really* alive and well and continuing "to do his thing" in the lives and bodies of his followers. I realized this with reassuring clarity on Easter Sunday, 2004:

> To celebrate Easter is to believe, to feel, to affirm that Christ is alive in and as me. All the discussions about the empty tomb, about the nature of the appearances, about the kind of body he had may have their importance. But centrally, decisively important is whether I truly believe that He as the Christ-Spirit is actually risen and alive in me. If he's not alive in me, which means in us the community, then so what if he stepped forth from the tomb, so what if he had a physical body.

But in suggesting that the risen body of Christ bears similarities to the enjoyment body of Buddha, we can't forget that they are, as it were, two *different* bodies. Just as the Three-Bodies doctrine of Mahayana Buddhism makes clear that Buddha's enjoyment body is related to his physical body, so too the risen Christ-Spirit can be understood and experienced only in reference to the historical Jesus. This I believe is the point of all the elaborate (and sometimes contradictory) stories of the Easter appearances in the Gospels. The early Jesus-followers wanted to make it clear, to themselves and to those who would follow, that this risen Christ-Spirit is the same Jesus-Spirit that walked the hills of Galilee and streets of Jerusalem. Again, we're back to a defining characteristic of Christianity (which it inherited from Judaism): whatever is universal and available to all peoples and all religions has to be anchored in the concrete particularities of history. This is what makes the one, universal Spirit to be the truly different Spirit in the different religions.

Therefore, the risen Christ-Spirit, because it is and remains the Spirit of the particular, historical Jesus, is both similar to, but really different from, the universal enjoyment body of Buddha, which for its part is related to the physical body of Gautama.

I was trying to put this into words back in July 1998:

> The Risen Christ, therefore, is an expression of that universal presence and power of the Divine that can be found in all religions. And yet, it is a very particular presence, unique, different from all others, with a difference that cannot be lost if the world is to be properly saved. The Christ-Spirit is essentially linked to the historical Jesus as to that which gives it its particular character. To know the "mind of Christ," to live the "law of Christ," to be

born and grow into the image of Christ, we must keep our historical moorings in Jesus of Nazareth, and in the records that we have of him.

And on Easter Sunday 2004, I felt the need to make clear what these "historical moorings" call for:

And what or who is this Christ-Spirit? How does this Christ-Spirit differ from the presence of Spirit in followers of Buddha or Muhammad or Krishna? Jesus embodied a Spirit that underwent crucifixion because of a driving concern for compassion and justice. We Christ-Spirit-people are part of the Divine that empties itself into suffering for others, especially for those who don't count. This does not in any way make us better than Buddhists or Muslims or Hindus. But it sure can make us different.

And so, at the end of these passings over and back between Gautama the Buddha and Jesus the Christ I venture to say, cautiously but firmly, that my relationship with Buddha has clarified and deepened my commitment to Christ. I trust that it can do the same for many of my Christian sisters and brothers.

6

PRAYER AND MEDITATION

In this chapter we're going to be talking about practice. That's basically a Buddhist term. I've often heard my Buddhist friends talk about their "practice," or ask each other, "What's your practice?" What they're talking about is something that applies to, or can be found, in all the religious traditions of the world.

A loose definition of "practice" would be all the things people do to maintain, nurture, and give growth to their spiritual lives. "Practice" would be everything a person tends to in order to keep his or her spirituality in good shape. Although a person doesn't have to be religious – i.e. a member of a religious tradition or community – to be spiritual, in this chapter I'm talking about people who are part of a tradition or community, that is, Buddhists and Christians. And I'm examining their practices; all the things they do to make sure that their religion remains spiritual.

So one's practice would embrace all the things that one's religious tradition recommends in order to keep in touch with the core experience or experiences that gave birth to the tradition itself and that have been passed down through the centuries to keep the tradition alive and well. One's practice is what one does to assure that the heart of one's religion is also one's own heart; it makes sure that one is personally plugged into whatever it was that got this religious tradition going and that keeps it going. Practice, more concretely, is all the things that a Buddhist or a Christian does to keep connected with the experience of Gautama or Jesus, and to make sure that the energy of this experience grows, adapts, applies, and holds tight in all the rough times of life.

One's spiritual practice, essentially, would be the daily meals that are necessary to maintain our spiritual health and wellbeing. In our spiritual lives, if we're not eating properly, we're going to get sick.

Naturally, Buddhist and Christian practices include a lot of different things for different people or for different historical times. But I think that most of the experts would agree that if we want to point to the main ingredients of what would be Buddhist or Christian practice, we would best talk about, for Buddhists, the last three pieces of the Eightfold Path: right effort, right mindfulness, right concentration, all of which constitute what can be called right meditation. And for Christian practice, the pivotal place would have to go to prayer, in both its liturgical and its personal forms.

Thus the title of this chapter: prayer and meditation. Or, the *words* that are essential for prayer, and the *silence* in which meditation takes place. In what follows, I hope to figure out for myself and describe for others why and how Buddhist meditation has helped me deal with some of the struggles I've experienced with Christian prayer.

MY STRUGGLES: WHAT AM I DOING WHEN I PRAY?

Before I spill out my prayer problems, a little cautionary reminder is in place. In talking about practice and prayer, I'm dealing with matters that are intensely personal – even more so, I think, than the topics of the previous chapters. The difficulties I laid out regarding "God," "Afterlife," "Christ" were primarily (though not exclusively) conceptual, even philosophical: how to image God, how to understand life after death, how to explain the divinity or saving role of Jesus. But in dealing with prayer, we're exploring not so much "what makes sense" but "what works." Although the two are intimately connected (what makes sense should work; what works should be based on good sense), they're different. Among honest, open-minded people, it is not impossible to achieve general agreement about what makes sense; but there's a lot more room for diversity about "what works." I feel that what makes sense for me should make sense for you. I'm not so sure I can say the same thing about "what works."

So, in describing my personal problems with prayer, I don't want to imply that these necessarily are or should be problems for other Christians. In what follows, I just want to set forth, as honestly and clearly as I can, what in Christian practice doesn't work very well for me. And I invite others to ask themselves if they feel any similar difficulties. If they do, the rest of this chapter will, I think, be helpful. If not, I hope it will still be interesting.

A difficult conversation

Christian prayer, for the most part, has been understood and practiced as a conversation with God. It's the part of our relationship with God in which we not only connect with the Divine, we also communicate with the Divine. In prayer, I stand here, in a church or amid nature; God exists there, in heaven or in my heart. And we communicate with each other. The communication usually takes place by means of words, but it can also be through gestures or ritual or song. We talk, God listens, and we expect, or hope, that God responds in some way or another. Although prayer is certainly different from human forms of conversation (one of the participants is divine), it still remains essentially an interacting in which both sides communicate with each other.

And there lie my problems. Now I know that Christian prayer-as-conversation can be a very deep and satisfying experience for many people. But as I've grown older, especially as I entered my middling years, my prayer-conversations have become strained. Both in liturgical prayers, as I try to join the community from my pew, as well as in my personal prayer, as I sit quietly in my room, I just can't get into the flow of words directed to God. It's not that I have intellectual problems that I am consciously aware of. I just can't do it. When I try to talk with God, the words falter, or feel flat, or forced, or simply inappropriate.

As a pious student at St. Joseph's Grammar School (I was an altar boy and you had to be pious to make the cut) and throughout my high school and college years in the seminary (during which years we would on average spend three hours every day in chapel) I could talk with God pretty much the way I would talk with my mom (Dad talked a lot less than Mom). But I can't anymore. Maybe it's because of the psychological maturation in which we realize that our parents cannot play the role of God, as well as because of a spiritual maturation in which we realize that God is so much more than a parent.

Receiving and giving

So much of Christian prayer, it seems, follows an all too human parental model. We receive from our parents what we need. And, as we grow older, we give them what they need. Most of prayer-as-conversation with God has to do with either asking for something for ourselves or giving something to God: we either petition God or we praise God; we speak words or we offer worship.

I wonder just what percentage of Christian prayer could be classified under the heading "petitionary." We do a lot of that kind of praying. That's because we have a lot of needs. We let God know about them, in the expectation that he will do something. Essentially, we're asking him to intervene, to step in and make a difference. For me, one of the main problems with this notion of a God who steps in to help us is that all too often it ends up discriminating against someone else. Good weather for our Sunday picnic is bad weather for the farmer's parched fields. If God cures my sister's cancer, why doesn't he do it for everyone's sister, especially if others are praying for their sisters as hard as I am for mine?

Also, when I ask that God step in to fix something, or save the situation, or even to help me, I have the itchy feeling that I'm either asking God to do things God is not responsible for or things for which I'm really responsible. Does God really change the weather? Will God help me in an exam, especially if I slacked off during the semester? Such "make it better" or "change this" kinds of requests I made of my parents when I was a kid, and appropriately so. But not any more. Such requests of parents are generally inappropriate for adults. I think this applies to our relationship with the Divine as well.

We refer to our liturgies or services as "worship." We gather to worship and praise God. That's the main reason for our gathering. But I find myself asking: does God really need our worship? Why do we have to spend so much time singing his praises and bowing down before him? Does God really need to be told again and again how great he is? (Many women might respond: "If God is really a 'he,' yes!")

The frequent answer to these questions is that we're not doing it for God but for ourselves. God doesn't need to be worshipped, but we need to worship God. But I still have to ask: why? If God really doesn't need it, why do we have to give it? Or, if worship is fitting as a reminder to us of our difference from God, then I would still have to ask: why do we have to do so much of it? Why do we have to keep reminding ourselves that God is different from us, greater than us, transcendent over us? Such a stress on difference creates distance. Big difference makes for big distance.

This depiction of the God of Christian prayer as "distant" provides the stepping stone to move from description of the problem to its diagnosis.

Diagnosis: Too Worshipful and Too Wordy

The tangles I encounter in trying to pray as I was taught to pray are really the practical upshot of the problems I have with traditional ways of speaking about God that I outlined in the early chapters of this book. "God-talk" (a term we theologians threw around a lot during the 1970s) is at the root of my prayer problems: if I have serious problems in the way I talk *about* God, I'm definitely going to have problems in trying to talk *to* God.

Drawing on those early chapters for help in trying to diagnose the reasons why I find myself so often shifting uneasily when I try to pray with my fellow Christians, in either liturgical or friendly settings, I think there are two primary causes of my uneasiness. Christian prayer is generally too worshipful and therefore dualistic. And it is too wordy.

Dualistic

With so much of Christian prayer occupied as it is with praise and petition, or worship and appeal, it is evident that the diagnosis of my problems with Christian theology or imaging God (especially in Chapters 1 and 2) applies just as much to my problems with the Christian practice of prayer: the God to be worshipped and petitioned remains the transcendent Other and the Super-person. The God I am called upon to "pray to" remains "the other" who stands outside me or opposite me, and who then has to enter or intervene into my life or the life of the world. This God is a person, a "you" with whom I am to have a relationship in which I communicate and speak.

If such images of God don't fit my thinking or feeling about the Divine, if, rather (as I described in the early chapters), the image or symbol of the Divine that I have refocused with the help of Buddhism is that of the inherent, connecting Spirit – not a Person but a personal energy – who lives and acts and has its being not just within but *as* each one of us creatures, if this Spirit is not simply an "other" facing me but a creative, sustaining vitality that is one with my vitality, or in

Paul's words if it is truly "not I who is doing the living of my life but the Christ who lives as me" – if my relationship with the Divine is truly *non-dualistic*, if the Christ-Spirit and I are not two (but also not one), then I'm going to need spiritual practices, or forms of prayer, that enable me to express and feel this thoroughly unitive, non-dualistic relationship. And there's the rub. I can't seem to find such practices readily at hand in what I have been taught about prayer in my Christian life and formation. So much of my Christian practice relates me to a God-out-there. Dualism.

Wordy

So often in Christian liturgies I find myself gasping for breath because I'm suffocating with words! Christian prayer, especially liturgy, is so verbose. This sense of suffocating amid words comes from what I've tried to describe in Chapter 3 – the growing awareness among us Christians that God is Mystery and must remain so – that the unknown part of God is much, much larger than the known part we are expressing in our prayers and services. Our words don't seem to respect that Mystery not just in their quantity but also in their quality.

We use a lot of words, but it's the way we use them that feels inappropriate, even disrespectful of the Mystery that is the Divine. We use them so facilely that it feels like we're using them literally. It sounds and feels like the Divine really and literally is "an Almighty Father who grants our prayers," or that Jesus will literally "come on the clouds at the end of time," or that we have to implore God "to accept our sacrifice."

Maybe I'm overreacting to this problem of literal words. The solution for such problems is to remind myself and my liturgical community that all our words are symbols and that we have to take them with a grain (or a spoonful) of hermeneutical salt. Okay. But that doesn't get at what I think is my deeper problem with the place of words in my Christian practice. Words are not only always inadequate in expressing the Divine Mystery, but they can be actual *impediments* to experiencing the Divine Mystery. Therefore, it's not just that we have to take them symbolically; sometimes we may have to set them aside. Stop using them.

What I've come to realize – and maybe here I'm getting ahead of myself and would have to thank the Buddha for this – is that the reality and the Mystery of the interconnecting Spirit, precisely because it is Mystery, has to communicate itself or be felt through other ways than through words. Indeed, maybe the deepest experiences of this Mystery can take place only without words. If my use of words becomes an addiction of words, perhaps I am missing other, or deeper, ways of feeling or waking up to the reality of the mysterious presence.

I'm talking about the need for *silence*. If the Divine is truly a Mystery that is beyond all human comprehension, beyond all human ideas and words, then any spiritual practice must make room – lots of room – for "the practice of silence." And that is what is missing in my Christian practice. That is certainly evident in the constant clamor of words or songs or music in Christian liturgies. The only time in Catholic Masses when no one is talking at all are the moments of reflection after Communion, and if the priest is in a rush, they don't last very long! In my Christian liturgies, I have realized that I pine for silence.

Also in my own personal practice of prayer I have grown to feel the need for silence. But here too I must say that I haven't had much help in my Christian education and training in learning how to make use of silence.

What about Christian contemplation and meditation?

But aren't I forgetting or neglecting something? What about the rich tradition throughout Christian history of contemplation and meditation? What about the guidance for methods of meditation and use of silence that I can find in the great Christian mystics – Teresa of Avila, John of the Cross, Meister Eckhart, Julian of Norwich, Ignatius of Loyola? These are the masters of unitive prayer, the architects of and guides through the silent corridors of mystical castles. So, in my search for a more non-dualistic, silence-filled diet of Christian prayer, am I complaining of hunger when there is plenty of food in my own spiritual pantry?

There are, no doubt, abundant mystical provisions in the Christian pantry. I will try to identify and open some of them in the last section of this chapter. For the moment, I offer two observations, one positive and easy to state, the other negative and harder to pin down. First, there is a broadening recognition within the Christian churches of North America and Europe (the churches I know best), both Catholic and Protestant, that the mystical provisions in the

Christian pantry of spirituality have not been readily available to the "ordinary faithful" on this side of the pulpit, perhaps because they weren't available (or of concern) to the pastors in the pulpit. Over the past thirty years or so, this mystical or contemplative aridity has been recognized and addressed.

One of the very first students I met at Xavier University back in 1975 has gone on to exemplify what is taking place in multiple sites throughout the States. Paul Peterhans, working out of Seattle with Father Thomas Keating, O.C.S.O., has organized the "Contemplative Outreach," which uses practices like "centering prayer" to convince laypeople that they can be contemplatives even though they have a nine-to-five job and a car full of kids. Such efforts toward a "mystical renewal" of Christian practice can only help address the problems with prayer that I, with many of my fellow Christians, face.

Now comes my second, and more slippery, observation. I'm not sure whether the resources of Christian mysticism are able, all by themselves, to deal adequately with the nagging pains of chronic dualism and dependency on words that I and other Christians suffer from. In an attempt to focus what I mean, let me reflect briefly and selectively on my own spiritual training.

As I alluded to above, I had a lot of it. My years in the seminary and religious life provided me with a prolonged, explicit training not just in Christian prayer, but in meditation. My spiritual formation in the Society of the Divine Word was modeled on the proven, profound, and practical spirituality of the Society of Jesus. That meant I had two years of novitiate, which is a kind of spiritual boot camp in which, at that time, a sergeant-like German novice-master trained us carefully and then tested us rigorously in the many practices of the spiritual life. During those novitiate years, we twice did a thirty-day silent retreat in which all our energies were devoted to the meditative exploration of the Spiritual Exercises of St. Ignatius. Throughout my twenty-three years as a member of the Society of the Divine Word, we had a yearly eight-day retreat and monthly days of silent recollection.

And every morning from 5:15 to 6:00 we practiced formal, personal meditation (in preparation for Mass that followed). The meditation took place in chapel; you could either kneel or sit – and if you found yourself dosing off, stand. (I marveled at – and occasionally envied – two of my classmates who perfected the ability to sleep while standing!) Throughout the day we were encouraged to "practice the presence of God," and as an aid thereto the bell would ring every fifteen minutes and we would all join in a brief "Quarterly Hour Prayer." All of these practices were intended to keep us in touch with and therefore responsive to what was called "the divine indwelling."

This rigorous routine loosened up a good bit after the Second Vatican Council (which loosened up and broadened the vision of the Catholic Church in general). But a daily round of silent meditation and liturgical prayer, together with ongoing spiritual counseling and spiritual reading, remained essential ingredients in my Christian practice. And it was all basically good. I'm sure that today I'm a better person for having had this training and kept to this practice. But as the years moved on, while I was still a priest and especially after I left the ministry and tried to continue my spiritual practices while teaching at Xavier University, the methods of meditation I was trained in just weren't working as they should, or as I needed them to. The main problem, I would say now, was that my sense of God was changing and becoming more non-dualistic, and my spiritual practices, as I had learned them, couldn't make the adjustment.

As I look back now, I think I know why. The methods of meditation and contemplation that I learned, though they insisted on silence, filled that silence with so many unspoken words and images. The silence wasn't really silent. To describe the problem technically, the methods of meditation that I learned were essentially *discursive*. Even though we literally "kept our mouths shut," we were still working with ideas, images, concepts – or unspoken words. To give an example, for our meditations we were generally asked first to picture for ourselves a "*compositio loci*" – a particular, concrete scene in the life of Jesus and imagine ourselves within it, in relationship to him. We were instructed to stir up our "affects," our feelings toward Jesus or God the Father. In these different ways, we were trying to enter into and feel the reality of a personal relationship with the personal God. And in the end of each meditation, we were to voice our conclusions, our resolves, our requests.

Some experts in Christian spirituality might observe: this is meditation, not contemplation. This is still the preparatory work that leads to the real thing. Meditation is still looking from the outside into the unitive experience of God. Contemplation is looking from the inside out – from within one's oneness with the Divine, for which there are no adequate words. Yes, I understand that the goal of Christian practice is such contemplation and its sense of being united with God. But my frustration was, as I look back now, that all my meditative spadework never produced the fruit of contemplation. Of course, part of the reason for that was my lagging efforts during those early morning hours. (Maybe real contemplation isn't possible without coffee – or green tea!) But I really think that my lack of success in contemplation also had to do with the inherent difficulties we Christians have in leaving the terra firma of words behind and soaring into the groundless space that is real contemplation.

I say those difficulties are inherent because as long as an aspiring contemplative is operating, consciously or subconsciously, with an image or symbol of God as a "being" or entity that exists or can exist as an "other out there," by itself, an entity that has its being beyond or independently of our being, and, finally, an entity that – I mean, who – is a "you" who stands outside and addresses my "I," then I'm afraid it's going to be very difficult, if not impossible, truly to get beyond images and words. The understanding of God as the Transcendent Someone who created the music somehow gets in the way of us really letting go of all words in order to be the music.

A deep well with leaky buckets

The earlier admonition I gave myself needs repeating: these are my difficulties, not every Christian's. Maybe my problems with contemplation result from my not being a contemplative. That concern was somewhat mitigated by an observation made to me by a friend who has had a lot more experience in hardcore Christian contemplation than I. Father Michael Holleran, who spent twenty-some years in a Carthusian monastery and is now a parish priest in New York, commented in an email in June 2007: "In my long experience of our Christian tradition, I have found that we are high in inspiration, but low on technique; long on ideals and content, but short on method."

That confirms my own experience of Christian practice. But it also gives me hope for my Christian practice. The Christian tradition and its spirituality is a well that contains waters of deep mystical, non-dualistic experience of the interconnecting Spirit and of the Christ who lives and acts within the community of believers. The Christian mystics attest to the depths of this well. But for many of us (even for contemplatives like Michael) the buckets that we have at our disposal to draw up those waters have holes in them. At least most of them seem to. For me, they're not working as well as they need to.

So while the well remains the same, the buckets can be repaired; maybe some of them can be replaced with newer, remodeled buckets. Buddhism has helped me do that – or begin to do that. Buddhism has some mystical methods that we Christians might take a good look at and make good use of in repairing or remodeling our own. For me Buddhism has been a rich, indeed an indispensable, aid in renewing and expanding the repertoire of my Christian practice. That's what I hope to explain in the third part of this chapter.

But first we have to take a closer look at how Buddhists go about their practice.

PASSING OVER: THE POWER OF SILENCE

It's not an exaggeration, I believe, to say that Buddhism was born as part of a search for a spiritual practice that really worked. Gautama, like many of us today, was a frustrated practitioner. Frustrated with the forms of public ritual and prayers that were available within his Hindu tradition, he decided to go out in search of a religious practice that could deliver the necessary goods – one that would enable him to deal with the sufferings of life, and that would foster a life lived in tune with the way things really work.

In carrying on his search, Gautama was part of a reform movement that recognized the inadequacy, or the impropriety, of much of the then current Hindu practices embodied in what has been called Brahmanism. It was believed that for the universe to function properly, humans had to carry out certain rituals, usually rites of sacrifice. These prayers, incantations, ceremonial sacrifices had to be done in a very precise manner, with very precise formulae; only the priests knew the proper actions and words. So, God or the gods required sacrifice; sacrifice required priests (Brahmins); and the priests required a price. (For older Catholics who remember $5.00 Mass stipends, this sounds uncomfortably familiar.) For Buddha and others, it was as much an insult to one's intelligence as to one's pocketbook.

So, as we heard, Gautama left his palace and his family (both well cared for) and started his search for the perfect, or at least an effective, practice, one that did not have a price-tag and one that actually helped deal with the sufferings of life. For some six years, he studied under and followed the recommendations of recognized masters of practice. These were the experts in mind-control and meditation. He learned a lot. But what he learned didn't pass his pragmatic test of enabling him to deal with suffering and to figure out who he really was. Finally, on his own, he planted himself under what was to be called the Bodhi Tree. And that's where it happened.

Right meditation

As we know, Buddha discovered Enlightenment or Awakening under the Bodhi Tree. But he also discovered a practice that worked – a way of waking up. So while Buddha's great contribution to humanity is the assurance that we can all wake up and see things as they are, maybe his greater accomplishment was to instruct people, in engaging detail, about what they have to do in order to find what he found. He not only announced a goal, he provided a map. He not only made a preposterous promise (You too can be a Buddha!), he offered the means to test the promise. In the image I'm using, he discovered a new well, and provided the buckets.

It's all right there in what came to be called Buddha's Eightfold Path. The three main components of this Path are slickly defined and provide a neat sequence of intermeshing components:

Trust Take Buddha's message seriously; try it and see if you like it (Right View and Right Intention).
Morality Buddha's practice will lead you nowhere if you are unnecessarily hurting others (Right Speech, Right Action, Right Livelihood).
Mental discipline You've got to work with your mind, in silence (Right Effort, Right Mindfulness, Right Concentration).

The spiritual core – or the core of the spiritual practice – in the Eightfold Path is embodied in those last three directives. Practically, and somewhat loosely translated, they call us to work hard at it (Effort), to be truly and fully aware of what is going on in us and around us right now, right here (Mindfulness), and to sit tight and let happen what will happen (Concentration). Really, what Buddha was urging, on the basis of his own experience and with his own personal and practical insights and emphases, is his own version of the Hindu tradition of Yoga – time-tested methods of working with your body in order to work with your mind in order to deepen your awareness of yourself and your world.

What these three directives add up to is what Buddhists through the centuries, as well as we today, call *meditation*. That term packs a variety of meanings – from the naked, wrinkled gurus on their mountain tops to the naked, bronzed Californians next to their swimming pools; from old age to New Age. Now certainly, as we will see in a moment, even among Buddhists there is no one orthodox way of meditating. But there are many unorthodox ways, especially among those whose contemplation is focused on the financial rewards of the meditation business.

So let me boldly venture a description of meditation that I think will receive the endorsement of most Buddhist teachers: formally but broadly, meditation is an intensely personal and individual practice (though usually done under the guidance of a teacher and often with others) by which we seek to move (or be moved) beyond words and concepts and our usual ways of thinking in order to grasp (or be grasped by) reality as it really is. Meditative practices generally stress bodily postures that keep us alert and allow us to breathe naturally. And they generally take place in silence, both physical and mental. (Sometimes this silence is sought after through words or sound, such as rhythmic chanting.) The proven outcome is that the more we can remove the screen of thinking and of identifying reality with our thoughts and feelings, the more we can see things beyond thought that we never saw with thought. Or, as I have put it for my undergraduates in terms inappropriate for the Awakened One: "Shut up and you just might wake up!"

Now Buddhist teachers can get pretty tough in their insistence that if Buddhist practice is going to work, if the Buddhist path is going to lead you anywhere, you're going to have to commit yourself to the practice of some form of meditation consistently, regularly, faithfully – and that generally means daily. If St. Paul urged us "to pray always" (Eph. 6:18), Buddha would make it "meditate always." Perhaps this is one of the sharpest, but also one of the richest, admonitions that Buddhists gently offer Christians: for any spiritual practice really to bear its potential fruit, for any spirituality to go as deep as it can go, some form of regular meditation – or some practice by which we silence our usual way of thinking and speaking – is literally a *sine qua non*. Without it, nothing really happens.

So although, as already pointed out, for Buddhists there is no "one and only" way to meditate, let me try now to describe some of the forms of meditation I have experimented with and how they might help us to calm down and wake up.

Different ways to practice silence

Despite the sometimes bewildering variety of Buddhist meditational practices, one can safely say that they all have but one intent: to help us realize that we are what Buddha said we really are, *anatta*s or no-selves, or as one of my Buddhist students recently urged me to put it, "selfless selves." All Buddhist practices, like Buddha himself, seek to transform human beings from selfish selves into selfless selves, or more philosophically, from self-centered beings to other-centered beings. To wake up to one's true nature, to one's identity as a selfless self, is to realize, and to live accordingly, that one's identity or one's wellbeing is really not one's own but is shared with all of reality. My own self, my real happiness, is really and truly and mysteriously also your self and your happiness. Really to know and live that truth is to be Awakened.

Now it seems to me that according to Buddhist teaching there are two significantly different but thoroughly complementary ways of coming to this realization of one's selfless self. One can look *into* one's self and happily realize that there's nothing there to claim as one's own. The more one peers within, the more one discovers that there is no-thing or nothing substantial to see. What one finds instead is something that is not a "some-thing;" it therefore cannot be described. It is, rather, a Groundlessness and an Inter-being-ness that sustains and constitutes one's existing. This is what the Buddhists call *prajna* – the wisdom of seeing things the way they really are.

Or, instead of looking within, one looks *beyond* oneself to all the other "things" that make up the universe, and when one witnesses the suffering that also marks their existence, one also feels the *claim* they make on oneself or the *responsibility* one experiences for them in their suffering. In looking beyond ourselves, in sensing the way others call forth our caring and concern, we feel, once again, the InterBeing that vibrates between all of us and constitutes all of us. Because of the way all of the "I's" lay claim on my "I," I sense that in some very real but mysterious manner they are part of my "I" and I am part of theirs. I therefore care about their "I" as much as I care about my own. This is what Buddhists call the dawning of *karuna* – the compassion for all sentient beings that reveals our selfless selves.

So, corresponding to these two manifestations of our natures as selfless selves, there are two broadly different but mutually enforcing types of Buddhist meditation: those that promote *prajna* or wisdom, and those that promote *karuna* or compassion. In both forms of meditation, we existentially and experientially feel and become aware that our true being is to be part of a larger interconnected picture and that being part of this larger picture means feeling compassion for all sentient beings.

Let me now sketch how the assembly of commonly recognized forms of Buddhist meditation might line up according to these two general categories.

Wisdom-filled silence

1. *Vipassana meditation*

Theravadan Buddhists would hold that this is perhaps the oldest form of Buddhist meditation, therefore the one closest to Gautama's own practice. Literally, it means "seeing clearly" – that is, seeing accurately, seeing what's really there, not what you think or feel or what you're told is there. Nowadays, therefore, it's often called "insight meditation" – the kind of meditation that can provide new discoveries about the world that enable new ways of living in the world.

The primary aim of Vipassana meditation is its essential method: to be totally aware of, present to, in tune with whatever it is you're looking at. The intent is to allow whatever it is you are regarding to reveal itself to you before you can impose on it your preconceived or socially determined ideas or preferences. To enable this to happen, the meditator is called upon totally and almost ruthlessly to do nothing else but observe. Just keep looking, observing. Whenever other thoughts start buzzing around, swish them away as gently as you would a fly, and return to looking.

A workable starting place is your own body, and so practitioners of Vipassana often begin with a kind of "body scan" – moving with full awareness and observation through all the parts of your body, trying to feel and be present to the top of your head, your eyelashes, your fingertips, down to your toes. Even if you can't find anything to feel in a particular part of your body, be aware of that. Or, you can be aware of your breathing, allowing yourself to feel the movement of the air through your nose, within your lungs, out through your nostrils. Just feel it; be present to it; let it be present to you.

By means of this concentrated and disciplined attention to what is happening, especially within one's very body, an awareness of the way things work, and the way one's very self is part of this working, grows. One starts to realize that "reality" is greater than our mind and its concepts and can't be controlled by our thinking. Better to allow our thinking and feeling to follow the lead of, and even to give ourselves over to, the flow of reality. Doing this, our awareness can deepen into relaxation and peace and freedom. We grow into the realization – or better, it grows into us – that everything is changing and we are changing with it, and that our real identity is to let the change happen and move with it.

2. Zen

We might say that "Zen" (or "Chan" in China) is what happened to Buddhism when it moved into China around the sixth century CE and adapted to, as well as adopted from, Chinese culture and spirituality, especially Taoism. The particular form of meditation that developed within China and then moved into Korea and Japan, where it sank even deeper roots into Japanese culture, has been called *Shikantaza* – "just sitting." And that's pretty much all we should say about Zen meditation. One is called upon to do nothing else but sit. Don't let anything else occupy you or concern you but sitting, just sitting. So while other forms of meditation might be pretty heavy on instructions, Zen is definitely instruction-lite.

Its dominant intent is to move beyond thought. For Zen, thoughts are the fundamental problem. Why? Because there is another way, besides thinking, of knowing and understanding the reality of the world and of oneself. This other way operates without, or beyond, thinking. In fact, thought gets in its way. The whole purpose of Zen meditation, therefore, is to clear the ground so this other way of perceiving-without-thinking might make its appearance.

Zen meditation is a constant process of catch and release: notice what is going on, notice the thoughts and feelings, and then let them go. The same applies to the breath. For Zen, observing one's breath is not an end in itself. Rather, watching or counting our breaths is a tool that we use to let go of our thinking. When thoughts or feelings push their way through the front door of our awareness, we return to observe our breath as a way of ignoring them and allowing them to leave through the back door. Counting one's breath is a tool for discounting one's thoughts. But ultimately, the Zen meditator wants even to drop the tool of watching or counting breaths; he or she wants to "just sit" without thinking about sitting or breathing.

But we have to be careful here. As the famous Zen master Eihei Dogen admonished us, Zen meditation does not aim at "not-thinking" but at "non-thinking." Zen is not about achieving a completely blank mind that would be an inert, directionless mind. "Non-thinking" means that when thoughts and feelings come, as come they will, we don't cling to them, we don't insist on them, we're not determined by them. And the more we don't try to control or master life with our thinking, the more we find that we are, as it were, embraced or held by life. An awareness grows that we are not so much living life as life is living us. We let go in order to let life. Or in more traditional Zen language, we gradually (or suddenly) become aware of that which is beyond all thought and comprehension – the Reality of ever-changing, always creative Emptiness or InterBeing. We are it. And it is us.

And the more we are aware of the embracing presence of InterBeing or *Sunyata* as we sit on our meditation cushions, the more we will be aware of it throughout the rest of the day, wherever we go, whatever we do – washing dishes, cutting grass, sitting on the toilet.

3. *Vajrayana visualization*

Vajrayana, as I pointed out earlier, is the Buddhist tradition that, like Catholic or Orthodox Christianity, delights in smells and bells, sights (*mandalas* or *tangkas*) and sounds (*mantras*). And so it offers a form of meditation in which audiovisuals play a central role. But unlike its Christian counterparts, the goal of the images and sounds is *prajna*, not prayer – that is, an experience of oneness in which differences are bridged between the pray-er and the prayed-to.

Meditation based on visualization can take many forms in Vajrayana practice (it is also found in some Pure Land Buddhist practices). The template would include the following. The meditator/ practitioner selects his or her *yi-dam* – a particular holy being, Buddha or Bodhisattva, who, the practitioner feels, embodies his or her own needs and aspirations. Then, in a first stage of the meditation, called Generation, one attempts to generate or create in one's mind as graphic, detailed, and enchanting a picture of the deity as possible –

one's *yi-dam*, as it were, on the big screen, in Technicolor. This can be done by visually absorbing an image of the deity, often located in an intricate painting called a *mandala*. Chanting *mantras* can also help (sounds or particular sayings associated with the deity). All of this is intended to produce a graphic and particularized image of the holy being that fills and delights one's mind whether one has one's eyes open or shut.

Then comes the next stage, called Completion, in which the deity and the meditator merge. All the particular energies and qualities of the *yi-dam* – courage, peace, wisdom, creativity, equanimity, compassion – are realized to be one's own. All the particular details of the deity's image are felt to be residing in one's own image. The image "out there," with all its energies and virtues, now becomes one's own image "in here." They are different, but they are also one.

The final recommended phase of this visualization practice is to drop it all and let it dissolve into Emptiness so that one does not become attached to it. (Sand *mandalas*, hours in the painstaking and meditative making, are brushed away with a sweep of the broom!) Thus, when dropped or brushed away, the visualized image makes room for the meditator's direct, non-conceptual experience of what the Dzogchen tradition calls "the Great Natural Perfection" – the peacefulness and restfulness of things just as they are.

Images in such visualization-meditations are powerful vehicles, even necessary vehicles, but only means to an end, fingers that show us the moon.

In the end, then, there is *prajna* – the wisdom of realizing that one's own existence is not one's own but is unfolding within the existence and interconnectedness of everything. What one visualizes is what one already is.

Compassion-filled silence

What we've called the "wisdom-filled" forms of Buddhist meditation are the ones that most people think of (if they think of anything) when Buddhism comes up in conversation. Less known, the "compassion-filled" meditation practices can be more easily and briefly described, perhaps because they are more user-friendly and to the point. The "point," of course, being the discovery that our true selves are selfless selves.

1. Metta *meditation*

The purpose of this meditation practice is to stir up or uncap *metta* within one's whole system of seeing and feeling so that as soon as one *sees* anyone or anything one feels *metta* for it. Usually translated as "loving kindness," *metta* designates a love that is both hot and cold. It's cold insofar as it is unconditional and unattached – it gushes as soon as the spigot is touched and it pours out without any bills to be paid. But it's hot because it comes from the heart, with all the heart's heat, and it embraces the loved one just as he or she is, beauty or beast. Buddhism actually believes that every single human heart is a reservoir of such *metta*, such loving kindness. *Metta* meditation is a means of opening that reservoir and assuring that its waters flow freely.

A *metta* meditation unfolds in stages, each intended to widen the channels through which the waters of loving kindness can flow. Sitting with your back straight on your cushion or in your chair, relaxed and breathing deeply and naturally, you start by sending thoughts or feelings of loving kindness to yourself. A fairly standard formula for doing this is something like the wish: "May I be well and happy. May I be free of difficulties and trouble." After some moments of trying to feel that this love is really flowing out of you and is really being received, you move on to doing the same thing for someone you love or feel close to – your spouse, partner, children, friends. "May Moira be well and happy ..." With the waters flowing freely, you broaden the channel, and in the next step direct it toward people you feel indifferent toward – the faces in the subway, the doorman you said hello to this morning. The next step might require you to turn up the water pressure as you direct it toward people who, to be honest, you wish weren't part of your life or this world – a nagging boss, a self-ish politician, the "self-centered bas****" who cut you off this morning. With a little extra effort, you can actually feel yourself sending them, maybe even embracing them with, the wish that they be happy, well, without suffering.

Some *metta* meditation teachers suggest that for some of us, if we want to put the most difficult person to love at the end of the process, we should finish, rather than begin, with ourselves. However we arrange these steps, one of the earliest descriptions of *metta* practice (in chapter 9 of the *Visuddhimagga*) adds two more. In a fifth movement, we gather all four recipients of our love – ourselves, loved ones, strangers, foes – around one table and embrace them all, collectively, with the warmth of our love and good wishes. And then, in an open-ended sixth step, we let our loving kindness flow out freely and gradually into the whole universe, to sweep over all sentient beings, all mountains and vales, all plants and planets.

2. Tonglen *meditation*

Found among schools of Tibetan Buddhism, this type of meditation seeks to reap the spiritual benefits of the basic meaning of the Tibetan word *tonglen*: taking and giving. Like *metta*-practice, *tonglen* reaches outside the self to others, but while *metta* meditation is a kind of universal love policy, *tonglen* is on a rescue mission searching for those in special need. It starts where Gautama started – with suffering. Its basic process is to find someone who is suffering (that's the easy part), and then to visualize taking that suffering into oneself, and then giving to those who are suffering one's own happiness and peace. So as you sit in silence, you breathe in the very particular suffering of whoever it is you wish to help. It can, of course, be someone you love but, similar to *metta*-practice, it can also be the suffering of someone you don't like, only here you're not just sending that person good wishes, you're taking on his or her suffering. And then you visualize yourself, as you exhale, breathing out warmth, strength, confidence – whatever it takes in order for the person to deal with and remove his or her pain.

Tonglen practice is grounded on the Buddhist conviction that suffering can actually provide a way of connecting us, or of reminding us of our connectedness; more so, the suffering of others can be the means for popping the cork on the natural compassion and love (*metta*) that we have for others but that for so many of us is stopped up. Thus suffering becomes a means of overcoming suffering. By eliciting our natural loving kindness, it stirs us to feel our connectedness, and by doing this to help both others and ourselves.

Pema Chödrön, who is a much-acclaimed teacher of *tonglen*, expands on how this process can work. It can actually be shifted into reverse and run just as well backwards as forwards. In those moments when you yourself are the sufferer – when you're caught in the tight grip of anger, despondency, fear, revenge – *tonglen* in reverse starts with your own particular pain but then asks you, immediately and before you let yourself sink into that pain, to connect it with all those thousands, perhaps millions of people throughout the world who are aching under the very same kind of suffering. Simply, you remind yourself that your particular pain entitles you to membership in the universal club of sufferers. And you send out warm wishes of well-being, of patience, of love, of strength to all of them, including yourself as one of all of them.

And here, as my wife tells me, is where the magic of *tonglen* sets in: by connecting with others, but setting your own suffering within the suffering of others, by wishing well to others as a way of wishing well to yourself – marvelously, you find yourself able to deal with your own suffering. It's not just that "misery loves company." But the company is actually a remedy for the misery.

And yet, given the way Buddhists understand the world and the way things work, there's really no big mystery to the way *tonglen*, and *metta*, meditation can instill us with peace and strength. That's precisely the way "compassion-filled silent meditation" is supposed to work. By connecting with others through wishing them well or taking on their sufferings, we are simply doing what our true nature as "selfless selves" calls for: in *metta* meditation we are making the wellbeing of others to be as important as our own, and in *tonglen* practice we are actually placing the happiness of others before our own. But in doing precisely that, we are discovering our own happiness and the ability to love and take care of ourselves. There is really no difference between our wellbeing and theirs. To realize that is to realize the InterBeing that contains us all. Such realization is Awakening/Enlightenment.

The key role of mindfulness

Within these different recipes for Buddhist meditation, there is a particular required ingredient that provides the yeast without which nothing rises. It's been implicit, or mentioned in passing, in the previous descriptions. I need to explain it more clearly since it's an ingredient not easily found in most Christian pantries – or, if found, used too sparingly.

I'm talking about *mindfulness*. Especially with the "wisdom-filled" forms of meditation, the silence and the sitting take place within an atmosphere of mindfulness. Mindfulness sets the stage, and then becomes the stage, for the practice of meditation. Indeed, according to the meditation master Thich Nhat Hanh, if we are truly mindful we are truly meditating: "to meditate means to be aware of what is going on ... what is going on in your body, in your feelings, in your mind, and in the objects of your mind, which are the world." What he is saying is profound, but especially for a Western Christian like myself, it can also be very difficult.

The awareness that Thich Nhat Hanh says constitutes mindfulness includes a lot more, and makes more demands, than I first imagined when I started my study and limping practice of Buddhist meditation back in the early 1980s. It's not just a matter of realizing what is happening; that's only the first step. Two other steps have to follow: one must fully *accept* what is happening but at the same time not *cling* to what is happening.

Pema Chödrön has helped me tune into what are the demands and the promise of mindfulness-practice. In her *The Wisdom of No Escape*, she lays out three progressive steps that can enable us both to be mindful and to act mindfully:

Precision Really face, don't ignore or run from, what is going on in you or around you. Be precise, be honest, and face it in all its beautiful or ugly detail. If you're feeling fearful, angry, depressed, joyful, satisfied, envious, or if someone just said something really nasty to you, or if you've just witnessed on TV the horror of some natural catastrophe or human violence – recognize it, don't deny it, let it be there in the form and feeling of whatever it is.

Gentleness This goes a step further than facing what is happening. It means being kind toward it, even embracing it. Hold it gently and lovingly, not necessarily because it is good (as it may be), but because it is there. It's what's happening. Don't just tolerate it; accept it. Even if it is something downright awful, hold it gently, and if you can't love it, at least be nice to it.

Let go Having faced whatever fact or feeling is there, having accepted and embraced it, we now release it. It's like taking a firm hold on the collar of a prancing puppy, tickling it under its chin, and then releasing our hold to let it go its way. We don't shout at or shoo it, we just loosen our hold on it – and allow to happen what will happen.

And at this point there can take place what Thich Nhat Hanh calls "the miracle of mindfulness." It's miraculous because it's uncanny, happily weird. In truly being mindful of the thoughts or feelings that the world around us stirs up within us, we find that we are able to deal with whatever the world throws at us. By acknowledging honestly, accepting lovingly, and then releasing gently whatever positive or negative emotion an event or a person or a memory may arouse within us, we find ourselves free to deal with it or respond to it in a way in which we, not the emotion, are doing the responding. Mindfulness is a bit like one of those security machines that you have to walk through at airports: it identifies and then removes what it is that can threaten both your own and all your fellow passengers' wellbeing. Mindfulness prevents us from being hijacked by our emotions or opinions.

But that's only half the miracle. Mindfulness also enables us to respond to those emotions in an appropriate way. Having as it were disarmed the feeling or thought of its immediate intensity (either negative or positive) by identifying and then letting it pass through, we find ourselves able to do with it what needs to be done. "What needs to be done" is vague, I know. But that's part of the wondrous workings of mindfulness. It frees us, or enables us, to act rather than react. And whatever that "action" will be – whether to walk away or to confront, to oppose or repose – it will be done peacefully and compassionately from an inner composure and an outer caring for both friends or opponents.

In a journal entry from June 1998, I tried to detect the source of this miracle of mindfulness:

> In being mindful, no matter what the feelings or thoughts are – no matter how intense the anger, deep the hurt, confusing the sense of inadequacy – they will tend to take care of themselves. Or better, they will be dissolved in the light and warmth of the fundamental unity, of the interconnecting Spirit, that is the most fundamental fact of existence.

It doesn't always work that way. But so often, miraculously, it does.

PASSING BACK: THE SACRAMENT OF SILENCE

What I have discovered in my efforts to pass over to Buddhist practice, and what I'd like to suggest to my Christian community, is basically this: we Christians need an additional Sacrament (for Catholics that would make eight, for Protestants, three). It's the Sacrament of Silence – or, the Sacrament of Meditation. Further, I believe we Christians need to receive this Sacrament regularly and frequently, as frequently as every day. (Fortunately, it's a self-administered sacrament, so we don't have to go to church.)

What I'm recommending in the remainder of this chapter is not a substitution for Christian forms of prayer and liturgy. It is an *addition*, and, I believe, a necessary addition. By the Sacrament of Silence I mean, essentially, the kinds of spiritual practices that make use of silence – both verbal and mental – in order to hear the deeper, inner meaning of the words we say we believe. The Sacrament of Silence seeks to administer a way of knowing that goes beyond thoughts and words. If Mystery is the goal and content of all religious experience, then Silence is a necessary means of letting Mystery speak.

As I recognized earlier in this chapter, such a use of meditative silence has certainly not been excluded from Christian practice; but neither, I believe, has it been sufficiently included. Nor has it been meaningfully and engagingly taught to the Christian faithful. Buddhism, I believe, can help Christians rediscover, or "re-member" and reconstruct, neglected contemplative ingredients of their own tradition.

It has certainly helped me. My exploration of Buddhist practice has enabled me to understand and make use of the Sacrament of Silence in my Christian practice. I can honestly say that without these Buddhist practices, without this Sacrament of Silence, I don't think I'd be able to pray as a Christian. Buddhist practices have helped to clarify my understanding and to facilitate my use of Christian prayer and ritual. Personally, I pray differently now. Ritually, I feel the language of liturgy differently. I'm not saying that this can or should happen also for others of my Christian family. But it might. And I suspect it would be good if it did.

Using a Buddhist bucket in a Christian well

I'm talking about practices that will help us Christians draw on the mystical contents of our faith. Buddhism can help Christians to be *mystical* Christians. It can help us respond to the need that we identified in Chapter 2 and that Karl Rahner summarized when he declared that for Christianity to survive into our contemporary age it will have to reappropriate its mystical depths.

To pick up the analogy used earlier in this chapter, Buddhism offers Christians a bucket that can draw up the mystical depths of the Christian well. It provides a help, for some a decisive help, to realize and enter into the non-dualistic, or unitive, heart of Christian experience – a way to be one with the Father, to live Christ's life, to be not just a container of the Spirit but an embodiment and expression of the Spirit, to live by and with and in the Spirit, to live and move and have our being in God.

So I'm proposing a Buddhist means to a Christian end – Buddhist tools for a Christian project. Here, some people – especially some of my colleagues in academia – might object. Isn't this a category mistake? Or more directly: isn't this like using baseball strategies to achieve football ends? True, what Christians are after is different from what Buddhists are after. For Christians it's identification with the Christ-Spirit. For Buddhists, it's realizing their Buddha-nature. And yet, both of these very different experiences have something in common: they are *unitive, non-dualistic, mystical* experiences in which we find that our own identity is somehow joined with that which is both more than, and at the same time one with, our identity.

This is what the Buddhist practices are so good at – achieving such unitive experiences in which the self is so transformed that it finds itself through losing itself. And that's where I believe Christians can learn a lot from Buddhists. By watching how Buddhists go about achieving their "goals," Christians can better "come home" to their own.

But there still may be a source of uneasiness: isn't this exploitative of Buddhism? Might it be another, more subtle, example of Western Christians falling into their colonial propensities to take advantage of other cultures and religions for their own benefit? No doubt, that's a proven propensity and a real danger. But exploitation happens when one side of a transaction is left impoverished or harmed. What I'm "taking" from Buddhism isn't in any way diminishing Buddhism; in fact, the Buddhist teachers I've known have been happy to give it away.

What I'm doing is, rather, an example of the giving and taking between religions that we call dialogue. Raimon Panikkar describes it as the "mutual fructification" that can and must take place between the religions. We all have a lot of different things to learn from each other. Maybe some day a Buddhist will write a book with the title *Without Christ I Could not be a Buddhist!*

So let me now try to describe some of the ways in which I have added – I trust I can say integrated – Buddhist recipes into my Christian practice: how Buddhism has enabled me to understand and daily receive the Christian Sacrament of Silence.

Receiving Christ in the Holy Communion of silence

If for St. Paul and for Christians through the centuries to be a Christian means "to be in Christ Jesus," if the substance and decisive meaning of the resurrection is, as we tried to say in Chapter 5, that the Christ-Spirit that animated Jesus continues to live on in, and animate and direct, those who call themselves followers of Jesus, then the heart and the ongoing heartbeat of Christianity is a mystical union with the Christ-Spirit. This is what the Sacrament of the Eucharist or the Lord's Supper intends to keep alive. As we Christians bless and consume the bread and wine, our bodies take in and become his body; he lives in us and we in him. That's why the Lord's Supper is a Sacrament that all Christians – Protestant, Orthodox, Catholic – regard as essential to the ongoing life of the community.

I believe that what I am calling the Sacrament of Silence is, for a growing number of Christians, just as essential. For the mystical experience that the Sacrament of the Eucharist seeks to bring about through words and symbols, the Sacrament of Silence seeks to bring about without thoughts or things. The two sacraments, I can say from my own experience, need each other.

Meditation, understood and practiced with help from Buddhism, is a much-needed way for Christians to get beyond the words and conceptual coatings that so often obscure the Mystery at the heart of Christianity – the Christ-Spirit breathing in the community. In meditation, without using words or concrete images, we simply sit with this Spirit. Silence is a means of recognizing it, letting it be, opening oneself to it. I am communing by simply being. The silence enables my being, which is a "being in Christ," to express itself, to make itself felt. It's not only that I become aware of the Christ-Spirit in me; I find myself to *be* the awareness of the Christ-Spirit. I'm not doing the living: as Paul put it, Christ is.

In a journal entry of July 2003, I tried to express it this way:

> To sit in silence is for me to sit in awareness of "Not I, but Christ" – or as a Buddhist teacher once told me, an awareness of "I ... Christ." In my sitting, I want to get beyond techniques of counting breaths, watching my thoughts, identifying "thinking, thinking ..." – as important and essential as such techniques are. What I really want to do is allow Christ to be Christ in and as me. This is a reality, something as real as the next breath I will draw – the living Christ, the Spirit

of Christ, breathes in me and as me. In sitting, I want to sink into and be surrounded by that reality.

I have found that, sometimes, instead of counting breaths – a method suggested by Buddhist teachers especially at the beginning of meditation – I can use a Christian mantra to mark my breaths: "Not I" on the intake, "Christ" on the out-breath. Again, I'm not trying to think of the meaning of the words; in a sense, I'm trying to let them think me.

When I sometimes use the *metta* or *tonglen* practices described earlier I find they take on particular Christian energy when I feel the compassion that I am sending out to others to be the compassion of the Christ-Spirit living as me. In a journal reflection of March 2005, I realized that as I try to carry this practice into the day, every time I feel called to compassion, I can be made aware of the Spirit:

> I am constantly reminded of being the Christ-Spirit – precisely by the steady procession of people who are the natural part of living. Especially when some of them come with sharp edges, or when I judge them to be sources of greed or injustice – I have an ever-reliable, constantly sounding bell that calls me to relate to them with loving kindness, even when I have to confront them and tell them that I am in opposition to what they say or to what they do.

Another way in which Christians might make use of particular Buddhist practices in order to awaken to the transformative power of "being in Christ" is through the Tibetan recipes for visualization. After all, one might define a Christian as someone who has chosen Jesus the Christ as her or his *yi-dam*. The person and the story of this Jesus contain what Christians feel they need and what they want to be. So in a Christian form of Vajrayana visualization meditation, I start with the techniques that I learned way back in 1957 in the novitiate: I visualize Jesus, perhaps in a particular scene from his life, or I gaze on an image of him, perhaps the crucifix, in order to "see" and feel the scene in all its vivid particularities. But then comes something different from what I learned in the novitiate: instead of talking or praying to Jesus, instead of neatly identifying the virtues of Jesus that I want to learn for my own life, I at this point move beyond words or thoughts and feel, or allow to come to awareness, that that which I am picturing in front of me is the reality within me. This Jesus, as Paul keeps reminding us in his epistles, is the Christ who now lives in us and as us. The external visualized picture becomes the internal image-less reality of my non-dual unity with Christ.

There's a final step and final difference from traditional forms of Christian visualization-prayer: I let my picture of Jesus go. I as it were remove or move away from it. The external form of the Jesus of history must not impede the birthing of the Christ-Spirit in my being. Buddhism has helped me touch what I think is the content of Jesus telling his disciples that "if I do not go away, the Advocate will not come to you; but if I go, I will send him to you" (John 16:7).

Worldlessness reveals Groundlessness – the God beyond God

In the Christian adaptations of Buddhist meditational practices that I have explored so far, I have still been using, to some extent, words (*mantras*) or images (*mandalas*) in order to get beyond words and images. But in my efforts to make use of Buddhist practices for Christian purposes, I have discovered that I also have to follow, regularly and steadfastly, a more strictly Zen practice and, as the Zen people say, let all words, thoughts, pictures *drop away*.

Don't make use of any particular technique, don't even count your breaths or try to be aware of breathing. Don't even have any thought of what you are trying to be aware of (e.g. the presence of the Spirit, the Christ living as me). If thoughts come, as they will, just let them go. Don't cling. Don't force. Just sit there. Just breathe. Just be. And let happen what happens, without expecting anything to happen.

What can happen is that we begin to sink more deeply into the unitive, non-dual mystical experience that feeds all religions, but will be felt and expressed differently in each religion. There's no one, neat way to talk about this kind of grounding mystical experience. But the way Pema Chödrön describes how it feels can, at least for me, reveal the full meaning of what we Christians call "faith." Chödrön informs us that the grounding mystical experience is *groundless*. For her, the practice of meditation – which is really the practice of daily living – is a letting go of everything and allowing oneself to be carried by "vast openness," or "Groundlessness."

Carried by Groundlessness? How can what's not there carry and sustain us? There's no answer to that question or explanation for how we can be carried by Groundlessness. But that is what happens – if we allow it to happen. Or, in my Christian terms, if we *trust* that it will happen.

And that is what faith calls us to do. A regular practice of wordless, silent meditation can make powerfully and existentially clear to

Christians that faith is, in its essence, trust. Trusting what? The usual answer is God. In meditation we can begin to comprehend – no, not comprehend, but sense or intuit – what that means. To experience God is to let oneself be carried, as it were, by Groundlessness.

During a retreat in August 2004, for which I was reading Pema Chödrön's *When Things Fall Apart*, I felt the peace and the strength that comes from realizing that God is Groundlessness and faith is trust:

> To stand on Groundlessness means that we are really trusting … Trust means that we "accept" what is, let go to what is, and trust that that's the best way of dealing with it. More, that's the best way to keep things going, the best way to "do God's will" or to be part of the dynamic, ever changing, but creatively interconnected process of *pratitya-samutpada* [InterBeing].
>
> For me, and perhaps for many Christians, the hardest part of such a life of faith or trust is the accepting of reality as it is. Acceptance, of course, doesn't mean approval or affirmation. It means allowing that to be what it is so that it, with us, may become what it can. What will it become? That we can't say. That's the invisible part of faith. That it will become we're certain of. Why? Because we have faith, we trust … Against the odds, without encouraging data, with no sign of success on the horizon – we trust that all manner of things will be well. That takes spiritual guts.

Earlier, in 2001, I had realized that Pema Chödrön's talk of Groundlessness and Karl Rahner's emphasis on Mystery were two different fingers pointing to the same moon:

> This is what Rahner talks about as 'Mystery.' Recently I read a comparison by Leo Lefebure [in *Revelation, the Religions and Violence*] on the similarities of Rahner's understanding of Mystery and Masao Abe's notion of Emptiness or Groundlessness: for both of them, to feel the Reality of Mystery or *Sunyata* means to let go of self, to trust totally in what both of them call infinite openness. Openness to what? To what is, to what's going on right now, in the trust that what is going on is what I am a part of and what will sustain and lead me, moment by moment. Only moment by moment. There are no grand visions promised here. Just a mindful trusting of each moment as it comes, with what it contains, with its confusion or inspiration, with its joy or horror, with its hope or despair. Whatever is there, this suchness right now, is the breath of the Spirit, the power of Mystery, the connectedness of Emptiness.

Later that same year of 2001, it hit me that:

> Merton was getting at the same thing: "Suspended entirely from
> God's mercy, I am content for anything to happen" [Merton's jour-
> nal, November 19, 1952] … It's the Buddhist notion that everything
> is perfect right at this moment, in precisely what this moment is.
> *Tathata* – suchness. The suchness of each moment is the infinite
> Mercy of God.

So the regular practice of the Sacrament of Silence can lead us
Christians into a deeper experience of what it means to have faith. To
move beyond words is to move beyond clear knowledge; to step into
silence is to step into Groundlessness. Just as the silence is full, so is the
Groundlessness sustaining. What Buddhist practice is telling us
Christians is something that our religion-built-on-words can so easily forget: that really to have faith, really to trust in God requires that
we really don't know what we are trusting. Trust requires not knowing. If we know, we don't have to trust.

That's what my teacher Bernard Lonergan, S.J., meant when he
told us that faith is a falling in love without being sure of what one
loves. Faith, like love, tells us what we don't really know; it reaches
beyond knowledge. The danger for us Christians is that, with all of our
words, we are too clear about what we are trusting when we trust. Yes,
for us words are important. But if we make too much of them, if we're
too certain about what we're trusting, we will miss both the challenge
and the rewards of what faith really is, what it requires, what it makes
possible.

By trustingly stepping off the cliff into the thin air of the groundless we can experience the strength and the peace of knowing that
the Groundlessness, the Mystery, is carrying us. So when we
Christians say "Let go and let God" the letting go includes letting go of
words and the certainty of knowledge. Only then are we really "letting
God." God as Mystery speaks most clearly and most powerfully in
silence.

The importance of being mindful

There is one more ingredient in Buddhist practice that I think we
Christians need to integrate into our practice of the Sacrament of
Silence. As we saw in our section on Passing Over, in all forms of
Buddhist meditation – both those aimed at wisdom and those aimed

at compassion – mindfulness is the point of departure. I have found in my own prayer and meditation that introducing the practice of mindfulness, as outlined in the previous section, can protect me, and perhaps other Christians, from real dangers in the way we pray or try to connect with the Divine.

I'm talking about the danger of not really bringing the reality of who we are or what is going on in our lives and world to our efforts to open ourselves to the presence of Spirit. Christian prayer, I have found in my own life, can all too easily become a way of not facing reality – my own internal reality or the world's. I've realized that prayer can become the occasion for a good bit of unintentional dishonesty with myself, or maybe an escape from my own messy reality.

What I'm trying to get at can easily happen among us Christians. We turn to God before we really look at ourselves. We ask for solutions before we frankly face, and properly understand, the problem. In too readily reaching out to God we fail to hear what the Spirit might be saying and doing in the immediate situation of our lives. The solutions we're looking for may be in the very problems we're facing. But we don't see them because we are not sufficiently mindful of the problem – of where it's coming from, why it arose, what it is stirring within us.

That, I think, is what Buddhists recognize when they insist on the importance of mindfulness-practice. To put it tritely but accurately, they have found that all we need in order to deal with each moment is to be found in each moment. In their language, we can find our Buddha-nature, we can know how our Buddha-nature is to respond, right here, right now, nowhere else but now-here. Translated into Christian terms, the Spirit can be felt or "heard" in what is actually going on in whatever situation, whatever question, whatever problem is facing us right now. But to know and feel this Buddha-nature or Spirit, we have to be mindful of the moment.

Pema Chödrön's three movements of mindfulness practice that I outlined earlier (Precision, Gentleness, Letting go) really simmer down, I think we can say, to two ingredients: we are to *acknowledge* what is going on as honestly as we can, and then *accept* it as fully as we can. Some Buddhist teachers really press the acceptance part and call for surrender to what is going on. We let it be; we don't try to control it; indeed, we embrace it. Now this doesn't mean that we agree with it, or approve of it, or encourage it. But we do allow it, accept it, yes, even hold it close – even when it is horrible or frightening or what we would call "evil."

And if we can do something like that – if we can truly be mind-ful of what is going on in us or around us – that's how we can find or feel "the Spirit" in it. Then our response to the situation will be originating from the Spirit rather than from our knee-jerk feelings of fear or anger or envy. And whether the response is to endure bravely or to act creatively, it will be done with *understanding* and *compassion* – which means it will be life-giving or life-creating.

It all sounds a little mysterious, maybe even a bit kooky, I know. That's why, as I already mentioned, Buddhists speak of "the miracle of mindfulness." That's also why mindfulness must make up an essential part of the practice of the Sacrament of Silence. The first step in receiving this Sacrament is the practice of mindfulness. We bring such mindfulness, such acceptance of reality, to our silent meditation in order to allow it to disappear into the silence.

In March 2000 I tried to connect the practice of mindfulness with my being in Christ: "It works both ways – in being in touch with or mindful of the moment, I am finding Christ in what is right here, in this world. But in finding the Christ in this moment, the moment no longer has power over me." Only in this way can the incarnation of the Christ-Spirit continue in the world without being overwhelmed by the world.

Taking silence to church

But as wonderfully necessary as the Sacrament of Silence can be for deepening or expanding my Christian practice, as a Christian I'm still stuck with words, with lots of words. Christianity in its very incarnational being is a religion of ritual. (That, of course, is more true of Catholic and Orthodox Christians than of Protestants.) To sustain and to live out our religious experience we Christians gather communally, and when we do so, we talk, we sing, we pray together. And the language we use to do this comes from sacred and liturgical texts ("sacramentaries" or "books of common prayer") that originated in very different historical and cultural settings. Such language, as we examined in the first part of this chapter, can be heavily and oppressively dualistic and anthropomorphic, seemingly directed to God, the Super-person, out there.

So how does the unitive, non-dualistic, mystical Sacrament of Silence fit with all the other sacraments and rituals of Christian practice? I guess I'm asking whether Silence is a personal sacrament that we administer to ourselves in the privacy of the "cave of the heart," or is it a sacrament that we bring to church with us and can share communally.

To answer that question directly and simply: I've been able to bring the Sacrament of Silence – or more accurately, its fruits – with me into Sunday Mass and into our daily worship services at Union Theological Seminary. And it has made a qualitative, dare I say life-saving or faith-saving, difference in the way I'm able to participate in those rituals. My regular practice of silent meditation has enabled me not just to bear with the torrent of liturgical words but also to be swept up by their power.

There's no one clear way to explain why this happens. But I'm sure it has to do with the way the practice of silence keeps me aware that the content of the liturgy, like the content of all Christian doctrine and dogma, is ultimately a matter of Mystery. And Mystery, by its very nature, both needs words but always remains beyond the reach of words. So as I raise my voice to sing "Glory to God," as I declare that "I believe in God the Father Almighty," as I make my confession to "all the angels and saints of heaven," my practice of silence has helped me feel that all these words are as true as they are inadequate. They are symbols. And they are true precisely because – dare I say only because – they are symbols. To know that all our liturgical and ritual words, gestures, hymns are symbols releases their power.

While the words and images that make up the liturgical life of the church inform and guide my values and hopes and actions, I know that there is so much more than what they tell me, so much more I can know, so much more I'll never know. So I hold and cherish these words – time-honored, treasured words passed down in the tradition of my community. But I do not cling to these words. They are true. They are never the *Truth*. By not clinging to them, they can touch me even more deeply. In knowing that they are fingers, I can see the moon!

One particular practice of Tibetan Buddhism has been especially helpful in tapping the power of my Christian liturgical language. This became clear to me during a ten-day Dzogchen retreat that I took during the summer of 2008 when I was working on the final revisions of this book. In all of the sessions of this retreat, we would start with invocations of various Buddhas and Bodhisattvas (especially the female Tara); we would chant (sometimes with the fervor of Pentecostal Christians); we would invoke and call down blessings and assistance; we would imagine ourselves being held and loved by our "spiritual benefactors;" we were invited to "absorb the healing radiance of their wish for your happiness into every cell of your body."

But then, after so lavishly and with total abandon being swept up in the language and images of this ritual, we were invited to "drop the visualization and just relax into the oneness with the loving luminosity, releasing all frames of reference. Deeply let be into that gentle, luminous wholeness beyond separation of self and others. Enjoy just being – at ease, at rest, complete."

These Dzogchen meditation experiences invited me, in my passing back to Christian practice, to abandon myself even more deeply into the language and content of Christian liturgy. For many religious practitioners (like Christians and Tibetan Buddhists) this is not only a helpful exercise; it is a necessary, powerful way of eliciting our imagination, indeed our body, and enabling it to feel the presence of Mystery and Spirit in our very corporeal, emotional fibers. But this Tibetan practice adds for me something that had been missing in my Christian practice: the reminder to be able to "let it all go," to "drop" the words and images, and "relax" into the Mystery that is both communicated by and remains essentially beyond all the necessary smells and bells, words and gestures. So now, while at Mass or services, I make use of or find for myself moments of Silence (I wish more were provided) where I can let it all go and feel the Mystery behind the words.

In different ways, I have found that this process of "hearing" the words of liturgy and ritual with ears tuned to silence can work and reinvigorate most of the language I hear in church on Sunday mornings. But not all of it. There are some fingers in my inherited Christian liturgy and language that just don't point, no matter how much I drench them in silence. But in these cases it's not because they are overly anthropomorphic or suggestive of dualism. It's because they're wrong, or false, or inconsistent with the message of Jesus. I'm speaking especially of patriarchal language that so stresses the power of God that it puts God's love in jeopardy.

So when liturgical prayers or hymns present me with a God who has enemies whom he vanquishes, or a God who gets so angry he damns or destroys, I just clam up, both spontaneously and in protest. And as much as I can, and as sensitively as I can, I let my fellow parishioners and the pastor know of my discomfort and protest. It takes time to change the language of institutions and tradition.

To petition is to connect

In general, then, my practice of the Sacrament of Silence helps me deal with and be inspired by the language of liturgy. That even includes one of the biggest ritual stumbling stones: prayers of petition. Yes, it remains true that I just cannot get myself to answer "Lord, hear our prayer" when what we're asking for would require God to prefer our needs – our nation or team or picnic or church – over those of others. Confronted with such "me first" forms of petitions, again, I lose my voice. But regarding petitionary prayer more broadly, I believe that my daily reception of the Sacrament of Silence has helped me see and feel not just the validity but the value of bringing our requests to the Spirit.

If what we become aware of in silence is real – that is, if we, each one of us, are part of the interconnecting Mystery that we call Spirit and that has its life in us – then prayers by which I express my concern and good wishes for you are ways in which I can act out, as it were, what I know in silence: my Spirit-grounded connections with and compassion for all other beings, especially those in need. That's how Buddhists understand *tonglen* and *metta* practice to work. That's how I can understand our prayers of petition to work. When I feel compassion for others, I am "practicing" what I am. I am letting the energy of the Spirit connect me with others.

And when I do this, I am sure it is good for me – because it is connecting me with you. Just how much it will be good for you, just how much the energy that I feel and send out from my end will arrive and affect your end, that I don't know for sure. For sure I know it's good for me. I trust it will be good for you.

In any case, when we pray for each other in this way, it is not a form of requesting divine interventions. It is a way of enabling the connecting Spirit to emerge rather than invade; it's activating the Spirit that is already there, rather than asking it to intervene from out there. Petitionary prayers, we might say, make us aware of – and therefore more active agents of – the Buddha-nature that contains all beings, or the Body of Christ of which we are all parts. To petition is to connect, really though mysteriously.

In all these instances of finding meaning in liturgical praise and petition, I have, as it were, been bringing silence with me into church. But if we Christians are going really to integrate the Sacrament of Silence into the marrow of our Christian practice so that it can be part of our liturgical and communal life, we will have to create *more* silence in church.

Here there is much work to do. As beautiful and inspiring as Christian liturgies can be, they are still, for me and I know for many of my fellow churchgoers, too noisy, too busy, too wordy – and that means not sufficiently respectful of what liturgists call the "*Arcanum*," the wordless Mystery that is at the core of all successful ritual.

To put it bluntly but also imploringly: we Christians need more silence in our services and liturgies. Just how this might be realized, just how we can blend and balance silence into our talking and praising and singing will have to be worked out as part of the ongoing liturgical reform that was launched, for Catholics, after the Second Vatican Council.

I do suggest, however, because I have personally experienced, that in this area Western Christians have a lot to learn from Asian Christians. Because of their conditioning in Buddhist and Hindu cultures, many Asian Christians take it for granted that silence must be part of Christian ritual. In participating in Father Aloysius Pieris's "Buddhist Mass" in the small chapel of his dialogue center in Tulana, Sri Lanka, or in being part of the large congregation celebrating an "Indian Eucharist" at the Catholic Dialogue Center in Bangalore, India, I have personally witnessed how the use of communal silence can be integrated into and enrich Christian liturgy. Such rituals are the results of liturgical passing over to and passing back from Eastern spiritualities. And they bring hope by providing examples for the entire Christian church.

In sum, passing over to Buddhist spiritual practice has taught me, and can teach my church, that all our words, whether in Christian theology or Christian liturgy, must arise from and lead back to Silence. Only then do they have something to say.

7

MAKING PEACE AND BEING PEACE

"In this chapter, we're going to be talking about practice." That's the first sentence of the last chapter. Then, we were using the word "practice" in its Buddhist sense – the daily exercises that one follows in order to stay in good spiritual shape. In this chapter we're talking about "practice" more in its Christian meaning – the activities one performs in order to live out one's spirituality in the world, local and global. Generalizing grossly, what Buddhists mean by practice is more interior and personal, while what Christians mean is more external and social. Or as Aloysius Pieris puts it, in their practice Buddhists stress *prajna* or wisdom, and Christians stress *agape* or charity.

Of course, as both Buddhists and Christians acknowledge, each needs the other: wisdom calls for compassion, and compassion requires wisdom. In this chapter, however, as befits the nature of this book and its author, our focus is on how Buddhist spirituality might assist – that is, clarify, ground, direct, inspire – Christian engagement in the world.

This means that the issues in this chapter are much closer to the surface of my life and of the social and political (maybe also economic) life of the world. Although the struggles I'm going to try to describe all have theological roots, they have sprung up in the soil of what might be called "activism." Certainly, as I look back over the four decades of my professional life, the main hat I've worn has been that of an academic. But especially since the mid-1980s (after I readjusted the direction of my life and moved from the "singular" blessings of being a priest and settled into the more complex blessings of being a professor, husband, and parent) I've tried to make sure that my intellectual pursuits have been properly mixed and challenged by engagement in concrete social or political projects.

Besides the general activities and frustrations involved in trying to be a concerned citizen of the U.S.A. and a responsible member of a political party, the two organizations that have claimed most of my activist energies over the past decades have been Christians for Peace in El Salvador (known by its Spanish acronym, CRISPAZ) and the International Interreligious Peace Council. As already mentioned in an earlier chapter, CRISPAZ is an ecumenical group that has been working for peace with justice together with churches and Non-Governmental Organizations of El Salvador since the mid-1980s (the bloody years of the civil war) up to the present. My wife Cathy and I were members of CRISPAZ's Board of Directors from 1988–2002. The Peace Council gathers prominent leaders from the major religious traditions of the world and, with the help of its Board of Trustees, meets every year in a situation of conflict and violence in order to make an interreligious contribution toward a non-violent resolution of the discord. I've served on its board since 1996. Most of the struggles that I'm about to lay out have surfaced in my work with CRISPAZ and the Peace Council.

To paint an even broader picture of the context for these struggles, I can say that they have all arisen for me in my efforts, shared with all Christians, to promote the project that directed the life of Jesus of Nazareth (and ultimately got him into big trouble with the authorities) – that is, the project the New Testament calls the "*Basileia tou Theou*," which I'm translating as the Kindom of God. That's the symbol for Jesus' vision of a world so organized as to urge and enable human beings to respect and care for each other and so to promote the wellbeing of everyone (and today he would add the wellbeing of the planet).

Working for the Kindom project, one invariably bangs into many problems, in both planning and execution. Buddhism has been for me a big, big help in dealing with these problems. In fact, while Jesus has provided me with the original vision and commitment to the Kindom, Buddha has been indispensable in my struggling and dealing with all the problems I've faced as I've tried to understand and implement this vision and commitment over the years. I guess I'm saying that without Buddha, I could not be a Kindom-builder with Jesus.

MY STRUGGLES: GOD'S KINDOM – WHEN? WHERE? HOW?

What can we hope for?

One of the most troubling questions that, like a recurrent cold virus, has so often infected and therefore weakened my efforts to work for the better world envisioned in Jesus' image of the Kindom of God has been "What can we really achieve? What can we hope for?"

Such a question came to a particularly painful focus for me in our efforts to make a difference in El Salvador. CRISPAZ, as mentioned, had been working with the churches, with teachers and union organizers, with human rights groups, throughout the horrendous years of military massacres, disappearances, death squads. So when the Peace Accords were finally reached in 1992, when the daily rumble of war ceased, we were, with all the people of El Salvador, elated. And there was also the sense of achievement, maybe tinged with pride, that our efforts to non-violently overcome injustice and violence had borne their hoped-for fruits.

But as we returned to El Salvador during the ensuing years, as we visited the still-impoverished urban communities and villages, as we witnessed how the rebel forces of the F.M.L.N. were "integrating" into the political system, the new and different corner we thought we had turned revealed an all too familiar landscape. Poverty remained pervasive; economic power once in the hands of the notorious "fourteen ruling families" was transferred to invisible globalized agents; political corruption, even among F.M.L.N. guerrillas now in business suits, remained; military violence mutated into gang and police violence; and the leadership of the Catholic Church, once typified in the courageous martyr Archbishop Romero and the patient but persistent Archbishop Rivera y Damas, passed, by Vatican decree, into the hands of an Opus Dei prelate determined to uproot liberation theology. All of this, after so much suffering, so much blood (70,000 civilian deaths in a country of 5 million), so much hope. The pain and confusion of it all was captured in the exasperated comment of a Salvadoran friend: "*Era mejor cuando era peor*" ["It was better when it was worse"].

In the intensity of its particular time and place, El Salvador is unique. But in its concentrated clarity, it captures a lurking question that unsettles, maybe even disables, many a person, religious or secular, whose "basic values" include a commitment to change this world of suffering and injustice. Simply and sharply stated: Is it possible? Can we really make a difference? Can we really bring about lasting change for the better? Or do we all belong to the church or movement called "Sisypheans?" Like the fabled Sisyphus rolling his stone up the hill, when we reach the top, we can sigh in relief and accomplishment. But the boulder soon rolls back downhill. Though life in the valley may have been a little smoother for a while, nothing really changes. Boulders keep rolling back and crushing people.

So can I – do I – really have hope that things can be different in this world of violence and injustice? The "do I?" part of that question gives me the shivers. It slapped me in the face some years back when Elise Boulding, one of the Interreligious Peace Councilors, asked with her typical gentle frankness: "Do peacemakers really believe that peace is possible? Do they really believe that we humans can reach a point in our history where we will resolve our conflicts no longer through violence and bloodshed but through conversation and compromise? If peacemakers really don't believe this, why are they doing what they're doing? And *how* are they doing it?" I continue to wince at that question. Do I really believe that peace is possible?

Such practical, personal questions (especially for people like myself who think too much) lead to, or are fed by, deeper philosophical and theological questions. To be honest, even though I'm a paid Christian theologian, I'm sometimes not sure just how traditional formulations of Christian beliefs really help me deal with these harassing questions. What can I really hope for?

To try to find answers to that question in the broad expanse of Christian beliefs and theology, one would have to google "Christian eschatology." "Eschatology" marks the files that contain what Christians are supposed to believe about "the last things:" the end of the world, the life to come, the final destination of all creation, the purpose of history – simply, homecoming. All Christians believe, fundamentally, that the world is going somewhere, that there's an end-station. Further, they believe that what's going on now – what people choose to do in their limited appearances on the stage of history – determines, to some degree or manner, what that final destination will be. In other words, there is a causal linkage between the present and the future, between human history and the final state of affairs with the Divine (called "heaven" or "hell").

But in Christian belief this linkage works both ways. Not only is the present able to affect the future, the future can also influence the present. In fact, Christians believe that what God has prepared for the end of time is already present in these best and worst of times! Now this is a notion that is perhaps just as difficult to comprehend as to believe. Theologians, perhaps illustrating their ready ability to complexify the complex, refer to this as "realized eschatology" – the "last things" can be *realized*, at least to some extent, right now.

New Testament scholars are, I think, more helpful and engaging when they make their case that if we carefully analyze how Jesus in the New Testament records referred to the *Basileia* or Kindom of God, we come to the realization that it was an "*already/not yet*" presence and power. Certainly, the Kindom for Jesus, in all that it meant and was, was *not yet here* since it was still *out there* in the future. But at the same time, it was *already here*, already arrived, especially in his mission and person. We don't have to wait until the end of history – until heaven – to experience the Kindom of God. Jesus instructed his followers to remember this every day when they pray "Thy Kindom come, thy will be done, on earth [right now!] as it is in heaven [still to come]."

So this balancing of "already and not yet" in Christian beliefs about the "last things" should help me answer my question: "What can I hope for?" I can hope that what is still to come can already be realized.

But my questions persist, not just philosophical questions, but those borne out of my experience in places like El Salvador, or for that matter (and more seriously) in Washington, D.C. Nothing really seems to change. The poor before the war are the poor after the war. Misguided, life-destroying policies in El Salvador are repeated in Iraq.

These gnawing doubts about whether things here on earth can ever be *really* different, really changed, are corroborated, it seems, by certain Christian beliefs. Balancing, or maybe contradicting, the heartening good news that the Kindom of love and justice can be realized right now is the sobering bad news that we human beings are sinful and remain so. Or, as my undergrad students responded every time I hung out the hope of a new economic order: "You can't change human nature!"

We remain sinful. That means selfish. That also means that the boulder that we have so laboriously pushed to the top of the hill doesn't just roll back on its own. There are always some sinful human beings who push it down! And, according to what Christian doctrine says about our sinful natures, there will *always* be such individuals. So how can the Kindom already come among societies of humans who are always sinful and selfish? Will the boulder, or at least some boulders, ever stay at the top?

Such questions seem to receive a rather discouraging answer through another fundamental Christian belief: Christ's Second Coming. The imagery and the interpretation of that symbol suggest – or do they declare? – that it will be only in the last act of history, or better, when the play is over, that Jesus will really bring about his Kindom and turn it over to the Father. This means that only then, only after history has run its course, will things really be different. Only then will sin and selfishness and violence and injustice really be blotted out. Only then will the boulders stay on the top of the hill and allow true, lasting peace in the valley.

But what does such an interpretation of the Second Coming mean for our hopes to realize the Kindom *now*? A quick reply would be: simple, it means that nothing's perfect until the end. The Kindom, or a world of compassion and non-violence, can be realized on this earth only partially, never fully. But both the philosopher and the activist in me finds such replies too facile. What does "never fully," "never perfect," "always sinful" really imply?

My gadfly questions come down to something like this. When we Christians believe, as our Jewish heritage and all the Jewish prophets including Jesus tell us, that we can and must try to *fix the* world (the Hebrew is the resounding *Tikkun Olam*), that "fixing" can mean either to *tinker with* or to *transform*. Tinkering means patching up problems that are only going to recur, fixing a leaky pipe that will start leaking again next month. Such tinkering certainly makes life more livable because we do fix the problems as they continue to pop up, but the house remains what it is: dilapidated. Transforming would mean that we can actually build a new house, or construct new additions, which are not perfect but definitely improvements over the old ones.

Are we on this earth called by Jesus' vision of the Kindom to tinker or to transform? With this pinpointed question I'm facing the even more deep-reaching, fundamental question: after all, what is the value of this world, this planet? Does it provide the building materials out of which, and dependent on which, the Kindom of God is taking shape? Or, in the end, will it all be swept away to make room for something entirely new? Or the same questions put more personally and existentially: are we humans on this earth to transform it and ourselves into something different, something really more just and compassionate and sustaining? Or are we here mainly to earn our passage to another world that will essentially leave this one behind in its enduring sinfulness and self-seeking – and final annihilation?

Such questions and uncertainties are not just the grist for philosophical or theological musings. They arise from and more importantly they determine what I'm trying to do as an activist. They determine how I answer Elise Boulding's question, "Do you really believe that peace is possible?"

Action and contemplation

The struggle I want to describe in this section is contained in a conversation I had with a Zen Master back in the 1980s. It was the summer of 1987, a few weeks before my wife Cathy and I were to leave for another of our trips to El Salvador to keep connected with our CRISPAZ associates and volunteers. In New York for academic business, I decided I needed a short retreat, so I spent some days at the Riverdale Zen Community under the direction of Tetsugen Bernard Glassman. After three relaxing but intense days of sitting Zen meditation, I had my "*dokusan*" or short conference with Roshi Bernie. Rather uneasily and stumbling over words, I informed him that I felt a strong need to go to El Salvador to do my little part in trying to stop the death squads (then particularly rampant, especially targeting church workers). But at the same time, I felt just as strong a need to sit in meditation. What was unclear for me, I tried to explain, was how these two "necessaries" fit together.

Glassman responded with typical Zen cool: "They are both absolutely necessary. You have to sit. You have to stop the death squads." And then he leveled a Zen zinger at me that I'm still trying to figure out: "But you won't be able to stop the death squads until you realize your oneness with them." And he gently dismissed me.

In a sense, the Roshi was telling me something I already knew, but he was inviting me to plunge into it more deeply. Throughout my training with the Divine Word Missionaries and my long years of studying and working with the Jesuits, I had been convinced of the vital connection between *action* and *contemplation*. The reason for this vital link, as was explained to me, was essentially contained in the dictum my German novice-Master, Father Glorius, used: "*nemo dat quod non hat*" – nobody gives what they don't have. You have to have before you can give. You have to know what you're talking about and know it not just intellectually but personally. Further, the transfusion of lifeblood that comes from contemplation will strengthen and sustain you in the demands and hardships that are part of the ministry of announcing and working toward the Kindom of truth and justice. So contemplation – regular practices of spirituality – is necessary both to have a product to deliver and to have the energy to deliver it.

Roshi Bernie would basically agree with all this. But he was, I believe, saying something more. He was not talking about appropriating the message and acquiring the stamina to deliver it. He was talking about *changing the messenger.* And he intended a particular kind of personal, subjective change – one that would enable me to "realize my oneness with the death squads." Here I was baffled. This seemed to be beyond the reach of what I had learned in my Christian training. Was he calling for a different kind of contemplation or spiritual practice that would foster a different kind of personal change or awareness than what I had been striving for in my Christian practice?

Such questions, stimulated and led on by my experience at the Riverdale Zen Center, nagged but also nurtured me during an intensely activist period of working with CRISPAZ in El Salvador during the later 1980s and early 1990s. I knew that what we were trying to do was right. We had to do something about the immense suffering of the Salvadoran people caused by the economic, political, and military policies of the Salvadoran government and ruling classes, which were sustained vitally by the economic, political, and military policies of the United States government. But a feeling gradually was seeping into my awareness that the way we were going about our efforts to change things was not entirely right, or not adequate. Something was missing in our "action," or in what we were bringing to our actions. I wasn't sure what it was, but I sensed it had to do with the gentle admonition that Roshi Bernie had given me.

As I look back, I realize that there were multiple stimuli for this emerging uneasiness that I was doing the right thing but not in the right way. In retrospect, they clustered around the growing discomfort I felt in both the *attitude* we brought to our work and the *tone* in which we carried out our work. Regarding attitude, although we were very clear that as foreign "gringos" working in El Salvador we were there to accompany and learn from the Salvadorans, still, we arrived with pretty clear plans and agendas. We had, after all, followed the methodology of "liberation theology" and done our "social and political analysis." We knew the causes of suffering and violence (unjust economic policies) and we knew the basic solutions (structural changes in political agendas and even in governments). We knew who were the good guys (the struggling poor and those who were struggling together with them – us!) and the bad guys (the oligarchy, the military, the Reagan Administration, of course the death squads – them!).

And this "clarity" of analysis and plan affected our tone. Though unintended, there was a certain smugness, a better-than-thou-ness, in the way we informed civic and parish groups in the States about the awful things their government was doing in El Salvador. There was even a sense of chosenness when we found out that Cathy and I were being investigated by the F.B.I.! Clearly, we were the good guys.

We were convinced about the rightness of our projects. And we were angry about the wrongness of the Salvadoran and American governments' projects. This conviction and this anger introduced a certain violence into our words and sometimes our conduct, never physical, but nonetheless harmful. I remember the hatred I felt in a restaurant in Santa Ana when we saw a death squad enter and take a table next to us (we knew their telltale features: Cherokee S.U.V. with darkened windows, civilian clothes, toting automatic weapons). I recall the disdain in our questions and comments at the American Embassy. I recollect the contempt that seeped into our conversation with American Evangelicals who came to El Salvador "just to build churches." Also, I can look back now and note the violence we did to ourselves as we stressed and strained, and forgot how to smell the flowers, in our determination "to make things better." Thomas Merton once said that some of the most violent people he met were social activists, in what they did to themselves.

I vaguely sensed all this then. I see it much more clearly now. As I'll explain below, Buddhism has provided me with the glasses with which to see.

Peace – justice – violence?

Again, to get at the issues I'm struggling with in this section, let me reach back to particular activist experiences, this time, two contrasting experiences.

On our very first trip to Central America in 1984, Cathy and I were with a U.S. delegation from G.A.T.E. (Global Awareness through Experience) in the small town of Ocotal, Nicaragua, on the border with Honduras. The town had been attacked by U.S.-supported

"Contras" the previous week. (The Reagan Administration was in staunch opposition to the socialism of the Sandinistas governing Nicaragua at the time.) The Contras had destroyed the Sandinista radio station and burned alive the two young radio operators, but were repulsed in their efforts to blow up the day-care center built by the Sandinista government with money from Sweden. We were talking in the evening with a group of Maryknoll Sisters who were working in the local parish and in what were called "basic Christian communities." At one point in the conversation, two of the Sisters checked their watches, went into an adjacent room, and came out bearing AK-47 rifles! Evidently uncomfortable, even pained, at what they held in their hands, they simply stated: "Time for our turn on the night watch ... We have to do our part and stand with our people."

Twelve years later, Cathy and I were in Chiapas, Mexico, with the Interreligious Peace Council at the invitation of Bishop Samuel García Ruíz to help him work out a non-violent resolution to the conflict between the Zapatistas and indigenous people on one side and the Mexican government and military on the other. It was the second-last day of our visit. We had spent more than a week meeting with representatives of both sides. Now we – peace councilors and trustees – were all gathered around a big table in Don Samuel's house, trying to formulate a public statement for the press that would articulate our multi-religious contribution to resolving the tensions and violence. Having witnessed the sufferings inflicted on the indigenous peoples by the economic and political policies of wealthy landowners and government officials (who were taking full advantage of the recently declared North American Free-Trade Agreement or N.A.F.T.A.), we Christians were loud and clear in our insistence that we must denounce the economic and political policies of the Mexican government and of N.A.F.T.A. After all, one of the pillars of our liberation theological approach was that in order to *announce* the truth of the gospel we often had to *denounce* the power of the oppressors.

The room still quaked with our righteous declaration when one of the Buddhists at the table calmly raised his hand, and even more calmly stated: "I'm sorry, but we Buddhists don't denounce anyone." At this point, all I can say is that the "interreligious dialogue" that followed was some of the most sobering and inspiring that I have ever experienced. I'll report on it in the final part of this chapter.

But there you have it – on the one hand, Catholic nuns painfully picking up a gun to defend their people against the violence of injustice, and on the other, a group of Buddhists, in the face of the very same kind of violence, refusing even to denounce verbally the oppressors. In this contrast are embodied both the commitment and the confusion I have felt over these past decades as I've tried to apply the vision of the Kindom of God to the brutal realities of this world.

My confusion and uneasiness gravitate around a commitment that lies at the heart of the Christian (as well as the Jewish and Muslim) experience of the Mystery we call God. It's embodied in the admonition of the prophet Jeremiah to the king building his palace on the backs of the poor: "To know God is to do justice" (Jer. 22:13–16). If one is not acting for justice, defending and taking the side of slaves and marginalized, one does not really know the God of Jesus (and of Moses and of Muhammad). So, while charity and love of neighbor are central in that one cannot love God unless one is loving one's neighbor, Jesus would add: and if your neighbor is suffering from injustice, you can't really love him or her unless you are doing something to overcome the injustice, which requires confronting the perpetrators of injustice.

And so the resounding call that fills the hearts and guides the hands of Christian activists (and adorns many of their car-bumpers): "If you want peace, work for justice." This is a powerful statement. I believe that it was the primary inspiration for me to "get involved" back in the 1980s and it has directed my involvement throughout the past decades. Its implications are broad and demanding.

My Christian understanding of justice reminds me that there will be no peace in a neighborhood, society, or the world when some of its members, despite their efforts to work hard, cannot feed their children, or provide them with medicine, or offer them an education. Justice tells me that there is something wrong with the world, something that impedes peace, when some individuals or nations have more than they need, while others do not have what they need.

Justice requires that in order to have reconciliation between offended and offending parties, "I'm sorry" isn't enough. Where opportunities, property, and life have been taken, something must be *restored*; and if circumstances are such that this is in no way possible, then some form of public accounting must be made and forgiveness requested.

Justice also means that to set things right it is usually not enough to "change hearts." Structures, too, must be changed. Often, a change of structures must precede a change of heart. As liberation theologians remind us, injustice, originating in the human heart, takes on its own identity and power in economic, legal, political structures. Enlightened beings who meditate daily buy running shoes made in sweatshops.

This staunch commitment to and understanding of justice guided me then, and still guides me now, in the way I act in the world, in the way I analyze what I read about every morning in the *New York Times*, in the way I try to bring my society and my world a little closer to Jesus' vision of the Kindom. No peace without justice!

But … but … over the years – already then in El Salvador working with CRISPAZ and still today in New York working with the Poverty Initiative at Union Theological Seminary – I've sensed that something was wrong, or better said, something was missing. The staunchness and clarity of our commitment to justice seems to be the cause, or the occasion, for the superior attitudes and the harmful tones that I tried to describe earlier.

As I now try to figure out this simmering uneasiness, it seems that a lot of it hovers over the question of *violence*. The energy of my total commitment to justice often produces – spontaneously or reluctantly or even necessarily – violent feelings, words, actions. The picture of those Maryknoll nuns holding rifles (thank God, they never had to pull the trigger) still haunts me, for I suspect that in their place I would have done likewise. I'm haunted, too, by memories of the time in 1990 when our CRISPAZ delegation managed to visit the F.M.L.N. rebel headquarters in Perquin, where we had a clandestine, candlelight conversation somewhere in the jungle with Father Rugelio Poncel, who was serving as chaplain to the rebel forces. "These brave young men and women have tried every possible non-violent means, and still have seen their parents, siblings, friends tortured or disappear. In doing what they need to do, in taking up arms, they ask for, and they deserve, the spiritual support of their Christian faith. As a priest, I cannot turn my back on them. I must support them." Again, I suspect that I would probably have done likewise.

But in this feeling of having to do so, I also feel that something is not right. I fear that to the principle "If you want peace, work for justice" we have to add "And if you want to work for justice, be prepared to do violence." I sense that it doesn't have to work that way. But so often it does. Why? Is it simply unavoidable in this imperfect, always ambiguous, sinful world that we live in? Many point out, for example, that without the military resistance of the F.M.L.N. guerillas, the

Salvadoran and U.S. governments would never have come to the discussion tables and agreed to the Peace Accords. Our non-violent ways in CRISPAZ were noble but inadequate. I can't deny that. But today, while we have the Peace Accords in El Salvador, we do not have peace, nor justice.

So these are the questions I've been struggling with over the past decades. Is violence – whether the violence of physically pulling a trigger or the violence of verbally denouncing an oppressor – simply unavoidable in order to achieve justice? If structures have to change, *how* do they change? Which is more important, changing hearts or changing policies? And the deeper question: if justice is *necessary* for peace, is it *sufficient* for peace? Or: if we need justice in order to have peace, what do we need in order to have justice? Something has been missing in the way I've understood and gone about my activism for the Kindom of God.

As I'll try to explain in the Passing Back part of this chapter, Buddhism has been essential for me in raising these questions, and in trying to answer them.

PASSING OVER: "DON'T JUST DO SOMETHING! SIT THERE!"

In trying to summarize how Buddhism has helped me figure out whether and how I can engage the world and "fix" it, I should first point out that over the past five decades or so a growing number of Buddhists have consciously and creatively been trying to do the same thing. They're part of a movement called "Engaged Buddhists." Roughly speaking, they are seeking to do with Buddhism what liberation theology has tried to do with Christianity – rediscover and revivify the resources in the teachings of Buddha that will convince and animate their followers to do something about the suffering of poverty, exploitation, violence that some human beings are inflicting on other human beings, and on the planet. Engaged Buddhists and liberationist Christians are fellow travelers (who perhaps don't know each other as well as they should).

I have learned from, and been deeply inspired by, the example and the writings of Engaged Buddhists such as Thich Nhat Hanh (Vietnamese), Maha Ghosananda (Cambodian, member of the Peace Council, recently deceased), Venerable Dhammananda (Thai, member of Peace Council), Sulak Sivaraksa (Thai), Joanna Macy, and

Stephanie Kaza (Americans). But in this section of the chapter I want to do what all of these people generally try to do – specify *traditional, foundational* Buddhist beliefs, attitudes, and practices that are helpful and necessary for understanding how we can engage and change this world of suffering and violence.

As will be evident, just about all the Buddhist attitudes or beliefs that I will take up are "counter-intuitive" (putting it mildly!) to basic Christian beliefs and attitudes that play centrally in liberation theology. Indeed, they sometimes appear to be out-and-out contradictions. But as I will try to show in the final Passing Back section such differences between Buddhist and Christian views, precisely in their stark contrasts, turn out to be complementary rather than contradictory. And that means they can challenge and transform the way Christians go about their efforts to build the Kindom of God on earth.

The world isn't going anywhere

Here we bump into one of the starkest contrasts between Buddhism and Christianity: Buddhists get along without any kind of an eschatology! For them, the world isn't going anywhere. And it doesn't have to. They don't believe, or they have no need to believe, in an end point for history, a final chapter when we will have reached our destination, when loose ends will be tied together (or discarded), when questions will be answered, yes, when accounts will be settled. Buddhists don't have a happy ending for the drama that is human history.

And even more bewilderingly for Christians, this all means that without a belief in a happy ending, Buddhists get along without the *hope* that things are going to get better – that all the ambiguities, all the losses, all the frustrations of life will, at least eventually, be resolved. But for a Christian, that simply seems – well, unjust! Without an end point, without some kind of a final resolution, all the people who have died in struggling for a better world (or just died in misery) will have died in vain! All the blood, sweat, and tears that were poured out heroically but ended up down the drain of empire and power, all the martyrs, all the little people who were stepped on and then kicked aside – how can their sacrifices receive any kind of meaning, any kind of justification, if there is no end point? Sure, Buddhists will talk about the law of *karma*. Selfish acts, they remind us, produce painful results – but most of the pain seems all too often to land on the heads of others, while the selfish actor receives a state funeral.

Buddhists don't seem to have answers to these questions. In fact, it appears they don't feel the urgency, the pain of such questions. This is where for a Christian, passing over to Buddhism becomes really uncomfortable and demanding. It requires real listening, real openness.

The discomfort swells when as a Christian I ask about the Buddhist concept of justice. They don't have one! Unlike the "God of history" of the Abrahamic traditions who is up to something in the flow of history and who urges God's people to engage in a historical project of bringing ever more justice and love into the world, Buddhist Emptiness or InterBeing doesn't seem to be up to anything. As far as I know, and according to what my Buddhist friends tell me, Buddhist tradition contains no explicit, extended "theory of justice," no calls for a more equitable distribution of the earth's goods, no demands to free slaves and "let my people go," no proclamations that the poor shall inherit the Kindom while entrance for the rich will be like a camel passing through the eye of a needle. Buddhists certainly are committed to promoting peace. But they don't seem to have much concern about justice.

If we can talk about Emptiness being "up to" anything, it would be, I suppose, to generate what we have learned are the two main ingredients of Awakening: wisdom and compassion. *That's* what Buddhists are about; *that's* their response to the horrendous sufferings of our world. Given the First Noble Truth about "*dukkha*," Buddhists stand alongside Christians in recognizing and being concerned about suffering, including the suffering that some humans unjustly inflict on others. But their response is first and foremost, maybe even exclusively, to foster a wisdom that leads to compassion, and a compassion that is full of wisdom. Just do that, really do that, and things will take care of themselves. No big plan. No final goal.

We're back to what we have heard so often in our efforts to pass over to Buddhist experience and teachings: *live in the moment*, be fully present to the moment, embrace the moment as mindfully as you can, respond to it with the wisdom of feeling your connectedness with everyone and everything, and then respond with the compassion that naturally results when you feel so connected – and the moment will both teach you and guide you. That, essentially, is all you need to do.

And that's why eschatology – talk about where it's all leading to and what we have to do to get there – may be not only unnecessary, it may be, for Buddhists, dangerous. Plans and programs and analysis can be dangerous if they prevent us from really being mindful of and responsive to what the moment contains and is trying to teach us. And even hope can be an obstacle, for if the value of our actions depends on hoped-for, divinely promised goals, the more threatened or tenuous or constantly postponed those goals are, the more difficult it will be to hang in there and keep acting. Buddhists are aware, it seems to me, that to make the value of any act depend too much (or at all!) on its hoped-for results runs the risk of devaluing the act – something like making the love we have for our children too dependent on the hopes we have for them.

So, inherent in the Buddhist persistent admonition to live in the moment with as much mindfulness as possible is the hidden but powerful presupposition that all the value of our actions is contained right here, in this moment. That pertains especially to the distinctive activity of a Bodhisattva – compassion. The value of acting compassionately is found in its being a compassionate act. It's valuable, it's right, it's sufficient because that's how we naturally act when we are wise and aware of our interconnectedness. No further reason is necessary, either in the past or in the future. Compassion needs no further justification or motivation or satisfaction outside itself. In this regard, Buddhists endorse one of the main, and most challenging, teachings of the Hindu Bhagavad Gita: we are called upon to act *without seeking the fruits of our actions*. Let the fruits come, as come they often will. But don't seek them. If you seek them, your compassion may be jeopardized.

This Buddhist ability to transcend incredibly and, for Christians, to transcend scandalously the past and the demands of justice and to focus all their mindfulness and responsiveness on the present moment was illustrated stunningly at a meeting of the Interreligious Peace Council in Israel/Palestine in 2000. We had spent more than a week listening to the grievances, the fears, the angers of both Palestinians and Israelis. We were gathered with students and teachers at Hebrew Union College in Jerusalem, on Holocaust Memorial Day, after an emotionally wrenching ceremony remembering the victims of Nazi terror. In our subsequent discussions we heard the Jewish participants talk of "the need to remember," never to forget, so that "never again" will such horrors occur. As the conversation flowed easily back and forth, Geshe Sopa, Tibetan monk and scholar, raised his hand and then quietly but forthrightly asked the Dean of the College: "But why do you have to remember?"

After an awkward, almost horrified, moment of silence, Geshe continued, "What would happen if you let go of such memories of suffering?" He went on to speak about the sufferings the Tibetan people are enduring from the Chinese, adding that what is important now, in the moment, is not to cling to memories of the past but to understand that the Chinese are acting out of the ignorance that results from bad *karma*. The reaction that follows such understanding is compassion. "The main thing is to have compassion for mistakes made from an egocentric viewpoint, from ignorance ... The Chinese are now earning terrible *karma* for what they are doing to us. We must feel compassion for *all* who are suffering, on both sides. We don't look at the Chinese as evil, but try to find a peaceful solution and make them happy and peaceful."

Unfortunately, but also understandably, there was no further discussion of Geshe's question and suggestion. It was so different, so unimagined, that it was, probably, not understood. A similar silence was the response a few days later when Geshe made a similar statement to the director of the Deheishe Camp for Palestinian refugees. To let go of angers from the past and fears for the future in order to be free of them and so fully present to the moment is something very difficult for us Christians and Westerners to understand. Or perhaps we're afraid to understand.

The priority of Awakening

So Buddhists are much more concerned about waking up to our innate wisdom and compassion (our Buddha-nature) than they are about working for justice. If Christians insist that "if you want peace, work for justice," the Buddhists would counter-insist, "if you want peace, *be* peace." That's the point Thich Nhat Hanh gently drives home in the little book that I'm sure has shaken up the lives of many a Christian activist as it did mine some two decades ago: *Being Peace*. His message is as simple and straightforward as it is sharp and upsetting: the only way we are going to be able to create peace in the world is if we first create (or better, find) peace in our hearts. Being peace is an absolute prerequisite for *making* peace. And by "being peace," Thay (as his followers affectionately call him) means deepening the practice of mindfulness, both formally in regular meditation as well as throughout the day as we receive every person and every event that enters our lives; through such mindfulness we will, more and more, be able to *understand* (Thay's word for wisdom) whomever we meet or whatever we feel, and so respond with compassion. Only with the peace that comes with such mindfulness will we be able to respond in a way that brings forth peace for the event or person or feeling we are dealing with.

This Buddhist insistence on the necessary link between being peace and making peace reflects Christian spirituality's traditional insistence that all our action in the world must be combined with contemplation. But in the Buddhist reflection, there is a sharper focus. Yes, both action and contemplation, both making peace and being peace, are equally important in our efforts to address the sufferings of this world. But the Buddhists are very clear: while both are essential, one holds a priority of practice. If action and contemplation form a constantly moving circle in which one feeds into the other, the entrance point for the circle is contemplation.

Now this does not mean that one has to be a saint or a fully Awakened being before one can step into the fray of the world. But it does mean that we must *begin* and be faithfully committed to whatever practices our spiritual tradition provides for transcending our ego-identity and transforming it into our Buddha-nature, or our "being in Christ Jesus." Only if we are in touch with, or able to return to, our center, our source, the Emptiness or Spirit in whom we live and move and have our being – only then will we have, or be, "the right stuff" to bring forth peace. Unless we are seriously and resolutely trying to "get our own act together" – or in more Buddhist terms to realize that our act is acting within a larger Act – only then can we be of service to others.

Why? Just why do Buddhists insist on the priority of Awakening over acting? Why do they want to "just sit there" before they "do anything?" Certainly, there are different ways a Buddhist might answer this question. But I believe that one of the recurring responses would be: to remove one's ego from one's peacemaking, so that one's actions will not be coming from one's ego-needs but from the wisdom and compassion that constitute one's true nature.

"Ego-needs" embrace a multitude of little devils – anger, fear, ambition, jealousy, stubbornness, self-importance – all the little and big things we need to affirm or protect our substantial self. How often in the meetings and deliberations of peace activists have I felt myself surrounded by, and one of, a gathering of starved or overweight egos! The Buddhists seem to be aware that such egos are not very good peacemakers.

In September 2002 I wrote out in my journal a quotation from Eckhart Tolle's book *The Power of Now* that explains in more explicitly Buddhist terms why we must be peace before we can make it:

> Your primary task is not to seek salvation through creating a better world, but to awaken out of identification with form. You are then no longer bound to this world, this level of reality. You can feel your roots in the Unmanifested and so are free of attachment to the manifested world.

We have to be "free of attachments" if we are to be truly able to "create a better world" according to its needs and not our own.

But Engaged Buddhists like Thich Nhat Hanh and the Dalai Lama seem to go a step further: if we first work at *being* peace, they propose, not only *can* we make peace in the world, but we *will!* "Being peace" is not only a means toward an end; it is already the end. It *is* the making of a peaceful world. This point is perhaps subtle, but I believe powerful. Thay and His Holiness are suggesting that the internal, personal transformation that constitutes being peace will inevitably become the external, social transformation of making peace.

Yes, structures will have to be changed. But they *will* be changed, naturally and necessarily, by people with changed hearts. Yes, justice will have to be realized. But it *will* be realized, because Enlightened beings, peace-filled beings, will naturally share and address the needs of those who have been exploited. True contemplation will automatically become action. People who *are* peace will surely *make* peace. If you spend enough time "just sitting there," you will stand up and do. So again, the priority, perhaps the only real requirement, for making peace in the world is to be peace in the heart.

First surrender, then act

There is an aspect of being peace, or more specifically of the practice of mindfulness, that I find myself resisting almost every time I hear a Buddhist teacher talk about it. For that reason, I suspect, it may be one of the most critical things Buddhists have to teach Christians about peacemaking. We've talked about it in the previous chapter. In order to be really mindful of anything, we first have to *accept* it. This acceptance means to let it be, not to resist it, not even to judge it, but to look it straight in the eyes and say "Okay."

When teachers like Pema Chödrön, Charlotte Joko Beck, Adyashanti spell out just what the acceptance of mindfulness means, I find myself squirming even more. As we heard in the previous chapter, acceptance calls for more than tolerance, more than letting things be while we hold our nose. Acceptance calls for *surrender* – the surrender not of capitulation but of embrace. We hug what is, no matter what it is. We hug it not because it is good and we're happy about it, but because it's there. Crucial to the practice of mindfulness, Buddhist teachers emphasize, is not to judge, not to declare something good or evil. You can't judge anything unless you first understand it. (That's what my teacher in Rome, Bernard Lonergan, used to harp on.) But, as I once heard a Buddhist teacher exclaim, "How can you understand anything unless you first accept it!" Judgments may follow. The first order of the day with mindfulness is to be with, accept, surrender, embrace what is. In the moment of mindfulness – some teachers put it this way – everything is okay the way it is. Don't change or fix anything!

Now Christians may be able to manage such non-judging acceptance when it's a matter of missing a train, flunking an exam, even losing a friend. But when the reality to be accepted is a starving child, a raped woman, a tortured captive, it's pretty darn difficult to say "okay." And it's just about impossible to embrace the rapist or the torturer.

But this is precisely what mindfulness calls for. You're not approving, you're accepting. You're not judging, you're understanding. You're not allowing, you're loving. This, Buddhists insist, is the way of responding to what is that will create peace rather than more discord. This surrendering to whatever happens opens the possibility of "understanding" – that is, of coming to the realization that the act of injustice or violence is what happens because of certain "causes and conditions" which in a person's particular life bring about ignorance, which brings about fear or greed, which bring about selfish actions, which bring about suffering, for self and others. If we respond with hatred or anger or violence, we're only going to make things worse. Only a response that flows not from our ego-needs but from understanding and compassion will change things. And such responses require the acceptance and surrender of mindfulness.

Precisely what the response should be, Buddhists add, can be discovered only through this process of acceptance and embrace. It generally cannot be known beforehand, in a prepackaged plan. Such was the reminder I received in a public discussion back in the late 1980s with my Buddhist friend Stephanie Kaza. It was in a session on "Social Action: Christian and Buddhist Approaches" at a meeting of the American Academy of Religion. We were talking about the raging civil war in El Salvador and the rampant disappearances and murders perpetrated by the death squads. "As a Christian, I feel I have to do something about this terrible loss of life. And I have to do it quickly!" I declared. Stephanie responded: "As a Buddhist, I feel the same urgency. But before I act, I wait for openings."

Wait for openings when people are dying?! At the time, it made no sense to me. But this is the Buddhist insistence: even in the midst of horrendous violence and hatred, we must, as in the Asian martial arts, act with and not simply contrary to the forces that we wish to overcome or convert. Indeed, we must *convert* rather than *destroy*. And to do that we must accept what is, understand "where it's coming from," and then allow this understanding to let flow a compassionate response. We have to watch for openings, and work with them. Otherwise, there may be only more deaths.

"We don't take sides!"

There's another line in Thich Nhat Hanh's *Being Peace* that is particularly stinging for Christian activists and liberation theologians: "If we align ourselves with one side or the other, we will lose our chance to work for peace." The sting becomes not just more painful but perturbing from a sentence in a more recent book: "I do not think God wants us to take sides, even with the poor." This is but a restatement of what my Buddhist partners on the Peace Council told us in Chiapas: "We Buddhists don't denounce." To denounce the Mexican government would be to take sides with the indigenous people and against the government.

In *Being Peace* Thay offers some very practical reasons why Buddhist peacemakers don't take sides – reasons that resonate with what one reads in contemporary manuals for non-violent conflict resolution: "Reconciliation is to understand both sides, to go to one side and describe the suffering being endured by the other side, and then to go to the other side and describe the suffering being endured by the first side. Doing only that will be a great help for peace."

But these pragmatic reasons for not taking sides are rooted more deeply in Buddhist experience and teachings. If our true nature is to be "no-selves" or selfless selves or, more positively, interconnected selves, then our peacemaking, if it is going to be effective, must flow out of our interconnectedness. That includes our interconnectedness with the people whose actions we have to oppose. That includes the death squads. And to act out of a sense of interconnectedness with the death squads is to act out of compassion for them. Now the verbal slap in the face that Roshi Bernie Glassman non-violently gave me at the end of my Zen retreat begins to fill with meaning: "You will be able to stop the death squads only if you realize your oneness with them." Only if I feel my actual connectedness with them. Only if I feel genuine love for them. Only then is there any hope for having peace with them.

This is why Buddhists don't take sides for some people and against other people. It's the same reason we heard in Chapter 2 why Buddhists don't want to call anyone evil. To pronounce them evil is to take sides against them, and to take sides against them is to cut off connectedness – and the possibility of understanding and feeling compassion for them. Once you do that, once you define anyone as an "evil-doer," there's little chance for peace. There's even smaller chance for justice.

So for Buddhists who are engaged in this world, all efforts to overcome the sufferings due to injustice, all labors for making and keeping peace, must be grounded in a sense of connectedness with and compassion for not just the oppressed but also the oppressors, not just the poor but also the rich, not just the victims of violence but the perpetrators of violence. For me, and I know for many of my students, one of the most powerful and halting examples of what this means is Thich Nhat Hanh's well-known poem "Call Me by My True Names." Its most daunting verse:

> I am the twelve-year-old girl, refugee on a small boat,
> who throws herself into the ocean after being raped by a sea pirate,
> And I am the pirate, my heart not yet capable of seeing and loving.

Unless our compassion can flow out and embrace "both sides," we will not be peacemakers.

Buddhists' refusal to denounce anyone, or to take sides against anyone, is an expression of their refusal to engage in any kind of violence toward anyone, whether physical, verbal, or merely attitudinal. Violence cuts off connectedness and compassion or renders them inoperative. Of all the religions in the world, I think Buddhism has the firmest doctrinal foundation for, and the most ongoing call for, non-violence. (Though, like all religions, it has not always lived up to its own beliefs and ideals.)

This aversion for violence is also why I believe we can say that for Buddhists there is no such thing as "just anger." Of course, we will feel anger. And it will motivate and direct our energies. But, for Buddhists, it will not determine what those energies lead to. We will not act out of anger. Rather, when anger surges, we will be mindful of it, and that means embrace it, be kind to it. Our anger will point us to those people or events which, through mindfulness, we will seek to respond to with understanding and compassion. Yes, we may have to oppose them, seek to stop them from their agendas of land appropriation or healthcare reduction. But our opposition will be one of non-violent resistance; that means compassionate resistance.

One of the most quoted verses of the *Dhammapada* is: "In this world hatred is not dispelled by hatred; by love alone is hatred dispelled. This is an eternal law" (vv. 3–5).

Standing back from this all too hasty review of Buddhist ways of acting in a world of suffering, a Christian like me concludes that for Buddhists compassion is more important than justice. In fact, I have to wonder whether they are that concerned about justice at all! Not because justice doesn't matter, but, rather, because justice will, as it were, take care of itself if compassion is truly present. Certainly, they are saying that without compassion there will be no justice. But are they going a step further and suggesting that if there is compassion, there will be justice?

I juggled the same questions in a conversation that some of us Christian/Western members of the Interreligious Peace Council had with Venerable Samdhong Rinpoche, counsellor and friend to the Dalai Lama, and since 2001 Tibet's elected Prime Minister. We suggested to him that despite the Tibetan government's official policy of non-violence toward the Chinese, the injustices perpetrated against the Tibetan people continue; indeed, they seem to have intensified. His response: "I guess we have not been non-violent and compassionate enough!"

PASSING BACK: IF YOU WANT JUSTICE, WORK FOR PEACE!

In this final effort of this final chapter to "pass back" to my Christian ideal of being a peacemaker after trying to "pass over" to the Buddhist ideal of being a "peacebe-er," I will inevitably be offering a selected review of this entire book. Both the theological contents of chapters 1–5 and the spiritual message of Chapter 6 will find their more practical payoff in this chapter. If, as they say, praxis is supposed to confirm theory, then this final passing over should, I hope, offer a further confirmation of the value of being a Buddhist Christian.

Our efforts to come to a more non-dualistic understanding of the relation between the Divine and the finite, our preferred symbol of God as the interconnecting Spirit, our view of Jesus as embodying and revealing the "Christ-Spirit" and so living on in his disciples, our proposal for an additional "Sacrament of Silence" in Christian spirituality and liturgy – all these reinterpretations and re-livings of Christian belief and life that Buddhism has helped me envision will play centrally in how I believe Buddhism is aiding me and challenging me to become a more effective Christian peacemaker.

"The Kindom of God is among you"

It sure does look like there is a contrast, if not a straight-out contradiction, between the way Buddhism seems to suck all of history into the present moment (the eternal now) and the way Christianity propels history forward toward a final conclusion (the end of the world and Christ's Second Coming). Now according to guidelines for inter-religious dialogue, what often looks like a road-blocking contradiction can turn out to be a path-finding revelation. That has been my experience from trying to sit with and open myself to this contradiction between the Buddhist "now" and the Christian "future." Buddhism has enabled me to understand more clearly, and to live more meaningfully, what I believe Christian belief about the future is telling us. It's offered me insights that go beyond what Christian eschatology has said in the past, and yet at the same time these insights renew what eschatology has always said. Let me try to explain.

Getting right to the pivotal point of what I think I've learned from Buddhism, it's this: the same kind of non-duality – that is, the same kind of essential unity within actual difference – between the Ultimate and the finite, or between God and the world, that we explored in Chapters 1 and 2 can apply to the relationship between the now and the future. As we have often heard before they are *not two* but they are also *not one*. The relationship between the present and the future is one in which they co-inhere, or have their existence, in each other. They're really different, and yet one cannot be found, or realized, without the other.

This is all pretty abstract and heady. Simply and practically, it is warning us that we cannot look for the future "out there." We may have some fingers (like the image of Jesus' Second Coming) that point to the future, but as for what they might mean, we have to look to, and fully engage, the present moment. Whatever the future is, or will be, can be known and it can be realized by what is going on right now.

That means we must engage the present moment with as much honesty, creativity, boldness, and yes, mindfulness, as we can. And we know that we *can* so engage the present moment; we know that we *can* "make something of" whatever suffering or failure may be contained in the present moment. Why? Because the "now" is not just the now. It is also the future. It is, as it were, pregnant with the future, able to bear the future. It already contains the future. But these contents of the future are not pre-determined. They're being specified, formed, by what is taking place now. What will come tomorrow is *already/not yet* present in what is done today.

I use that phrase, "already/not yet," deliberately, because, as I already noted, it is the term that New Testament scholars have been employing to describe what they think was Jesus' understanding of the Kindom of God. Jesus clearly believed that the "*Basileia tou Theou*" was still to come in the future. And yet, the Gospel of Mark opens with Jesus' ringing wake-up call: "The time is fulfilled. The Kindom of God is at hand" (Mark 1:15). And then there is the enigmatic way Jesus answered the Pharisees' question about when the Kindom of God was coming. "In fact, the Kindom of God is among you," he declared (Luke 17:20–21). In some paradoxical, mystical way, for Jesus the Kindom was both still to come and yet "among you," both present and future, both "already and not yet."

The way I, and I believe most Christians, have tried to figure out what this contradiction means is to conclude, rather assuredly and logically, that what Jesus of course meant was that the "future Kindom" is the full and final reality, whereas right now we have it partially, in promissory pieces. This assures us that the Kindom is certainly going to arrive, but, like a child thinking about Christmas, we just have to be patient and wait – and of course "we'd better be good" so as to enjoy it when it comes. Buddhism has helped me grasp that what Jesus experienced and revealed was probably not that logic-bound, not that neat. The Kindom he was announcing was really and truly both already *and* not yet.

Through my conversation with Buddhism, I've come to suspect that we Christians have so stressed the "not yet" that we have lost touch with the "already" (similar to the way we have so focused on Jesus' divinity that we have blurred his humanity). We're so fixed on, and we have so consoled ourselves by, what's to come that we lose sight of opportunities, and perhaps responsibilities, within what's going on right now. In concentrating on Jesus' assurance that "*then* things *will be* better," we miss his assurance that "*now* things *can be* better." Because we know that only in the future, when Jesus comes again, will things really be put right, we slip into an attitude that the mess of the moment has to be put up with. And so we find ourselves thinking, maybe even saying, "You can't change human nature … You can't fight city hall … Politicians will always be corrupt … That's what the market dictates." And so we content ourselves with tinkering with rather than transforming the world. We take it for granted that transformation is not yet here, that it will come only in the future.

Buddhists are perhaps more able to take Jesus seriously: transformation is already here. What the future contains can be realized right now because it is already present! In fact, whatever the future will be is being worked out, taking shape, right now, in the "already" part of Jesus' message. What we're after is already here. And therefore we can continue to go after it. This empowering paradox is captured in a pithy sentence of Dzogchen Lama Surya Das: "we're perfect as we are, and yet there's work to be done." Realizing that the perfection of the Kindom is already here, we are empowered to carry on with the work that stands before us.

Here I believe that Buddhism has pushed me deeper into what Jesus, paradoxically, was proposing: the assurance we have about the future "not yet" is meant to *prioritize* the present "already." What counts most is not to wait for the future that is to come but to recognize and shape the future that is present in the moment. So if we Christians want to affirm that the symbol of Jesus' Second Coming will bring finality, Buddhism – and I believe the message of the New Testament – tells us that this finality is being determined by what we're doing now.

In a journal entry of June 2002 I was trying to say something along these lines: "Buddhists are telling Christians that if they really hold that God reveals Godself in history, they had better pay attention not just to history but to the Now, because that's where history is taking place. Nowhere else!"

Lama Surya Das, in describing the heart of the Buddhism he practices, makes the same point even more pointedly and powerfully: "The secret wisdom of Dzogchen teaches us that whatever we are looking for, it is always right here. *We are usually elsewhere.* That's the problem."

This prioritizing of the Now makes clear why Buddhists sound their warnings about "the dangers of a plan." Plans are important and helpful, for by looking ahead to our goals, to what we want to accomplish in the future, we direct our energies as we work with the materials of the moment. But, if Jesus is correct that "the Kindom is already among you," and if Buddha is correct that all we need is already given to us, then whatever plans we have must be not only applied to the materials of the moment but, often, subordinated to these materials. If there is truly a non-dualistic relationship between the "already Kindom" and the "not-yet Kindom," then the future, not-yet-Kindom must be found within and it must grow out of the present-already Kindom. Plans that are too clearly drawn or too tightly held can prevent the now from becoming the future. Bottom-line lesson for us Christians: have plans, but don't cling to them – and always be ready to adjust, change, or jettison any plan. For type-A people like myself, that isn't easy!

Pretty much the same lesson applies to the question of hope, but with even more discomforting demands for Christians. Jesus' conviction that the Kindom is *already*, clarified through the Buddhist understanding of the present moment, tells us – I think I can put it this way – that we can have hope, but we really don't need it, and certainly our present actions should not be dependent on it. We don't need hope for the future because the not-yet future that we're hoping for is already here, in this moment. What sustains us, and what enables us to draw the "not yet" out of the "already," is given to us in the very situation that we are struggling with. This means we can trust, even though we can't get a clear fix on just what we are trusting.

This, as we said last chapter, is faith at its finest – when you trust without being able to see what you are trusting, when you love without having a clear comprehension of what you are loving. Maybe this is what St. Paul meant when he admonished the early Christians to "hope against hope" (Rom. 4:18), to hope even though it's a groundless hope. I tried to tell myself this in a journal entry of January 2006:

"So I can hope, even though I can never define neatly what I am hoping for, even though I can never control the future for which I hope."

So, with this Buddhist reappropriation of Christian eschatology and of Jesus' vision of the already/not-yet Kindom, how do I answer the question I started this chapter with: "What can we hope for?" I would want to formulate my answer along these lines: "I don't know what we can hope for. But I do know that we can hope." We can hope because human history, like every human being, is part of and at-oned with a larger, interrelated and interrelating activity that we have called InterBeing or the Connecting Spirit. And this Spirit, which filled Jesus to the point that it continues to fill his disciples, convinced Jesus that the vision he inherited from his Jewish ancestors of a world in which human beings would truly love and care for each other was really possible because the Spirit of God was already present.

This is what enables us to hope – the experience and the conviction that when we act in this world with wisdom and compassion and concern for justice, it is the Spirit acting in and through us. What this will lead to, we don't know. The Spirit and therefore the Kindom is present already. The not-yet will take care of itself.

So the value of our actions is to be found in the actions themselves, insofar as they are actions of the Spirit and therefore part of the already present Kindom. Whether they produce fruits or not – whether they bring about structural change in El Salvador or in the global market or not – they are what we do when the Spirit touches us, when we wake up to our Buddha-nature or our being-in-Christ. We cannot not do them. We act not to gain the fruits of our actions but because this is how the Christ-Spirit or our Buddha-nature acts, though we rejoice when our actions do bear fruit. The well-worn dictum applies: "We are not called to be successful, but to be faithful" to what we are, though we also know that if ever there is to be success, it will come out of such fidelity.

Tomorrow can be better than today

In concluding these reflections on the Kindom of God, I have to confess that there is an element of my Christian belief, based on my understanding of Jesus, that seems to be at odds with Buddhism and that I can't let go of (though I don't want to cling to it!). It has to do with the affirmation found in all the Abrahamic religions that history is real *and* that history can be better. Buddhists, insofar as they find change and impermanence at the root of reality, can be said, perhaps, to recognize history (insofar as history consists of change). A Buddhist friend recently gave me a T-shirt that announces, under a smiling Buddha-face, "Impermanence makes everything possible." But Buddhists don't affirm – at least not as clearly and centrally as Judaism, Christianity, and Islam – that things can change for the *better*. For them, as I already put it, history isn't going anywhere. And it doesn't have to.

Because as a Christian I believe in a Divine, a connecting Spirit that is "up to something" in history, I believe that history bears within itself the possibility – that does *not* mean the necessity – of improvement. In other words, I hold the belief that there can be less hatred, less violence, less injustice in the world tomorrow than there is today.

As we heard, if we should ask Buddhists whether Emptiness or InterBeing is up to anything, they might reply that it is bringing forth evermore Awakening among humanity – ever more wisdom and compassion. But they leave it there. As a Christian I want to add: and with and through this wisdom and compassion we can bring about real change in this world; we can transform social and political structures and so fashion a world in which it will be a little easier for people to attain wisdom and compassion. Never the final, perfect world, but a different, a better world.

In making this point that the world can improve and be transformed, I have to keep in mind the Buddhist warnings not to think I know or can predict just what these improvements will be. I also need to listen carefully to their reservations about thinking and expecting that there will be an end point where everything will be tied up and no more change will be possible or needed. Still, I want to hold to my Christian hope (which is always a groundless hope against hope) that not only human hearts but the world and its structures can and must change.

Back in November 2002, while I was reading Jon Sobrino's wonderful books *Jesus the Liberator* and *Christ the Liberator*, I came to an insight about what the symbol of Jesus' Second Coming might mean:

> This is what the "second coming" tells us: that things can be different, that they can change, improve. But that there will be a final completion, that the curtain will come down, and everything will be statically okay – that is not for us to know; and really, the more we think about such a final curtain call, the more it does not seem to fit a God of history, a God whose richness and creativity cannot be contained and finalized.

So here we may have a way of clarifying, even correcting, certain understandings of Buddhism and Christianity that really may be misunderstandings: the notion that Buddhism holds that there is no future, and the notion that for Christians, the future will some day run out in a final Kindom in heaven.

In other words, the symbol of the Second Coming, or the end of the world, means that we can expect "end points" where things will really be different. But no end point excludes further end points, further "not-yets" to be drawn from the "already."

So, as a Christian, with a good bit of help from Buddhism, I can offer an answer to Elise Boulding's question: "Do you really believe that peace is possible?" Yes, I do. That doesn't mean that peace will be perfectly, unchangeably realized all over the world so that there will be no violence, no hatred whatsoever. That doesn't mean that when we roll our peacemaking rock up the hill, other rocks will not tumble down into the valley. But I believe that some rocks *will* stay. I believe that we can bring more people to realize their true natures as inter-connected sources of wisdom, compassion, and justice, and that therefore there can be a little more peace in the world tomorrow than there is today. And I believe that this is so because my personal experi-ence has led me to trust what Jesus and Buddha have announced: that our deepest nature is the Buddha-nature of wisdom and compassion, and that the interconnecting Spirit that animated Jesus is still alive in the world.

But even if someone was able to prove to me (as I don't think any-one can) that peace is *not* possible, that things will never really change, that all rocks roll back downhill – even then, as Buddhism has helped me realize, I would still continue my efforts to be peace and to make peace. Why? Because that's what one does when one awakens to one's Buddha-nature, or when one comes to know that "it is not I who live but Christ who lives in me." Happily, I have no choice!

Being Christ and building the Kindom

Over the years, ever since Thich Nhat Hanh's little book *Being Peace* delivered its blow to my spiritual solar plexus, this simple but demanding conclusion has gained strength for me: he's right, and boy do I and so many of my fellow Christian activists need to take him seriously.

We're really not going to be of much help in making peace for the world unless we are seriously committed to making peace and being peace for ourselves. What the makers of peace end up making depends on what they are. Whether peacemakers are going to be able to achieve their goals of bringing at least a little more peace into this strife-filled world depends not on what they *do* but on what they *are*. If peacemakers *are* peace, then what they do will *make* peace. If they are *not* peace, then what they do will either be ineffective, or it will be counter-productive – that is, it will end up bringing more unrest or strife. My personal response to such admonitions, as I've indicated in the first part of this chapter, is a humbled one: "Been there. Done that." I have tried to make peace without being peace.

What Thay and other Engaged Buddhists are reminding me of is not just that as a Christian, in my efforts to build Jesus' vision of the Kindom on earth, I must keep a proper balance between action and contemplation, between time on the streets and time on my knees. In a sense, Buddhists are suggesting that there needs to be a certain *imbalance* between spirituality and activity insofar as they give priority to spirituality. As I put it earlier, action and contemplation have to form an ongoing circle, for one leads to and needs the other. But Buddhists remind us that meditation and spirituality are the entrance point where we are taken up into the movement of the circle. Even more: meditation provides the energy that keeps the circle turning and that prevents it from petering out.

This does not translate into simplistic formulae like therefore we must spend more time in prayer and meditation than we do in action and organizing. It doesn't mean, either, that we have to have bulging spiritual muscles before we start rolling rocks up the hill. But it does mean that we have to do a substantial amount of spiritual training and develop a basic store of the inner resources of wisdom, compassion, and mindfulness before we enter the fray and take up the exhausting and the always dangerous work of peacemaking and Kindom-building. Like deep-sea divers, we have to have an ample amount of spiritual oxygen in our tanks before we jump into the tasks below the surface. And as these labors exhaust and confuse us, our tanks are going to need regular refilling. In Thay's language, *making* requires *being* – and the job of nurturing our being peace is never over.

The Buddhist insistence that making peace requires being peace has pushed me even further. They're not just reminding me that contemplation is essential for action and therefore bears a certain priority over action. Buddhists are talking about a particular kind of spirituality that they believe is essential for effective peacemaking. When one examines what Thich Nhat Hanh and other teachers mean by "being peace" one realizes they are talking about the kind of spirituality that Christians would call *mystical*. My passing over to Buddhism has made clear to me that if I want to have any success as a Christian activist I'm also going to have to be, or try to be, a Christian mystic.

We're back to the theme that has sounded throughout this book: the fundamental, dynamic relationship between the Infinite and the finite – in Buddhist symbols, between Emptiness and form, or in Christian language, between the Spirit and the world – is one in which both exist in and out of each other; utterly different as they are and remain, they co-inhere, they "inter-are." (This is what we explored in Chapters 1–4.) And "salvation" and "spirituality" are a matter of waking up to this unity, this identity, this oneness-in-twoness, to feel it in our spiritual bones and to live it out in our daily lives (Chapters 5 and 6). Well, Buddhism has helped make it clear to me that just such a mystical, unitive experience must also form the source and direction for my activist efforts to bring this world a little closer to the ideals of the Kindom of God. Again, effective activism requires solid mysticism.

For me, the particular Christian realization of this unitive, mystical experience is contained in Paul's outburst in his letter to the Galatians: "I'm not alive. Christ is alive as me!" For this reason, I've sub-titled this section "Being Christ and building the Kindom." For Christians, "to be peace" is "to be Christ." So if we want to "make the peace" of Christ's Kindom, we first have to "be Christ."

It is precisely the effects of the mystical, unitive experience of being in Christ-Jesus that help remove one of the greatest obstacles to peacemaking: our ever-lurking egos. If it is "no longer I who am building the Kindom but Christ building in me" I will be less prone to being infected by the ego-viruses that contaminate the work of so many doers-of-good: the need for recognition, for success, for control, for superiority. The mystical experience of being in Christ-Jesus, like all unitive spiritual experiences, enables us to feel and so to know that our true identity is much larger than our self-identity and that we can find ourselves only outside ourselves.

And so our energies will be naturally shifted from centripetal self-centeredness to centrifugal other-centeredness. This means that the energies devoted to building the Kindom will be generated not by the formulated need to achieve certain goals or realize certain plans but by the natural need to have compassion and love. Further, this will enable us to be as firm in our commitments to the task of fostering the Kindom as we are loose in our way of going about this task. We will, as the Buddhists put it, have plans of action, but we will not cling to them. We will enter every situation usually knowing what might be done, but always with an even greater readiness to learn what is to be done. Clinging to nothing, we are open to everything – but with an openness guided by the wisdom and compassion of being-in-Christ.

When our peacemaking activities are so grounded and sustained in the mystical experience of being in the Christ-Spirit, when we have an abiding sense that all our efforts to transform the world are part of an InterBeing that embraces and constitutes everything that is going on in the world – then we will be able to act with an uncanny kind of freedom. It is the freedom to succeed, and the freedom to fail; the freedom not to cling to success and the freedom not to be crushed by failure.

There's a paradox involved in such freedom that evades words. We know and feel we have to act in order to deal with all the suffering suffusing our world. But at the same time, we sense that because our actions are not just ours but part of the broader, ongoing activity of the Spirit, they're not *that* important. Or better, their value or necessity is not determined by their outcomes. So we can make our efforts with utter seriousness and determination, but we can also step back from them and laugh. We can dance and play in the Spirit as vigorously as we toil and strain in the Spirit.

In my journal of September 2002 I quoted another passage from Eckhart Tolle's book *The Power of Now*, which I think expresses the power of this freedom more clearly and deeply than I can.

> He states that when "you feel your roots in the Unmanifested [which I call the Christ-Spirit] ... you are in touch with something infinitely greater than any pleasure, greater than any manifested being. In a way, you then don't need the world anymore. You don't even need it to be different from the way it is." You are free from having to change the world. Then, really only then, are you free and able to change the world! Tolle continues: "It is only at this point that you begin to make a real contribution toward bringing about a better world, toward creating a different order of reality. It is only at this point that you are able to feel true compassion and to help others at the level of cause.

Only those who have transcended the world can bring about a better world."

Or in Thay's terms: only those who are at peace in the midst of the injustices and brutalities of the world are able to bring peace to such a world. I suspect that only mystics can understand that, and act on that.

I, and I believe many of my fellow Christians, have much to learn from the Buddhist teaching that Awakening, or being peace, is both necessary for, and has a certain priority over, making peace. But I have to confess that I can't help my Christian uneasiness about the suggestion that all we have to do is "be peace" in order for the world to "have peace." As I pointed out, Buddhist teachers sometimes give the impression that personal Awakening and transformation will by itself bring about social transformation. All we really have to do is wake up ourselves and help others to do likewise ... I'm not so sure.

From my limited experience in encountering "the powers that be," whether in San Salvador or in Washington, D.C. or on Wall Street, I've come to realize that Christian liberation theologians are on to something very important when they remind us that besides personal sin there is also social sin. In Buddhist terms – and for me, terms that are more reflective of why this is so – the greed that results from ignorance becomes embodied in social structures, in economic and political policies, and cultural attitudes. And in this process social ignorance and greed take on a life of their own. Personal ignorance becomes social ignorance; personal greed, national greed; individual suffering, social suffering.

So while individual, personal Awakening and transformation are absolutely necessary to bring about social change (this is what Christians too often forget), it is not enough. Social, political, legal Awakening, and transformation are also necessary. (This is what, it seems, Buddhists too often forget.) We are dealing with not only individuals who harm others out of ignorance. We are dealing with socio-economic structures that harm others, even when they are populated by Awakened individuals. Besides personal *karma*, there is social *karma*. They both may have the same causes, but they inhabit different bodies.

Therefore, as a Christian, I feel that besides the personal introspection that is necessary to realize that all *dukkha* or suffering comes from *tanha* or greed, I must also engage in a social introspection to determine where greed is operating in economic or legal policies. While individual hearts and actions are the ultimate cause of social structures that produce suffering, we may often not be able really to understand and transform our hearts unless we also, at the same time, understand and transform social structures. Perhaps Gautama implicitly realized this when he formulated the fifth principle of the Eightfold Path and warned people that before they can be Enlightened they may have to change their job (right livelihood)!

But if as a Christian I feel I have to remind Buddhists that they need to do social analysis together with personal analysis, they in turn offer me important – maybe indispensable – help in doing such social analysis. If Christian liberation theologians insist that the transformation of society may require more than the transformation of individuals, Buddhism has valuable advice on how to transform social structures. In the next and final section of this final chapter, I hope I can make clear what I think I've learned.

No justice without compassion

The "conversion" that Buddhism has brought about in my understanding of requirements for building the Kindom of God is summed up in the subtitle I gave this "passing back" section: "If you Want Justice, Work for Peace." That's a flat-out reversal of what I have been taught, and what, over a couple of activist decades, I believed, preached, and tried to practice.

But the reversal is not a denial. Rather, it calls for the same kind of dynamic circle that I described regarding the relationship between action and contemplation. It's both/and. If you want peace, work for justice. And if you want justice, work for peace. And yet, as with the action/contemplation circle, Buddhism has persistently nudged me toward the realization that the point of entry for this circle, as well as what keeps it turning, is found in working for peace. Striving for peace through reconciliation, in other words, has a certain priority over striving for justice and, I must add, over striving for structural change.

This pivotal insight into the relationship between peace and justice that Buddhism has crystallized for me also clarifies the role of non-violence in all my efforts to transform this world. Thanks to Buddha, I have come to see – and more importantly I have come to feel – that non-violence is at the heart of Jesus' message. But also, thanks to Buddha, I can affirm this in a way in which I do not absolutize non-violence. Again, paradox is at play here. Let me try to bring it into focus in five steps, which really are five ways in which Buddha has helped me understand more deeply Jesus' action plan for the Kindom of God.

1. No greater commandment

First a hasty review. We've heard often in these pages that the two defining qualities of an Awakened being are *prajna* (wisdom) and *karuna* (compassion). Really they are two different expressions of the same experience-based realization. Wisdom indicates what one discovers *within* oneself, and compassion describes how one responds to the world *outside* oneself. As the story of Buddha's Enlightenment illustrates, the very first thing Buddha did when he got up from under the Bodhi Tree (the Tree of Awakening) was to head back to his buddies in Benares. He felt compassion for them; he had to share with them what he had discovered. Compassion therefore is the first, fundamental, dominant, we might even say the regulative energy with which a Buddhist views and deals with the world. However else a disciple of Gautama will understand and respond to the world, it will be inspired by and guided by compassion. A Buddhist, ideally, doesn't do anything in the world that is not spilling out of her or his compassion.

This compassion is universal. It embraces all sentient beings, no matter who they are or what they have done. Why? Because of what becomes clear in Enlightenment – that we are all so interconnected that we have our life in each other; we see and find ourselves in other selves, to the point that the "other" is just as much *my* self as an *other* self. We live and move and have our being in each other. So a Buddhist can love her neighbor as herself because her neighbor *is* herself!

I have come to the realization that what Buddha discovered about the natural necessity and primacy of *karuna* affirms, deepens, and makes even more demanding the core energy of Jesus' gospel. One thing that Jesus – and St. Paul after him – was absolutely clear about was that if we line up all the commandments in order of importance, the first place always goes to love, to *agape*. For Jesus, loving God and loving neighbor were two different ways of fulfilling the very same commandment, and he was utterly clear that "there is no commandment greater than these" (Mark 12:29–31). For Paul, love of neighbor "sums up" and "fulfills" *all* the other commandments (Rom. 13:8–10).

For both Jesus and Buddha, love of neighbor and compassion for all sentient beings is what their followers naturally do. Compassion flows from wisdom just as naturally as love of neighbor flows from love of God. For Buddhists, to experience Awakening is to experience the interconnectedness that makes us all one. For Christians, to experience the Divine as Love is to experience the source that makes us all "children of God" and therefore brothers and sisters to one another.

And this means that everyone and every sentient being is so connected and so related. No one is excluded, even those who have tried, as it were, to exclude themselves through ignorance, hatred, or greed. That's why Jesus said even those who would call themselves our enemies aren't really enemies. The neighbor whom he tells us to love as ourselves also includes our "enemies," for they too remain God's children. Nothing can remove them from the interconnectedness of what Buddhists would call InterBeing and what Christians call the family of God.

If this is so, if *agape* or love holds the same kind of centrality for Christians as *karuna* or compassion does for Buddhists, if love is truly the "greatest of commandments," then it must precede, or guide and determine, all our actions and attitudes toward our "neighbors," including those neighbors who look like or try to be our enemies.

This "prior" or "greatest" commandment, therefore, also precedes justice. Yes, Jesus wanted all people to be treated justly. But Buddhism has reminded me that he first of all wanted all people to love each other. I don't want to say that therefore love is more important than justice. But I do want to say, because I believe I have to say, that love precedes justice; or better put, it provides the necessary "condition for the very possibility" of justice. To paraphrase Paul: "Peace, justice, love. These three remain. But the greatest of these is love."

2. Love excludes the violence of hatred

If love and compassion, as the "greatest of the commandments," are both to inspire and regulate all of our efforts for the Kindom of God, including our actions for justice, then hatred can have no part in building God's Kindom. That, my undergrad students would define as a "no-brainer." Like water and oil, love and hatred just don't mix. That's clear, as well, in the message and actions of Jesus: he opposed, but he never hated.

But Buddhists go a step further and so have prodded me to look more deeply and honestly into the nature and demands of Jesus' "greatest commandment." For them, compassion excludes not only hatred. It also rules out anger, and the almost unavoidable result when anger gets out of its corral: violence. Actions and words that flow from anger are generally going to be violent, physically, verbally, psychologically. Their purpose will be to hurt. For this reason, Buddhists hold that if you're trying to combine compassion with anger, you're kidding yourself. Anger opens the door to violence. And once you're violent, you've cut off your interconnectedness and profoundly jeopardized your ability to love.

In ruling out actions that arise from anger, Buddhists, as we have seen, do not deny the reality of anger. In fact, they accept and even embrace it – as mindfulness directs them to do with everything they encounter. But in being mindful of their anger, they sever the direct current between anger and action before that current can flow. In recognizing and embracing their anger they do not allow it to control their response to whatever caused the anger.

Indeed, anger, such as we might spontaneously feel about the "collateral damage" on civilians in an unjustified military action, can serve as an alarm that alerts us to suffering, without however determining our response to suffering. Anger can stir up our energies without dictating how those energies are applied. In fact, the surges of anger that we spontaneously feel when we witness how cruel and unjust humans can be to each other can be used as "wake-up bells" that call us to return to the connecting Spirit within us and to respond from that Spirit, not from anger.

The reason that Buddhists are so wary of anger and the reason they want to transform it through mindfulness before it can impregnate their actions is because they realize, I suspect, that "just anger" so easily leads to "just war." Justified anger slips slickly into justified violence. Declared and hated "evil-doers" are one step, or one speech, away from declared targets.

Because Buddhists see an evident incompatibility between violence and their interconnected Buddha-nature, they offer a much more generalized and elaborated endorsement of non-violence than do Christians. The way they link "being peace" with "being non-violent" has convinced me that the same incompatibility exists between violence and Jesus' "greatest commandment" of loving one's neighbor as oneself. After all, I think that one of the things that Jesus wanted to tell us when he urged us "to love our enemies" was not to kill them! Buddha has faced me with the same question that I should have earlier heard from Jesus: how can we love our enemies and at the same time wage war against them?

But loving our "enemies" to the point of refusing to do violence to them does not exclude identifying them, opposing them, and doing so resolutely. This is evident from the well-known scene of Jesus cleansing the Temple. Clearly he was upset, and he felt anger. And though his actions were drastic – upsetting money tables, driving out sheep and cattle with a whip – there is no indication of hatred, or of physical harm to any of the vendors and money-changers. As the Gospel writer comments, he acted not out of hatred but out of "zeal for his Father's house" (John 2:13–18).

But in following the dictates of non-violence given by Jesus and Buddha, what is really dictating is not non-violence but *agape* or *karuna*. If I may put it this way, the "absolute" in this case is not non-violence, but love. In Jesus' Jewish vocabulary the "commandment" we're talking about is love, not non-violence. While I cannot, in any way, conceive of exceptions to the spontaneous, natural law of loving all my neighbors and all sentient beings, I cannot say the same regarding the principle of non-violence. If someone was to show me that love of neighbor can, in some extraordinary situation, be compatible with doing or speaking violence to my neighbor, I would have to be open to that … But I don't think anyone can. Or no one has yet.

3. An option for the oppressed cannot be an option against the oppressors

To Thich Nhat Hanh's gentle criticisms of Christian liberation theology's "preferential option for the poor," I would have to respond gently that such an option is part of the distinctive way Jesus the Jewish prophet experienced the Spirit of InterBeing, and therefore part of the distinctive contribution that Christianity can make to Buddhism and to the interreligious conversation. Yes, Thay is correct: God does not have preferences in the sense of loving some people more than others. The embrace of the universal Spirit does not exclude anyone, nor does she give bigger hugs to some over others. The Compassion that moves the sun and the stars falls upon the sufferings and needs of all sentient beings.

But according to Christian experience and belief, the incarnation of the Spirit of Compassion in Jesus of Nazareth reveals that this universal Spirit moves us toward a particular pressing concern for those sentient beings who are not only suffering like everyone else, but who are suffering because of what other, more powerful sentient beings are doing to them. Again, we're talking about the suffering that results from the ignorance and greed of injustice. There's a difference between the suffering I impose on myself because of ignorance and the suffering I impose on others because of ignorance. The reminder that "Hey, everyone is suffering, rich and poor" is certainly true, but it can also be a distraction from, or a camouflage for, the role I play in causing the suffering of others.

To extend a Christian symbol for Divine Love, Jesus experienced his Parent-God to love all her children, but with a prior concern for those who were being harmed by others – like a father who turns momentarily from the three hungry kids he is preparing lunch for to tend to the hurt of the child who enters the door beat up by the school bully. So a "preferential option" for the excluded or enslaved or marginalized is not exclusive of others, but it does direct our attention and clarify our responsibilities.

Hoping that my Buddhist friends will understand my point regarding a preferential option for the oppressed, I do understand (or I think I do) their point – the one that the Buddhist members of the Interreligious Peace Council made in Chiapas when they declared "We don't denounce anyone." If as a follower of Jesus I feel I have to pursue a preferential concern for the oppressed, the followers of Buddha remind me that such a concern cannot involve an option against the oppressors. This, I have found, isn't easy to pull off. But I have also come to be convinced that it is absolutely necessary. If my option for the oppressed leads me to an option against the oppressors, things are only going to get worse.

But how to "take the side" of the oppressed without "taking sides" against the oppressors? How to oppose without denouncing? How to "be with" without "being against?" No neat answers are possible. But I have found help from Gandhi's example of *ahimsa* and from the ongoing practice of mindfulness-meditation. Gandhi's program for non-violence was, I believe, precisely what we are talking about: he stood firmly with the colonized people of India, but he never hated, or humiliated, or spoke ill of the British colonizers. Thus, he never broke off his connections with them. They knew he opposed them, but they did not feel he was against them. Indeed, they knew he respected and cared for them.

Gandhi opposed, but he also embraced. To do that, one must be acting from a well-nurtured spiritual center. This is another reason why all our liberating action must arise out of our uniting contemplation – why, as Roshi Bernie Glassman told me, I'll never stop the death squads unless I realize my oneness with them. The more we practice mindfulness while sitting, the more we will be able to practice mindfulness while acting. And such mindfulness or centeredness will enable us to accept the reality of oppression, to view the oppressors without judging them to be evil, and so to feel our "oneness with them" and our love for them. And then, perhaps only then, will we have the wisdom and compassion to oppose them effectively.

When our opposition to those we have judged to be the oppressors is so animated by wisdom and compassion, our opposition to what they are doing will always contain an option for their wellbeing. So a preferential option for the poor is also always part of an option for the oppressors. We are also seeking to promote the wellbeing of the oppressors, their happiness, their peace. We know they are oppressing others not because they are inherently evil or inherently selfish, but because they have not yet realized who and what they really are – God's children, bearers of Buddha's nature. In opposing them, we wish to help them realize their essential goodness. To oppose oppressors is to embrace oppressors.

My primary example of such an ability both to oppose and embrace your "enemies" is Jesus. I realized this in a journal entry of November 2004, after a presidential election in the U.S.A. that both depressed and angered me:

> Jesus was both prophet and non-self. He spoke boldly, boldly enough to get himself executed. But he spoke selflessly, lovingly, dialogically enough to allow himself to be executed.
>
> I need to be more in touch, more mindful, of this prophetic-kenotic Christ-Spirit living and acting in and as me. In my criticisms, in my denunciations of the harm that this Administration is doing – better, that I think it is doing – I want also to be animated by two pieces of mindfulness: a) my connectedness with and therefore my embrace of those whom I am opposing; and b) the limitation of what

I know, of my assessment and evaluations of the situation. I always have to learn more and see more; and perhaps those I am opposing can help me do that.

Resistance and embrace – prophetic proclamation and self-opening dialogue – these are the energies that I need to allow to move through me during these difficult days – probably during these next four years.

4. Just social structures require reconciled human hearts

As I tried to explain earlier, I do believe that Buddhists have something to learn from Christian liberation theology about the necessity of working for structural change as they work for personal change; personal transformation does not automatically lead to social transformation, and thus the need actively, consciously, intelligently to engage and re-form the world of politics and economics. While I truly believe this is so, I also know that we Christians have an even greater need to listen to the Buddhist admonition that although structural change may be an undertaking distinct from personal change, it will never really happen without personal change. If Christians insist that individual, personal Awakening or conversion is not enough, Buddhists might respond, okay, agreed, but personal Awakening must be *prior*.

Why? A clear response has been taking shape for me over these years of working for justice and structural change with CRISPAZ in El Salvador and with the Interreligious Peace Council in Mexico, Northern Ireland, and Israel/Palestine: I have come to see that justice and structural change cannot be imposed, they cannot be simply required by a new law from the government, or a new resolution from the United Nations. To seek social change solely through the imposition of law, or through required land-reform programs, or through punitive or re-distributive measures may introduce a transformation of society but it won't be able to sustain it.

Actions that impose or force change upon that which is denounced as unjust and evil are, in a limited but real sense, violent. And according to the laws of physics and the psyche, a violent force will bring forth a counter-violent force. For the human psyche, this is so because violence communicates hatred. If the oppressors feel that they are being hated, if they feel that they are not being listened to or respected, they will respond with the all-too-human reaction of violent self-protection or violent hatred in return. Even if those who are demanding justice and denouncing oppression do not harbor hatred in their hearts (that is indeed a big "if!") that will not be the message the denounced oppressors receive. Violence, willy-nilly, communicates hatred. And being hated reacts with violence.

The conclusion from all this is, I think, clear: the only way, or the only hope, that real social transformation will take place is if there is personal transformation and internal Awakening in the hearts of the oppressors. But doesn't that make things even more daunting? According to the *Dhammapada*, not really: "In this world hatred is not dispelled by hatred; by love *alone* is hatred dispelled. This is an eternal law" (I added the italics). If there is any chance that hatred will be appeased and that our enemies will be turned into our brothers and sisters, it will be "by love" only if we "love our enemies." And that includes those who are oppressing us or others.

Here, with Buddha's help, I draw the uncomfortable, sometimes dangerous, but liberating conclusion for us Christian activists: if hope for real change in social structures hinges on the personal Awakening and conversion of the oppressors, such a conversion calls for the prior Awakening and conversion of those who are committed to overcoming oppression. It will be Awakened seekers of justice who, because they can respond to hatred and injustice with love and compassion, have the best chances of waking up the oppressors from their state of ignorance and greed.

As Gandhi and Martin Luther King Jr. – and the Buddha and Jesus long before them – realized, our best "weapon" for changing the hearts of our oppressors or enemies is to love them. Jesus does not mince words: "But I tell you who hear me: Love your enemies, do good to those who hate you, bless those who curse you, pray for those who mistreat you" (Luke 6:27–28). Only in this way can we hope to bring an end to their hating and cursing and mistreating. Only then will hearts be changed. Only so will new laws and policies and structures work. Only in this way will liberation come not just for the oppressed but also for the oppressors.

This makes the work for justice and structural change much more demanding, especially for those who have been on the direct receiving end of injustice. It's relatively easy for me, a white, middle-class, American male to declare that we must love and forgive our oppressors if we hope to change their hearts. It's not so easy, indeed it is just about inconceivable, for a mother whose son has disappeared, a father whose land was appropriated, a teenager whose family was killed by a stray bomb. From a Christian perspective, to respond to hatred and harm with the non-violence of love is more than human. It is to be divine, interconnected, Spirit-born. (For Buddhists, this is to discover who we truly are.)

This realization lit up thunderously for me when I read a short passage from a book by Adyashanti. I copied the passage into my journal of March 16, 2007: "The truly sacred is the love of what is, not a love of what could be. This love liberates what is." I commented: "That last sentence is a spiritual bomb." When we love those whom we oppose as perpetrators of injustice *as they are*, not *for what we want them to be*, then, maybe only then, are we providing them a chance to become something different.

I have come to see that it was this "truly sacred," this "liberating love" that was revealed for us Christians in the way Jesus died.

5. *"The Law of the Cross"*

My passing over to Buddhism's emphasis on the non-violence of compassion as a condition for justice has enabled me to retrieve something from my "distant past" – from almost forty-five years ago, to be precise. I was sitting in the stuffy amphitheater-like classroom of Rome's Gregorian University in 1965. It was for a course on Christology ("*De Verbo Incarnato*" was its title) with the famous Bernard Lonergan, S.J. We were dealing with one of the last "theses" of the course, on the "the salvific efficacy" of the death of Jesus. Just why, or how, does Jesus' dying on the cross save the whole world? Only within the last ten or fifteen years, thanks especially to the help of the Buddha, have I been able to comprehend, appreciate, and try to live what Lonergan was telling us.

The thesis centered on the "*Lex Crucis*," the Law of the Cross. Lonergan was trying to move beyond, or offer alternatives for, an understanding of Jesus' death that, though it was one among many early explanations for how the cross saves us, came to dominate Christian consciousness: the so-called "Satisfaction Theory," which viewed Jesus' dying as the infinite satisfaction offered to God for the infinite offence of human sin. Lonergan was trying to get at the inner meaning (what he called the "intelligibility") of Jesus' death, which would help explain how it has the power or ability "to save us."

He found it in what he called "the Law of the Cross." By "law" he did not mean a dictate or commandment from God but, rather, a principle for the way things work, or can work – in this case, the way in which we can overcome (that is, diminish if not delete) the suffering that results from the selfishness that Christians call sinfulness (a selfishness that Buddhists would ascribe to ignorance).

Why, Lonergan asked, did Jesus end up on the cross? He didn't have to be executed. God did not decree his execution. Rather, Jesus died because of what he said and what he did. It all had to do with the core of his message and mission, the Kindom of God. In advocating a new social order in which people would truly care for each other as they care for themselves, in which this caring would be addressed especially to those most in need, the poor, Jesus knew that he would find himself, eventually but certainly, in trouble. What he had in mind with the Kindom of God was at odds with the policies of the Roman colonialists and their collaborators among the Jewish ruling classes. Like so many other prophets, Jesus was going to be called in to city hall to face the powers that be. It happened. They caught him. And the sentence was death.

It was at this point that Jesus felt himself claimed – perhaps unconsciously but certainly agonizingly – by what Lonergan called the Law of the Cross. Faced and threatened by hatred and violence, Jesus knew – or better, he felt – that the divine Spirit acting through him could not respond to hatred and violence with more hatred and violence. That is simply not how the Divine Love that animated him acts. But he also knew that if he didn't so respond, it was over. They would kill him. That horrified him. The Gospels report that he was so frightened that he sweat blood. He could neither avoid the issue by fleeing nor respond to it with violence. Somehow, having to die at this moment was part of his mission. Therefore, so be it. "Thy will be done."

According to the passion accounts in the Gospels, Jesus was firm on rejecting violence. To the rambunctious Peter, quick to seize his sword, Jesus spoke the words that are as memorable as they have been forgettable throughout the history of Christianity: "Those who resort to the sword will perish by the sword" (Matt. 26:52). The Gospel writer stresses the inappropriateness and ineffectiveness of swords by reminding us of the "twelve legions of angels" (all with swords!) that Jesus could appeal to in order to defend and promote his Kindom cause. But he made no such appeal. Throughout his trial and execution, there were no words of hatred or disdain for those condemning him or torturing him. Indeed, his final words about the perpetrators of his unjust execution show that non-violence is not just a refraining from physical harm but an actual feeling of compassion and love: "Father, forgive them, for they do not know what they are doing" (Luke 23:34).

But such love and such refusal to hate or act hatefully cost Jesus his life. It is here, precisely here, according to Lonergan, that Jesus revealed the saving power of "the Law of the Cross." It is really the law of love ready to die rather than hate. *It is such love, such refusal to hate, such non-violence that can change things* – not immediately but surely. In so loving, in so dying, Jesus reveals how we can stop or break the chain of hatred provoking hatred, violence begetting violence. On the cross, it was shown that this chain reaction that has tormented human history can be broken.

Out of such love, and out of such readiness to give one's life rather than hate, and also and even more paradoxically, out of such death, there comes life! Whether Jesus himself knew this clearly – from his complaint to God about "Why have you abandoned me?" it seems he did not – he trusted that in so dying and in so being faithful to his mission of confronting hatred and injustice with clarity but always with love, he was being faithful to his mission. "Into your hands, I commend my spirit." The God of compassion he believed in would, somehow, draw life out of his dying.

And in the resurrection, his followers realized that this is exactly what happened. Having confronted the powers that be, having embraced in love rather than in hatred these powers that be, and having died in doing so, Jesus was still alive with them and in them. His "cause," his vision of the Kindom of God, was still alive. His new body, what Paul called Jesus' mystical body, would carry on.

The "Law of the Cross" therefore saves us in that it engages and so empowers us to follow Jesus in seeking the justice of God's Kindom and the changes in social structures that it requires, but to do so, always, with a love that refuses the violence of hatred, even if this should cost us our lives.

The Law of the Cross saves because it affirms and embodies the "eternal law" that the *Dhammapada*, in a different context, also realized: "By love alone is hatred dispelled." Jesus would add: a love that must be ready to die rather than hate. Out of such love, and out of such death that this love can require, will hatred be dispelled. Hearts will be changed. And so will our world.

CONCLUSION:
PROMISCUITY OR HYBRIDITY?

An uncomfortable, but in the end I think helpful, question about this book took shape in that course at Union Theological Seminary that I mentioned in the Preface. This question offers a fitting conclusion to our efforts to pass over to Buddhism and pass back to Christianity.

Titled "Double-Belonging: Christian and Buddhist," the course used as its main text the first draft of this book. By the second week of the course the question that students found themselves wrestling with, and about which they wrestled with me, cut sharply to the quick: "Does religious double-belonging really work? Is it even possible?" Or as one of the more worldly students phrased it bluntly: "It looks like spiritual sleeping around!"

Blunt and unsettling as it is, the question raises a crucial point: is what I've been trying to do in this book really a kind of religious promiscuity? After all, one's religious identity and practice do bear striking similarities to a committed relationship such as marriage. I'm not talking about what "the law" (religious or cultural) says about marriage. I mean what it feels like when one falls in love. A religious experience and the decision to follow a spiritual path is, as I've recognized throughout this book, a lot like (maybe essentially the same as) falling in love. Whether it's the thunderclap of a sudden Awakening or the gentle rain of a growing awareness, when the Spirit enters one's life, one feels deeply and responds totally.

There's an inevitable all-consuming quality and a focused devotion to religious experience that by its very nature seems to exclude. "I choose you" means I'm not choosing someone else – at least not in the same way that I am choosing you.

So whether it's a case of the public declaration of marriage or the more private decision to "move in together," some form of monogamous practice or expectations result. Muslim scholars tell us that even when the Qur'an allows for polygamy, it also points out that it's practically impossible to pull off, since the prerequisite for having many wives is the requirement to love them all equally (4:3). No matter how large a marital bed may be, its occupancy is generally limited to two.

So does all the passing back and forth that I've described in the preceding pages end up, contrary to my intentions and awareness, as a form of *cheating*? Since I call myself a Christian, it would be cheating on Jesus. That's what a number of my theologian friends would suggest, though they use more academic terms: religious people raised in one tradition who try to identify with and nourish themselves also from another tradition end up, willy-nilly, in either diluting or shifting their religious commitments. They're Christians having an affair.

These are serious, very serious, concerns, not just academic but deeply personal. But having tried to take them as seriously and carefully as I can, I have to say here what I tried to say to my students: I honestly don't think these fears that double-belonging will lead to promiscuity or infidelity are accurate. I say that primarily on the level of what I feel: experientially, personally, I just do not feel that my "relationship" with Buddha has in any way lessened my relationship and commitment to Jesus, to gospel values, and yes, even to the teachings of my church and my tradition. On the contrary.

We're all hybrids

These feelings have been confirmed and clarified by the word that feminist theologians of religions like Jeannine Hill Fletcher use to describe a primary characteristic of religious identity. Our religious self, like our cultural or social self, is at its core and in its conduct a *hybrid*. That means that our religious identity is not purebred, it's hybrid. It's not singular, it's plural. It takes shape through an ongoing process of standing in one place and stepping into other places, of forming a sense of self and then expanding or correcting that sense as we meet other selves. There is no such thing as a neatly defined, once-and-for-all identity. Buddhists, indeed, are right: there is no isolated, permanent self. We're constantly changing and we're changing through the hybridizing process of interacting with others who often are very different from us.

So if we take the etymological meaning of "promiscuity" – the inclination to "mix it up," from the Latin *miscere* – we can say, with a dangerous stretch of words, that not only are we all promiscuous; we *have to be*! We have an identity, but that identity in its origins and in its ongoing life comes to be and continues to flourish only through mixing it up with others. Hybrids are stronger, live longer, and have more fun than purebreds.

But being religious hybrids doesn't mean that we don't have an identity. It doesn't exclude that some relationships that form our identity have a primacy or greater influence on us over others. Hybridity, I guess you can say, doesn't rule out monogamy.

That's what I've found in my lifelong relationship with Christ and Christianity and in my newly formed relationship with Buddha and Buddhism. For me, Christ has a certain primacy over Buddha. I suspect (though I am not sure) that what I have discovered in my process of Christian–Buddhist double-belonging characterizes many if not most other double-belongers: there is a core religious identity (which is often the tradition one grew up in) that enters into a hybrid relationship with another religious identity and tradition.

As I believe this book makes clear, my core identity as a Christian has been profoundly influenced by my passing over to Buddhism. Even though my primary allegiance is to Christ and the gospel, my Christian experience and beliefs have not dominated nor always had to trump what I learned or experienced through Buddha. There have been many instances in this book where I have recognized, often with great relief, that Buddhism can offer us Christians a deeper insight, a clearer truth. And yet, at the end of the day, I go home to Jesus.

As one of my more unreserved Union students blurted out in class one day: "Well, it looks like you love both Jesus *and* Buddha. But you sleep with Jesus." Uncomfortably inappropriate, the statement is also pretty accurate. There's a depth, a specialness, a history that I have with Christ that I don't find elsewhere – and that, yes, bears or requires a certain exclusivity that resembles the intimacy and exclusivity that I feel for my wife.

But this primary relationship with Christ has not only been profoundly influenced, enhanced, and preserved through my relationship with Buddha. My Christian faith has also served as the motivating, propelling force for my reaching out to Buddha. This is more difficult to explain. I believe I have discovered something that I suspect characterizes religious experience in whatever tradition or historical context: the more *deeply* one enters into the core experience that animates one's own tradition, the more *broadly* one is enabled and perhaps moved to enter into the experiences of other traditions. The more deeply one sinks into one's own religious truth, the more broadly one can appreciate and learn from other truths.

In my case, the more I have discovered what it really means to be "in Christ Jesus" the more I have felt the need and the ability to listen to and learn from the Buddha, and so to discover my Buddha-nature.

A big decision

At least, that's how it has worked for me. In writing this book, in looking back over my efforts during the past couple of decades to "pass over" to Buddhism, it has become clearer than ever that *Without Buddha I Could not be a Christian.* For me, not only does double-belonging seem to work. It's necessary! The only way I can be religious is by being interreligious. I can be a Christian only by also being a Buddhist.

And so I made a big, but also an easy, decision during the summer of 2008 when I was doing the final revisions of this book. It was at the end of a ten-day Dzogchen Buddhist retreat at the Garrison Institute on the Hudson River. After careful consultation with my teacher, Lama John Makransky (who is also Professor of Buddhist Studies and Comparative Theology at Boston College), I decided to "Take Refuge" and to pronounce the "Bodhisattva Vows" as part of the Dzogchen community in the United States. I was given the *Dharma* name of *Urgyen Menla* – Lotus Healer.

So it's official. I am now, you might say, a card-carrying Buddhist. In 1939 I was baptized. In 2008 I took refuge. I can truly call myself what I think I've been over these past decades: a Buddhist Christian.

Cutting edge or outer edge?

But is my being a Buddhist Christian an entirely personal matter? Or, is it something I can bring to and share with my Christian community, my church? For us Christians, that's a very important question, for given the nature of Christianity, if you can't share and celebrate and explore your spiritual beliefs and practices with your community, you may not really belong to that community. So, with my

Buddhist–Christian practice and hybrid identity, am I on the cutting edge or the outer edge of my Christian community?

Along with a growing number of Christian brothers and sisters who go to church on Sunday and sit on their cushions daily, I do believe, or I certainly hope, that it's the cutting edge. I do believe and hope that this "edge" is leading to what some call "a new way of being church" – a church that lives and finds life through dialogue. I do believe and hope that if Karl Rahner is right that Christians of the future will have to be mystics, they will also have to be *interreligious* mystics. I do believe and hope that Father John Dunne (theologian at Notre Dame University) was right when more than thirty years ago he predicted that "the holy man or woman of our time is … a figure like Gandhi, a man who passes over by sympathetic understanding from his own religion to other religions, and comes back again with new insight to his own … Passing over and coming back, it seems, is the spiritual adventure of our time."

Such an adventure can not only help renew the churches. It can also produce Christians better able to help renew the world.

A NEW CONCLUSION
JESUS AND BUDDHA BOTH COME FIRST!

As I announced in this book's Preface, one big reason for writing it was to find out whether I am a Buddhist Christian or a Christian Buddhist. I was concerned that my Buddhist practice might be diluting my Christian identity. Or, as I phrased the question in the book's original Conclusion: I was worried that I was having "an affair" with Buddha that made me unfaithful to Jesus.

In that Conclusion, I soothed my anxieties by determining that in my religious identity and practice I was "hybrid," not "promiscuous." I followed *both* Buddha and Jesus. And in that hybridity – this was particularly soothing for my Christian uneasiness – my *primary* relationship was with Jesus. Or, as one of my more eloquent, earthy students helped me phrase it, I loved both Buddha and Jesus, but at night, I went home to Jesus.

Now, some four years after writing the book, I'm not so sure.

During these ensuing years I've continued, and I think deepened, both my Christian and Buddhist practices. I've also given numerous talks and been challenged in numerous conversations about just what it means, for myself as well as for others, to say that "Without Buddha I Could not be a Christian." As I faced many new and probing questions, both from others and from my own ongoing experience with my practice, I felt that my answers were often wobbly.

What was wobbly was actually tilting in a new direction. That's what I realized when I read a recent book by a new scholar: Rose Drew's *Christian or Buddhist? An Exploration of Dual Religious Belonging*, New York: Routledge, 2011. From her ethnographic study of actual dual belongers, she found that a) some have a primary religious identity, b) some alternate between both primary identities, c) some cannot attribute primacy to either identity, and d) some are too bewildered by it all to say anything. As I pondered Drew's description and analysis of her interviewees' meanderings back and forth across religious lines, I realized that although when I finished my book I located myself firmly in Drew's first group, now I seemed to find myself in the third.

Buddhist or Christian: which comes first?

The reason I say that is because, as I have gone about my Christian and my Buddhist practices over these recent years, *I can't keep them apart.* It's not that they are blurring into each other and becoming just one practice. No, they remain clearly distinct. But unlike my good friend, Roger Corless, of blessed memory, I have not been able to honor their distinct identities by practicing them, as Roger apparently did, separately: being a Buddhist from Monday to Thursday, and a Christian from Friday to Sunday (and then waiting to see what would happen).

Rather, for me, when I'm at Mass, it's with Buddhist ears that I hear the words of the Scripture readings or of the sermon (though I usually resort to Zen mindfulness of my breath during many sermons). I feel the powerful symbols of the Eucharistic liturgy with Buddhist sensitivity. I'm constantly translating Christian into Buddhist and Buddhist into Christian but in what feels like a natural flow back and forth, like a conversation.

On the meditation cushion, whether daily by myself or during a retreat conducted by my teacher Lama John Makransky, the same conversation goes on. I generally begin with the "double triple-refuge" – first taking refuge in the Buddha, Dharma, and Sanga, and then in the Christ, Gospel, and Church (or in reverse order). I just feel that I have to do both. My awareness of the breath feels like awareness of the Spirit. The concepts I let go of are Christian concepts. When encouraged to sit like the Buddha, I find myself also sitting like the Christ. When Lama John leads us in a Tara practice, it becomes for me a Christ practice. In the guided meditations that are part of our Tibetan practice, I drift between both Buddhist and Christian images.

I can't keep my two practices apart, and yet they remain distinctly identifiable. That's why I suspect that I have moved from Drew's first category (dual practice with a primary identity) to her third group – those double-belongers who can't speak of primacy.

But then how to understand or speak about such a blended dual spirituality? In pondering that question, I found myself resorting to a perhaps inappropriate analogy that came to me from my past. I propose it to see if it might resonate with others who are trying to find their way on the path of religious double-belonging.

Two natures – one person?

In a course titled *De Verbo Incarnato* that I took with Bernard Lonergan, S.J. at the Pontifical Gregorian University way back in 1964, I spent many an exciting but also frustrating hour trying to follow his analysis of the Council of Chalcedon (451). The language and the images of Chalcedon and of Lonergan have stayed with me over the years – part of my Catholic theological toolbox, you might say. I found myself resorting to that toolbox as I pondered what was "double" in my religious belonging. I wondered whether the ancient language that the bishops finally formulated, and which has been kept alive down through the centuries through debates about its meaning, might actually help clarify what double religious belonging means. Here's the precise, sixteen-centuries-old language by which they described Jesus as having "two natures in one person":

> … two natures not confused, nor changed, nor divided, nor separated (*inconfuse, immutabiliter, indivise, inseparabiliter*), at no point is the difference between the natures taken away through the union, but rather the property of both natures is preserved and comes together into a single hypostasis.

If we take the classical understanding of *natura* (or in Greek, *ousia*) as the "*principium operandi,*" the operational principle or internal motor that determines how an entity acts, and if we hold to the conciliar understanding of *hypostasis* as the actual personal being expressing this activity, then maybe these concepts or images might be just as helpful in throwing light on the mystery of dual religious belonging as they are for trying to express the mystery of the "hypostatic union" in Jesus.

In the spiritual life of one double-belonging human being, two very different spiritual "operational principles" "come together in a single hypostasis or person" – but without being "confused or changed or divided or separated," for "the property of each is preserved." These images and philosophical distinctions of the fourth and fifth centuries might help explain how one person can be both Buddhist and Christian at the same time (maybe even more helpfully than they explain how one person can be both human and divine!). Just as Christian doctrine construes Jesus of Nazareth as one person who is acting both humanly and divinely, so too a double-belonger can be understood as one person acting both Buddhistically and Christianly.

The helpfulness of these categories increased for me when I was discussing them with a group of doctoral students at Union Theological Seminary. One of the students, Mr. Kyeongil Jung, astutely observed that the "hypostasis" or self in which these two activities commingle can be understood from a Buddhist perspective as a "*not-self.*" Then the hypostasis or personal center of a double-belonger (including the hypostasis of Jesus) is all the more engagingly imaged as an open, receptive space that cannot be defined by only one practice but can accommodate many. What is really empty has surprising capacity.

What's the difference?

More needs to be said. If, as the bishops at Chalcedon put it, "the property of both natures is preserved," how might I identify these differing properties in my own experience? What is distinctively Buddhist and distinctively Christian about my practice? Or, how might I describe, broadly, what each brings to the empty space of my personal center? Again, let me try to summarize what for me seems to be true, in the hope that it might make sense for other Christian double-belongers.

In the "hypostatic union" of my Buddhist and Christian practices, I've come to realize that Buddha supplies the "big picture," while Christ contributes the living color. Or, Buddha describes the broad energy field and Christ is a revealing instantiation of what happens when that energy takes form. Or, more philosophically, Buddhism provides the ontology and Christianity provides the particularity. Simply but I hope accurately: Buddha makes clear *what's* going on. Christ shows *how* it goes on.

Buddha's big picture

Here I'm taking up mainly Mahayana Buddhism's teaching on the non-duality between Form and Emptiness, Nirvana and Samsara. All finite or relative reality is grounded in the groundlessness of Emptiness – or as the Tibetans call it, open Spaciousness. Everything, absolutely everything, is contained in or gives expression to what is described, again in Tibetan traditions, as vast, aware, and compassionate Spaciousness or Emptiness. Absolute reality and Relative reality are distinct, but they are not separable. They co-exist by co-inhering. They dance together, distinct but both essential for the Dance. In this Dance, the relative forms (you and I, animals and mountains, pleasures and pains) are real. But Emptiness or Spaciousness is, in a sense, more real. The forms dance on into impermanence. Emptiness is the abiding music. This is a thoroughly non-dual understanding and perception of the relation between Finite and Infinite. They're not two. But neither are they one. That's the big picture.

Such a non-dual big picture, as it might be applied to the relation between God and creation, is generally not evident in popular Christian practice or traditional theology. But, as I've tried to argue in the first three chapters of this book, just because it's not evident does not mean that it's not present. Such a non-dual, or deeply unitive, view of God's being and our being is softly suggested, and sometimes loudly announced, in biblical writings like those of John and Paul who intrigue us with their talk of oneness with the Father, vines and branches, the Spirit moving invisibly as she will, Christ doing the living in us. Such a merging without blurring of the divine and the human is evident also in mystics such as Eckhart, Teresa of Avila, John of the Cross, Julian of Norwich – as well as in theologians such as Rahner with his notion of the supernatural existential (God's self-gift breathing in our very being) or Panikkar's image of reality as a dance between the divine, the human, and the material world (cosmotheandrism).

But if these different voices affirming the "big picture" of the co-inhering mystery of God and the world are indeed present on the Christian stage, they are found, for the most part, in the mystical wings. In the Buddhism I practice, they play center-stage. The ineffable experience of co-inherence or oneness between Emptiness and Form – or as Lama John Makransky puts it, between vast Space and our inner space – is at the heart of my Buddhist practice. What I'm calling the non-dual big picture is present much more centrally, clearly, effectively in Buddhism than, I think I can say, in Christianity.

So as far as this "big picture" is concerned, I'm primarily a Buddhist. Buddhism for me gets the big picture right much more lucidly, coherently, and centrally than Christianity does. In fact, if someone were really to prove to me that this non-dual Buddhist picture were incompatible with Christian experience and teaching (that hasn't happened, and I don't think it can), I would have to abandon Christianity for Buddhism.

Christ's living color

But in order to see clearly – that is, to know and feel – what can happen, or what needs to happen, when a human being truly wakes up to this non-dual big picture taught so centrally and so clearly in Buddhism, I have found that Jesus of Nazareth is not only helpful but vital. For me, Jesus the Christ is the embodiment, the instantiation, the realization – Christians use the term *incarnation* – of this non-duality between Form and Emptiness, divinity and humanity. He makes it real for me. I see it in him. I feel it through him. He embodies both how one needs to live in order to grow into the realization of non-duality or "oneness with the Father," and how one will carry on one's life after having awakened to this oneness. He is both the *way* that leads to the experience of co-inhering with the Divine, and also the *life* that results as this experience deepens and becomes more real. Thanks to Buddha, Jesus as "the way, the truth, and the life" (John 14:6) has taken on added meaning and power for me. What Buddha so clearly taught, Jesus so powerfully manifests.

When I say that Jesus embodies or incarnates the non-duality between Emptiness and Form, or between Abba and us, I'm talking about Jesus *of Nazareth*. I'm relating to Jesus in all his particularity, his historical concreteness as a Jew, a prophet, a victim of Roman imperial oppression, as crucified, as living on within his followers. This historical particularity is powerfully important for me in understanding and living into the "big picture" that Buddha makes so clear. The embodiment of Emptiness or Holy Mystery in the particularity of Jesus is for me a genuine revelation.

By that I mean that it's not just expressing what I already know. It's making clear, or revealing, to me the kind of *forms* that Emptiness *can take* in the relative world because it *has taken* this form in Jesus. But – and here I speak primarily out of my Christian conditioning – Jesus represents a form that Emptiness or Spaciousness *needs to,* or *intends to*, take in the finite, relative order. (I apologize if such language of "needing" or "intending" makes my Buddhist friends uncomfortable. These are topics for our ongoing dialogue.)

In stressing the revealing power of the particular Jesus for myself, in no way am I saying or even suggesting that he is the *only* or the *superior* embodiment or revelation of what a human being looks like, or what happens to a human being who has awakened, or in Christian language, who has been transformed by the Spirit. But I *am* saying – and I'm saying it because I'm feeling it – that what we see in this Jesus, or in this particular Form that Emptiness has taken – is important also for others. While it is central and most effective for me as a Christian, it is also relevant and maybe even urgent for others. What happened in this Jesus of Nazareth, and what continues to happen through him, is not at all *exclusive* of what has happened in other spiritual figures who have "awakened" or "been called." But it is *relevant* for these others.

But so is Buddha relevant for others who are not Buddhists and who don't intend to be Buddhists. Particularities matter. If Buddha and Jesus are both "forms" in which Emptiness or Spirit is particularly and powerfully present, and if they are very different forms, then they are important not just for their own followers but also for the followers of each other. In my own dual-belonging and in my Christian language, I know that Jesus "has what it takes" to "save" me; but my practice and study of Buddhism have also made clear that something is missing in this Jesus, or in how he has been understood. (And I make bold to ask whether Buddhists might say the same thing about Buddha.)

A coming together of two in one

So if Buddha, in his particularity, provides the big picture and Jesus, a particular, living out of that big picture, how do they, in the language of Chalcedon, "come together into the single hypostasis" of a double-belonger? Certainly, there is no one way to understand or describe such a hypostatic union of dual practices and visions. It will be experienced and known differently according to the "causes and conditions" (or "social construction") of the person and community doing the interpreting. But also, what Catholic theologians call "the signs of the times" – or the state of the world – will provide (or should provide) a guiding light in trying to understand what a Buddhist-Christian identity means.

So, given the social conditioning that liberation theology has exercised on me personally and on my Christian community generally over the past half-century, and given a world in which incredible injustice promotes incredible violence, I have identified the real but complementary differences between Buddha and Jesus in what I was trying to get at in Chapter 7 – the difference between "Being Peace" and "Making Peace. "

Buddhist Being Peace: I have found in my practice and study that Buddha teaches and embodies the path to *being* peace. In his teaching and analysis, Buddha offers me the possibility and the methodology for *transforming my sense of who I am.* If we will never be able to comprehend and put into words what Nirvana or Enlightenment is, we certainly can describe and identify what it looks like in others and feels like in ourselves. The "waking up" is a transformation of the self – a transformation in which we experience that what we really are is not what we think we are: what we are is both non-substantial and incessantly impermanent. If it's impossible to define what this "not-self" is, it is fairly easy, again, to state how we feel when we live as an *anatta:* we feel peace and freedom. There is a peacefulness that can sustain us no matter what happens, and that becomes the ground out of which we confront or embrace all the events and the beings that make up our lives.

Buddhist teachers such as Thich Nhat Hanh and Lama John Makransky stress that such "being peace" must be the precondition for all our efforts at making peace. Or in Aloysius Pieris's perspective, while *prajna* and *karuna,* wisdom and compassion, make up the two sides of one enlightened coin, for Buddhists *prajna* has a certain, perhaps we can say pragmatic, priority. While compassion is really nothing but the living out of the wisdom of interbeing – so that really they are two manifestations of one reality – still, if we are not actively nurturing our wisdom, our capacities for compassion are going to dwindle.

Hence Thich Nhat Hanh's thundering admonition to all activists: you need to *be peace* in order to *make peace.* Unless there is some level of waking up to our not-self reality, our ego-self is going to keep getting in the way of our activism and peacemaking. Whether it is clinging to our own plans, or wearing out when those plans don't materialize, or hating those who stand in the way of our plans – ego, or the lack of wisdom, can often make a bigger mess than the one we are trying to clean up.

This, then, is what I have experienced to be an essential, and an indispensable, ingredient in Buddha's particularity. In giving the big picture of non-duality, he announces the universally important message that we have to experience or realize our identities as not-selves within this big picture if we are going to be able to confront and remove the sufferings of sentient beings.

Christian "Making Peace": But if the big picture of Buddha reminds us that making peace must flow from being peace, the particularity of Jesus makes clear just what the job of making peace is going to require. If Buddha provides the *ability* to make peace, Jesus clarifies how *to do* it. If earlier I suggested that Jesus shows us how one lives after experiencing the non-duality between Emptiness/Form or Abba/Self, now we're filling in the picture of what such a life entails.

Because of his Jewishness, because of his participation in a tradition of socially engaged prophets, and especially because he lived and taught and experienced Abba at a time when the Roman Empire was brutally oppressing his people, Jesus' *mystical* experience of Abba was at the same time a *social* experience of the reality he called the *Basileia tou Theou* – the Reign of God. For Jesus, the two were much like the Buddhist understanding of wisdom and compassion: you can't have one without the other. A God without the *Basileia* of God – or an experience of Abba without an experience of the need for *Basileia* – was, for Jesus, an experience of a false God. As Aloysius Pieris sees it, if Buddha assigned what I've called a "pragmatic priority" to waking up to *prajna*, Jesus seemed to place a pragmatic priority on the *agape* of struggling to realize the *Basileia.* If you're going to the temple to pray and realize that you are in a rift with your brother, fix the rift before going to the temple (Matthew 5:23–25).

More particularly, or more concretely, the *Basileia* of God requires not only the transformation of the self but also the transformation of society; and that means social, political, economic and military structures. What was the case at the time of Jesus is the case throughout history: empires keep taking shape; some nations or classes of people (they're usually led by males) take advantage of and oppress others. The life and teachings of Jesus call all enlightened people to confront and seek to change such oppressive structures. The awareness of oppression – or the preferential concern for the oppressed – was a pivotal part of how Jesus experienced and lived out his oneness with Abba. So Jesus would remind Buddhists that the three poisons of ignorance, greed, and hatred are not just internal to the person; they are also embodied in social, political, and economic structures. And once so embodied, they take on an existence of their own, independent of their existence in the hearts of humans.

Therefore, while the transformation of the self into *being peace* is absolutely essential, it is not enough. *Being peace* will not, as it were, automatically or seamlessly *make peace*. To truly *make peace,* oppressive structures, and those who hold them in place, have to be confronted. This renders *making peace* a further step after *being peace,* a step that can be more complex and dangerous than *being peace.* It requires taking on what St. Paul called the powers and principalities. (Rom. 3:38; Eph. 6:12). This is what led to Jesus' crucifixion and to Paul's beheading.

So, I'm a Buddhist Christian but also a Christian Buddhist – one person with two religious natures or "principles of operation." Buddha provides the most compelling and transforming teaching and illustration of the non-dual big picture which enables me to *be peace;* Jesus offers the most compelling and transforming incarnation of how living in the big picture calls for *making peace* within this world. To have one without the other is to have neither.

August 15, 2012 (The Feast of the Assumption)
New York City

GLOSSARY

Amida (Pali); **Amitabha** (Sanskrit) The Buddha of "infinite light" (wisdom) and "infinite life" (compassion), who is present as a saving grace in our world.

Anatta (Pali); **Anatman** (Sanskrit) The negative prefix *an* plus *atta*, self or ego, is translated as no-self, no-soul, or no-ego. It points to the reality of who or what we are: non-individuals, inter-beings rather than beings.

Anicca (Pali); **Anitya** (Sanskrit) "Impermanence." It means that everything, both mental and physical, is without exception impermanent. We're constantly changing because we're essentially interrelated.

Arhat (Sanskrit); **Araha(n)t** (Pali) "Worthy One." Those, usually monks, who have attained the penultimate state of perfection.

Bhagavad Gita "Song of God," one of the greatest of the Hindu Scriptures.

Bodhi (Pali) "Awakening." The attainment of perfect clarity of mind in which things are seen as they really are.

Bodhisattva A Buddha-to-be. In the Mahayana tradition, a Bodhisattva is a practitioner who vows to attain Awakening for the sake of all sentient beings.

Bodhi Tree The tree (*ficus religiosa*) in Bodh Gaya, India, under which Gautama attained Enlightenment and became the Buddha.

Buddha-nature In Mahayana Buddhism, the true nature of all humans, because of which they have the potential to become Buddhas.

Dhamma (Pali); **Dharma** (Sanskrit) In the Hindu tradition

Dharma refers to cosmic law, order, and an individual's duty. In Buddhism, it is applied also to the teaching of the Buddha.

Dhammapada   One of the most popular texts of the Theravada canon.

Dharmakaya (Sanskrit)   "The Truth Body," one of the "three Buddha bodies" (*trikaya*), representing the formless and imperishable Ultimate.

Dukkha (Pali); **Duhkha** (Sanskrit)   *Dukkha* is most often translated as "suffering" and points to the fact that for most of us life is felt to be unsatisfactory, missing something.

Dzogchen (Tibetan)   "Great Perfection," part of the Nyingma school of Tibetan Buddhism, teaching that all we need to live life fully is given to us in the present moment; we just have to wake up to this fact.

Eschatology   In traditional Christianity, "the study of the last things" or the end of the world.

Karma (Sanskrit); **Kamma** (Pali)   Literally, "deed" or "action." The doctrine of cause and effect: our present experience is a product of previous actions and choices, and future conditions depend on what we do in the present.

Karuna (Sanskrit)   "Compassion," along with *prajna* (wisdom), is one of the two virtues universally affirmed by Buddhists. Basically, *karuna* is defined as the wish that others be free of suffering.

Koan (Japanese)   Literally, "public case." These are the usually enigmatic, frequently startling, and sometimes shocking stories and statements used in Zen to produce a sudden breakthrough of insight.

Magisterium (Latin)   The "teaching authority" in the Roman Catholic Church, usually referring to the Pope and bishops, but residing in the Catholic Church as a whole.

Mahayana   The Mahayana ("Great Vehicle") is the form of Buddhism prominent in Tibet, Mongolia, China, Korea, Vietnam, and Japan; it emphasizes compassion and wisdom, especially the Bodhisattva ideal.

Mandala (Sanskrit)   A symbolic pictorial representation of the universe, originating in India but prominent in Tibetan Buddhism.

Mantra (Sanskrit)   A power-laden syllable or series of syllables that manifests certain cosmic forces and aspects of the Buddhas.

Mara   Mara, whose name literally means "death" or "maker of death," is the embodiment of lust, greed, false views, delusion, and illusion. Paradigmatically, Mara attempts to stop the Buddha in his quest for Awakening.

Metta **meditation**   As a form of Vipassana meditation, *metta* (loving kindness) meditation is meant to soften our ego-edges and open our hearts to both others and ourselves.

Nirmanakaya (Sanskrit) Literally, "Transformation Body" is another of the "three Buddha bodies" (*trikaya*), referring to the Buddha in earthly form.

Nirvana (Sanskrit)   To attain *Nirvana* is to attain the Enlightened and Awakened state of mind that is free from suffering and from the cycle of rebirth; a state of mind that is free from craving and anger.

Performative language   Language that itself functions as an act and that serves to bring forth action not just knowledge.

Prajna (Sanskrit)   With *karuna* (compassion), *prajna* (wisdom) is one of two cardinal Buddhist virtues, and virtually all Buddhist traditions affirm that wisdom is a prerequisite to Awakening.

Praxis   Meaning "action," it is the starting point of the method of liberation theology; praxis leads to theory and theory clarifies and deepens praxis.

Pure Land   An untainted transcendent realm created by the Amida Buddha, to which his devotees aspire to be born after death and in which they can attain final *Nirvana.*

Sambhogakaya (Sanskrit) Literally, the "enjoyment body," another of the "three Buddha bodies" (*trikaya*). It is found in the forms by which the Buddhas or Bodhisattvas continue to be manifested and so enjoyed by their followers.

Samsara   Refers to our everyday cycle of constantly changing life, the cycle of birth, decay, and death. *Samsara* is characterized by suffering and the only escape from this cycle is through Enlightenment and attainment of *Nirvana.*

Soteriology   The branch of theology that studies "salvation" – what salvation means, how Jesus saves.

Sunyata (Sanskrit)   As the ultimate reality in Buddhism, *Sunyata* is translated as "Emptiness" signifying that everything is empty of independent existence and has existence in interdependency.

Supernatural existential   Karl Rahner's phrase that expresses the reality that our "existence" is supernatural because God's grace or self-communication pervades all that we are.

Tangka (Tibetan)   Tibetan paintings used for teaching and meditation.

Tathata (Sanskrit)   The "thusness" of things, signifying their true essence, their sharing in ultimacy just as they are.

Theodicy   The name Christian theologians have given their efforts to reconcile the goodness of God and the presence of evil in the world.

Theravada (Pali); **Sthaviravada** (Sanskrit)   Literally, "the Teaching of the Elders," this is the oldest of the Buddhist schools, found today in Sri Lanka, Burma, Thailand, Cambodia, and Laos.

Tonglen (Tibetan)   *Tonglen* is Tibetan for "giving and taking," and refers to a meditation practice of taking in suffering and sending forth compassion.

Trikaya (Sanskrit)   Refers to the Mahayana teaching about the "three bodies" of Buddha or the three levels of Buddhahood: *Dharmakaya* (the essence or absolute body), *Sambhogakaya* (the enjoyment body), and *Nirmanakaya* (the physical body).

Upaya-kausalya (Sanskrit)   "Skillful means" is a central Mahayana teaching according to which Buddha and Buddhist teachers adapt the particular contents of their teaching to the temperament and level of understanding of the audience.

Vajrayana   Vajrayana Buddhism, established in Tibet in the eighth century CE, is sometimes seen as the third major 'vehicle' of Buddhism after the Theravada and Mahayana traditions, and delights in smells and bells. Vajrayana meditation makes great use of audiovisuals such as *mandalas* and *mantras*. Its goal is *prajna*, wisdom, an experience of oneness.

Vipassana (Pali)   Often called "insight meditation," it stresses precise self-observation and introspection as a way of waking up to our true nature.

Zen (Japanese); **Chan** (Chinese)   A Mahayana school of Buddhism that developed when Buddhism moved from India to China in the seventh century CE and mixed with Taoism. It stresses direct realization, beyond theoretical thinking, through sitting meditation and the use of koans.

SOURCES AND RESOURCES

CHAPTER 1

Sources

"Passing over and passing back:" John Dunne, *The Way of All the Earth: Experiments in Truth and Religion*. Notre Dame: University of Notre Dame Press, 1978.

A summary of C.G. Jung's views on God and religious experience: Paul F. Knitter, *No Other Name? A Critical Survey of Christian Attitudes Toward the World Religions*. Maryknoll, NY: Orbis, 1985, ch. 4.

Bonhoeffer's views of a "religionless Christianity:" Dietrich Bonhoeffer, *Letters and Papers from Prison*, Eberhard Bethge, ed. New York: The Macmillan Company, 1956, in the letter of 30 April 1944, pp. 151–155.

Buddha's experience of Awakening and his first sermon: Walpola Rahula, *What the Buddha Taught*. New York: Grove Press, 1974.

On "InterBeing:" Thich Nhat Hanh, *Peace is Every Step: The Path of Mindfulness in Everyday Life*. New York: Bantam, 1992, p. 95.

Groundlessness: Pema Chödrön, *The Wisdom of No Escape*. Boston, MA: Shambhala, 1991.

Panikkar's notion of non-duality: Raimon Panikkar, *The Trinity and the Religious Experience of Man*. London: Darton, Longman & Todd, 1973, pp. 74–75.

Rahner on mysticism: Karl Rahner, *The Practice of the Faith*. New York: Crossroad, 1983, p. 22.

Rahner on "transcendental experience:" "Thoughts on the Possibility of Belief Today" in *Theological Investigations*, Vol. 5. London: Darton, Longman & Todd/Baltimore: Helicon Press, 1966, pp. 3–22; "Being Open to God as Always Ever Greater" in *Theological Investigations*, Vol. 7. London: Darton, Longman & Todd/New York: Herder and Herder, 1971, pp, 25–46.

Hick on religious experience as a shift from self-centeredness to Reality-centeredness: John Hick, *An Interpretation of Religion.* London: Macmillan Press, 1989, pp. 343–361.

Aquinas on participation: "Nothing has being (*esse*) unless insofar as it participates in the divine being (*divinum esse*)." I Sent. d.8, q. 1, a.2. Also: *Summa Theologiae*, Ia, 44, 1.

Rahner on the supernatural existential: Karl Rahner, *Foundations of Christian Faith.* New York: Seabury Press, 1978, pp. 116–133.

Tillich on God as the Ground of Being: Paul Tillich, *Systematic Theology*, Vol. 1. Chicago: University of Chicago Press, 1951, pp. 155–156.

Rahner on atheism and anonymous theists – people who believe in God without knowing it: Karl Rahner, "Anonymous Christians" in *Theological Investigations*, Vol. 6. London: Darton, Longman & Todd/Baltimore: Helicon Press, 1969, pp. 390–398; "Atheism and Implicit Christianity" in *Theological Investigations*, Vol. 9. London: Darton, Longman & Todd, 1972, pp. 145–164; "Anonymous and Explicit Faith" in *Theological Investigations*, Vol. 16. New York: The Seabury Press, 1979, pp. 52–59.

Elisabeth Schüssler Fiorenza on the earliest Christology in which Jesus is referred to as the Child of Sophia: Elisabeth Schüssler Fiorenza, *Jesus: Miriam's Child, Sophia's Prophet: Critical Issues in Feminist Christology.* New York: Continuum, 1995.

Dante Alighieri, *Paradiso: The Divine Comedy* (New York: Bantam, 1986), Canto XXXIII, line 145, p. 303.

Resources

Cobb, John B. Jr. and Ives, Christopher, eds., *The Emptying God: A Buddhist–Jewish–Christian Conversation.* Maryknoll, NY: Orbis, 1990.

Johnson, Elizabeth, *Quest for the Living God: Mapping Frontiers in the Theology of God.* New York: Continuum, 2007.

Keller, Catherine, *On the Mystery: Discerning God in Process.* Minneapolis: Fortress, 2008.

LaCugna, Catherine, *God for Us: The Trinity and Christian Life.* San Francisco: Harper San Francisco, 1993.

Thurston, Bonnie and David-Eckel, Malcolm, "Ultimate Reality" in *The Sound of Liberating Truth: Buddhist and Christian Dialogues*, Sallie B. King and Paul O. Ingram, eds. Surrey, England: Curzon Press, 1999, pp. 63–104.

CHAPTER 2

Sources

Addressing God as a "you:" Hugo M. Enomiya-Lassalle, *Zen Meditation for Christians*, trans. John C. Maraldo. LaSalle, IL: Open Court, 1974.

Buddhism and evil: David Loy, *The Great Awakening: A Buddhist Social Theory*. Boston: Wisdom, 2003, ch. 5, "The Nonduality of Good and Evil."

Pure Land Buddhism: Kenneth Tanaka and Eisho Nasu, eds., *Engaged Pure Land Buddhism: The Challenges Facing Jodo Shinshu in the Contemporary World*. Berkeley: Wisdom Ocean, 1998.

The many Buddhas and Bodhisattvas of Tibetan Buddhism: Stephen Batchelor, *The Tibet Guide*. London: Wisdom, 1987.

Buddhism and peacemaking: David Chappell, ed., *Buddhist Peacework: Creating Cultures of Peace*. Boston: Wisdom, 1999.

Buddhist wisdom and Christian love: Aloysius Pieris, S.J., *Love Meets Wisdom: A Christian Experience of Buddhism*. Maryknoll, NY: Orbis, 1988. See ch. 10, "Christianity in a Core-to-Core Dialogue with Buddhism."

T.S. Eliot's "we are the music:" Thomas Stearns Eliot, *Four Quartets*. New York, Harcourt Trade, 1971. See "The Dry Salvages," p. 44.

Levinas on God and the Other: Emmanuel Levinas, "The Word I, the Word You, the Word God and the Proximity of the Other" in Emmanuel Levinas and Michael B. Smith, eds., *Alterity and Transcendence*. New York: Columbia University Press 1999, pp. 91–110. Also; "Dialogue: Self-Consciousness and the Proximity of the Neighbor" in *Of God Who Comes to Mind*. Stanford, CA: Stanford University Press, 1998, pp. 137–151.

Karl Rahner on "the unity of love of God and love of neighbor:" Karl Rahner, *Everyday Faith*, trans. William J. O'Hara. New York: Herder and Herder, 1968, pp.106–117.

Rahner on freedom and grace: *Foundations of Christian Faith*. New York: Seabury Press, 1978, chs. 1 and 3.

Process theology and the persuasive power of God: John B. Cobb, Jr. and David Ray Griffin, *Process Theology: An Introductory Exposition*. Philadelphia: Westminster John Knox Press, 1976. See ch. 3, "God and Creative-Responsive Love."

Rabbi Kushner, *When Bad Things Happen to Good People*. New York: Avon, 1983.

Pema Chödrön, *When Things Fall Apart*. Boston: Shambhala, 2000.

Resources

Abe, Masao, "The Problem of Evil in Christianity and Buddhism" in Paul O. Ingram and Frederick J. Streng, eds., *Buddhist–Christian Dialogue:*

Mutual Renewal and Transformation. Honolulu, HI: University of Hawaii Press, 1986, pp. 139–154.

Habito, Ruben L.F., "On *Dharmakaya* as Ultimate Reality: Prolegomenon for a Buddhist Christian Dialogue." *Japanese Journal of Religious Studies* 12 (1975), pp. 233–252.

Kaufmann, Gordon D., "God and Emptiness: An Experimental Essay." *Buddhist–Christian Studies* 9 (1989), pp. 175–187.

CHAPTER 3

Sources

Christian mysticism: Bernard McGinn, ed., *The Essential Writings of Christian Mysticism.* New York: Random House, 2006; William Johnston, *The Inner Eye of Love: Mysticism and Religion.* San Francisco: Harper & Row, 1978.

The Mahayana view of language/words: Perry Schmidt-Leukel, *Understanding Buddhism.* Edinburgh: Dunedin Academic Press, 2006. See ch. 12, "Concept, Language and Reality."

A concise description of Zen: Huston Smith, *The World's Religions: Our Great Wisdom Traditions.* San Francisco: HarperSanFrancisco, 1991. See under the section title "The Secret of the Flower," pp. 128–139.

Thich Nhat Hanh, *Interbeing: Commentaries on the Tiep Hien Precepts,* Fred Epsteiner, ed. Berkeley, CA: Parallax Press, 1987.

Karl Rahner on Mystery: Karl Rahner, "The Concept of Mystery in Catholic Theology" in *Theological Investigations,* Vol. 4. Baltimore: Helicon Press/London: Darton, Longman & Todd, 1966, pp. 36–73.

On religious language as symbolic: Paul Tillich, *The Dynamics of Faith.* New York: Harper & Row, 1957. See ch. 3, "Symbol of Faith." Paul Tillich, *Systematic Theology: Three Volumes in One.* Chicago: The University of Chicago Press, 1967. See Vol. 1, pp. 122–126 and Vol. 3, pp. 57–62; Karl Rahner, "The Theology of the Symbol" and "The Word and the Eucharist" in *Theological Investigations,* Vol. 4. Baltimore: Helicon Press/London: Darton, Longman & Todd, pp. 221–252, 253–286.

The Buddhist understandings of the performative character of all religious language: Rita M. Gross, "Excuse Me, but What's the Question? Isn't Religious Diversity Normal?" and Sallie B. King, "A Pluralist View of Religious Pluralism" in Paul F. Knitter, ed., *The Myth of Religious Superiority: Multifaith Explorations of Religious Pluralism.* Maryknoll, NY: Orbis, 2005, pp. 75–101.

Resources

Barnes, Michael, "Expanding Catholicity: The Dialogue with Buddhism." *New Blackfriars* 88 (2007), pp. 399–409.

Fredericks, J.L., "The Incomprehensibility of God: A Buddhist Reading of Aquinas." *Theological Studies* 56 (1995), pp. 506–520.

McFague, Sallie, *Metaphorical Theology: Models of God in Religious Language.* Philadelphia: Fortress, 1985.

Merton, Thomas, *Zen and the Birds of Appetite.* New York: New Directions, 1968.

Panikkar, Raimon, *The Silence of God: The Answer of the Buddha.* Maryknoll, NY: Orbis, 1989.

CHAPTER 4

Sources

Is hell empty?: Karl Rahner, *Foundations of Christian Faith.* New York: Seabury Press, 1978, pp. 443–444.

Christian views of the praxis-based, or performative character, of all truth-claims: Terrence W. Tilley, *Inventing Catholic Tradition.* Maryknoll, NY: Orbis, 2000, ch. 2.

Andrew Greeley's statistics on Catholic beliefs about hell can be found at: http://natcath.org/NCR_Online/archives2/1999a/030599/030599p.htm

A Christian view of afterlife as beyond personality: Schubert M. Ogden, "The Meaning of Christian Hope" in Henry James Cargas and Bernard Lee, eds., *Religious Experience and Process Theology.* New York: Paulist Press, 1976, pp. 195–214.

Francis Thompson's poem, "The Hound of Heaven:" http://www.houndsofheaven.com/thepoem.htm

Karl Rahner, *On the Theology of Death*, trans. Charles H. Henkey. New York: Herder and Herder, 1961.

Rahner on reincarnation: *Foundations of Christian Faith*, p. 442.

"All manner of things shall be well:" Julian of Norwich, *Showings*, trans. Edmund Colledge, O.S.A. New York: Paulist Press, 1978. See "Long Text," ch. 32.

For a Buddhist (Tibetan) perspective on dying and on living, Sogyal Rinpoche, *The Tibetan Book of the Living and Dying.* New York: HarperCollins, 1994.

Resources

Gross, Rita M., "Impermanence, Nowness, and Non-judgment: Appreciating Finitude and Death" in Rita M. Gross, *Soaring and Settling.* New York: Continuum, 1998, pp. 140–151.

Harris, Elizabeth and Tsuchiya, Kiyoshi, "Life and Death" in Perry Schmidt-Leukel, ed., *Buddhism and Christianity in Dialogue.* London: SCM Press, 2005, pp. 29–83.

Ma'sumian, Farnaz, *Life after Death: A Study of the Afterlife in World Religions.* Oxford: Oneworld, 1995.

Moltmann, Jürgen, *The Coming of God: Christian Eschatology.* Minneapolis: Augsburg, 1996.

Sherbok, Dan Cohn and Lewis, Christopher, eds., *Beyond Death: Theological and Philosophical Reflections on Life after Death.* New York: St. Martin's Press, 1995.

Söelle, Dorothee, *The Mystery of Death.* Minneapolis: Fortress, 2007.

CHAPTER5

Sources

Rahner's "Transcendental Christology:" Karl Rahner, *Foundations of Christian Faith.* New York: Seabury Press, 1978, pp. 176–212.

For Cardinal Ratzinger's and Pope Benedict XVI's views of Jesus and other religious figures: *Dominus Iesus,* available at the Vatican website: www.vatican.va

Original blessing rather than original sin: Matthew Fox, *Original Blessing: A Primer in Creation Spirituality.* Santa Fe: Bear, 1983.

The variety of soteriologies in the New Testament and church history: Stephen Finlan, *Options on Atonement in Christian Thought.* Collegeville, MN: Liturgical Press, 2007. Also Gustav Aulen, *Christus Victor: An Historical Study of the Three Main Types of the Idea of Atonement.* New York: Macmillan, 1969.

On claims of "divine child abuse:" Dolores S. Williams, *Sisters in the Wilderness: The Challenge of Womanist God-Talk.* Maryknoll, NY: Orbis, 1993, pp. 161–167.

For Roman Catholic developments in views of other religions after the Second Vatican Council: Paul F. Knitter, *Introducing Theologies of Religions.* Maryknoll, NY: Orbis, 2002. See Part II, "The Fulfillment Model, pp. 63–106.

The resurrection in the New Testament and early Christian communities: Roger Haight, S.J., *Jesus Symbol of God.* Maryknoll, NY: Orbis, 2002. See ch. 6, "Jesus' Resurrection," pp. 119–151; Edward Schillebeeckx, *Jesus: An Experiment in Christology.* New York: Seabury Press, 1979, pp. 379–97, 516–44.

For the citation of Santideva: Santideva: *The Bodhicaryavatara: A Guide to the Buddhist Path to Awakening,* trans. Kate Crosby and Andrew Skilton, Paul Williams, ed. New York: Oxford University Press, 1995, pp. 20–21.

The multiple titles given to Jesus by the early church: Schillebeeckx, *Jesus,* pp. 399–515; Geza Vermes, *The Changing Faces of Jesus.* New York: Viking Compass, 2000.

Spirit and Wisdom Christology: Haight, *Jesus Symbol of God*, ch. 15, especially the section titled "Spirit Christology," pp. 445–465; Elisabeth Schüssler Fiorenza, *Jesus: Miriam's Child, Sophia's Prophet: Critical Issues in Feminist Christology*. New York: Continuum, 1995. See ch. 5, "Prophets of Sophia: Searching for Divine Wisdom," pp. 131–162.

Sacraments as symbols that make present and real what already is: Richard McBrien, *Catholicism*. Oak Grove, MN: Winston Press, 1981. pp. 734–740. David Power, *Unsearchable Riches: The Symbolic Nature of Liturgy*. New York: Pueblo, 1984.

John B. Cobb Jr.'s view of Jesus as the Way open to other Ways: John B. Cobb, Jr. "Beyond Pluralism" in Gavin D'Costa, ed., *Christian Uniqueness Reconsidered: The Myth of a Pluralistic Theology of Religions*. Maryknoll, NY: Orbis, 1996, pp. 81–95.

The "one and only" language of the New Testament as love language: Krister Stendahl, "Notes for Three Bible Studies" in Gerald H. Anderson and Thomas F. Stransky, eds., *Christ's Lordship and Religious Pluralism*. Maryknoll, NY: Orbis, 1981, p. 14.

On Jesus as "God's defense pact with the poor:" Aloysius Pieris, *God's Reign for God's Poor: A Return to the Jesus Formula*. Kelaniya: Tulana Research Centre, 1999.

The resurrection and the Holy Spirit: Luke Timothy Johnson, *Living Jesus: Learning the Heart of the Gospel*. San Francisco: HarperSanFrancisco, 1999, p. 15.

"Jesus Christ through Buddhist eyes:" see Rita M. Gross and Terry C. Muck, eds., *Buddhists Talk about Jesus, Christians Talk about the Buddha*. New York and London: Continuum, 2000, pp. 17–51, 59–86 (J.I. Cabezón, R. Gross, S. Machida, with Christian responses from M. Borg and J.D. Crossan).

Resources

Dunne, Carrin, *Buddha and Jesus: Conversations*. Springfield, IL: Templegate, 1975.

Gross, Rita M. and Muck, Terry C., eds., *Buddhists Talk about Jesus, Christians Talk about the Buddha*. New York and London: Continuum, 2000.

Haight, Roger, S.J., *Jesus Symbol of God*. Maryknoll, NY: Orbis, 2002.

Keel, Hee-Sung, "Jesus the Bodhisattva: Christology from a Buddhist Perspective." *Buddhist–Christian Studies* 16 (1996), pp. 169–193.

Knitter, Paul F, "Jesus and Buddha: A Conversation" in Brennan R. Hill, Paul F. Knitter, and William Madges, eds., *Faith, Religion, Theology: A Contemporary Introduction*. Mystic, CT: Twenty-Third, 1997, pp. 255–284.

Lefebure, Leo, *The Buddha and the Christ: Explorations in Buddhist and Christian Dialogue*. Maryknoll, NY: Orbis, 1993.

Nhat Hanh, Thich, *Living Buddha, Living Christ*. New York, NY: Riverhead, 1995.

Schmidt-Leukel, P., Köberlin, G., and Götz, J.T., eds., *Buddhist Perceptions of Jesus*. St. Ottilien, Germany: EOS-Verlag, 2001.

Yagi, Seiichi, "'I' in the Words of Jesus" in John Hick and Paul F. Knitter, eds., *The Myth of Christian Uniqueness:Toward a Pluralistic Theology of Religions*. Maryknoll, NY: Orbis, 1987, pp. 117–134.

CHAPTER 6

Sources

Basics of Vipassana meditation: Joseph Goldstein and Jack Kornfield, *Seeking the Heart of Wisdom: The Path of Insight Meditation*. Boston: Shambhala, 1987.

Basics of Zen meditation: Robert Kennedy, *Zen Gifts to Christians*. New York: Continuum, 2004; Ruben L.F. Habito, *Living Zen, Loving God*. Boston: Wisdom, 2004; Kazuaki Tanahashi, ed., *Enlightenment Unfolds: Essential Teachings of Zen Master Dogen*. Boston: Shambhala, 1999.

The Dzogchen tradition of Tibetan Buddhism: Lama Surya Das, *Natural Radiance: Awakening to your Great Perfection*. Boulder: Sounds True, 2005.

The practice of Tonglen: Pema Chödrön, *When Things Fall Apart: Heart Advice for Difficult Times*. Boston: Shambhala, 1997; *Tonglen: The Path of Transformation*. Halifax: Vajradhatu, 2001.

The quotation from Thich Nhat Hanh, *Being Peace*. Berkeley: Parallax Press, 1996, pp. 8, 111.

Practicing Mindfulness: Pema Chödrön, *The Wisdom of No Escape*. Boston: Shambhala, 1991.

Thich Nhat Hanh's understanding of mindfulness and meditation: Thich Nhat Hahn, *The Miracle of Mindfulness: A Manual on Meditation*. Boston: Beacon Press, 1987.

The reference to Panikkar's notion of "mutual fructification" can be found in: Raimundo Panikkar, "What is Comparative Philosophy Comparing" in Gerald James Larson and Eliot Deutsch, eds., *Interpreting Across Boundaries: New Essays in Comparative Philosophy*. Princeton: Princeton University Press, 1988, pp. 132–133.

Lefebure's comparison of Karl Rahner and Masao Abe: Leo Lefebure, *Revelation, the Religions and Violence*. Maryknoll, NY: Orbis, 2000. See ch. 8, "Buddhist Awakening and Christian Revelation: A Buddhist Christian Conversation," pp. 185–200.

Bernard Lonergan's explanation of faith as "falling in love unrestrictedly" and wordlessly: Bernard Lonergan, *Method in Theology*. New York: The Seabury Press, 1972, pp. 105–109.

Merton's understanding of how he is "content for anything to happen:" Lawrence S. Cunningham, ed., *Thomas Merton, Spiritual Master: The Essential Writings*. New York, Paulist Press, 1992, p. 352.

References to Dzogchen praying and then letting it all go are from John Makransky, *Awakening Through Love: Unveiling Your Deepest Goodness*. Boston: Wisdom, 2007, pp. 26–27, 80–81.

On what Western liturgy can learn from Asian liturgy: Aloysius Pieris, S.J., "An Asian Way to Celebrate the Eucharist." *Worship*, July 2007, pp. 314–328.

Resources

Clifford, Patricia Hart, *Sitting Still: An Encounter with Christian Zen*. New York: Paulist Press, 1994.

Corless, Roger et al., "Joint Practice." *Buddhist–Christian Studies* 14 (1994), pp. 13–96. (A series of papers and responses exploring double-practicing of Buddhist–Christian spiritualities.)

Cowan, John, *Taking Jesus Seriously: Buddhist Meditation for Christians*. Collegeville, MN: Liturgical Press, 2004.

Culligan, K., Meadow, M.J. et al., *Purifying the Heart: Buddhist Meditation for Christians*. New York: Crossroad, 1994.

Foster, N. and Steindl-Rast, David, *The Ground We Share: Everyday Practice, Buddhist and Christian*. Boston: Shambhala, 1996.

Gross, Rita M. and Muck, Terry C., eds., *Christians Talk about Buddhist Meditation/Buddhists Talk about Christian Prayer*. New York: Continuum, 2003.

Habito, Ruben L.F., *Living Zen, Loving God*. Boston: Wisdom, 2004.

Hand, Thomas G., *Always a Pilgrim: Walking the Zen Christian Path*. Burlingame, CA: Mercy Center Meditation Program, 2004.

Kennedy, Robert E., *Zen Spirit, Christian Spirit: The Place of Zen in Christian Life*. New York: Continuum, 1996.

——, *Zen Gifts to Christians*. New York: Continuum, 2004.

Mitchell, Donald W. and Wiseman, James, eds., *The Gethsemani Encounter: A Dialogue on the Spiritual Life by Buddhist and Christian Monastics*. New York: Continuum, 1998.

Pierce, Brian J., *We Walk the Path Together: Learning from Thich Nhat Hanh and Meister Eckhart*. Maryknoll, NY: Orbis, 200

Walker, Susan, ed., *Speaking of Silence: Christians and Buddhists on the Contemplative Way*. New York: Paulist Press, 1987.

CHAPTER 7

Sources

For Aloysius Pieris's contrasting of Buddhist *prajna* and Christian *agape*: Aloysius Pieris, *Love Meets Wisdom: A Christian Experience of Buddhism.* Maryknoll, NY: Orbis, 1988. See ch. 10, "Christianity in a Core-to-Core Dialogue with Buddhism."

For more on the central place that the Kingdom or Reign of God played in Jesus' life and preaching: John Dominic Crossan, *Jesus: A Revolutionary Biography.* HarperSanFrancisco, 1994; John Fuellenbach, *The Kingdom of God: The Message of Jesus Today.* Maryknoll, NY: Orbis, 1995.

For more perspectives on Christian eschatology: Carl E. Braaten, "The Kingdom of God and Life Everlasting" in Peter C. Hodgson and Robert H. King, eds., *Christian Theology: An Introduction to Its Traditions and Tasks.* Philadelphia: Fortress Press, 1985, pp. 328–352; Karl Rahner, *Foundations of Christian Faith.* New York: Seabury Press, 1978, pp. 431–447.

To explore a more current presentation of the sinfulness of human nature: Reinhold Niebuhr, *Moral Man in Immoral Society: A Study in Ethics and Politics.* Louisville: Westminster John Knox Press, 2002, pp. 51–82.

For more on the content and method of liberation theology: Robert McAfee Brown, *Liberation Theology: An Introductory Guide.* Louisville: Westminster John Knox, 1993; Leonardo Boff and Clodovis Boff, *Introducing Liberation Theology.* Maryknoll, NY: Orbis, 1987.

On Engaged Buddhism: Sallie B. King and Christopher Queen, eds., *Engaged Buddhism in Asia: Buddhist Liberation Movements in Asia.* New York: S.U.N.Y., 1996; Christopher Queen, ed., *Engaged Buddhism in the West.* Boston: Wisdom, 2000.

On the apparent lack of a concern for justice among Buddhists: Sallie B. King, *Being Benevolence: The Social Ethics of Engaged Buddhism.* Honolulu, HI: University of Hawaii Press, 2005, ch. 7, "Justice/ Reconciliation."

The words of Geshe Sopa in Jerusalem are taken from King, *Being Benevolence*, pp. 208–209.

The citation from Eckhart Tolle: *The Power of Now: A Guide to Spiritual Enlightenment.* Novato, CA: New World Library, 1999, p. 166.

On the meaning of Mindfulness: Pema Chödrön, *The Places that Scare You: A Guide to Fearlessness in Difficult Times.* Boston: Shambhala, 2001; Charlotte Joko Beck, *Nothing Special: Living Zen.* San Francisco: HarperSanFrancisco, 1994; Adyashanti, *Emptiness Dancing.* Boulder: Sounds True, 2006.

For Bernard Lonergan's thoroughly dense but thoroughly rewarding understanding of what it means to understand anything, see *Insight: A Study of Human Understanding.* New York: Longmans, 1958.

The references for Thich Nhat Hanh's refusal to "take sides:" Thich Nhat Hanh, *Being Peace.* Berkeley: Parallax Press, 1987, p. 70, and *Living Buddha, Living Christ.* New York: Riverhead, 1995, p. 79.

Thich Nhat Hanh's poem "Call Me by My True Names" is found in his *Call Me by My True Names.* Berkeley, CA: Parallax, 1993, pp. 72–73.

The quotations about the perfection of the moment is from Lama Surya Das, "The Heart Essence of Buddhism Meditation." *Tricycle,* Winter 2007, pp. 35–36. Also: Lama Surya Das, *Awakening the Buddha Within.* New York: Broadway, 1997, p. 70.

The quotation from Eckhart Tolle is in *The Power of Now,* pp. 166–167.

The quotation from Adyashanti is in *Emptiness Dancing,* p. 79.

For a lucid description of Lonergan's Law of the Cross, see William P. Loewe, "Lonergan and the Law of the Cross: A Universalistic View of Salvation." *Anglican Theological Review* 59 (1977), pp. 162–174.

Resources

Chappell, David, ed., Buddhist Peacework: Creating Cultures of Peace. Boston: Wisdom, 1999.

Gross, Rita M., *Soaring and Settling: Buddhist Perspectives on Social and Theological Issues.* New York: Continuum, 1998.

Kaza, Stephanie, ed., *Hooked! Buddhist Writings on Greed, Desire, and the Urge to Consume.* Boston: Shambhala, 2005.

King, Robert H., *Thomas Merton and Thich Nhat Hanh: Engaged Spirituality in an Age of Globalization.* New York: Continuum, 1999.

King, Sallie. B., *Being Benevolence: The Social Ethics of Engaged Buddhism.* Honolulu, HI: University of Hawaii Press, 2006.

—— and John P. Kennan, "Social and Political Issues of Liberation" in Sallie B. King and Paul O.Ingram, eds., *The Sound of Liberating Truth: Buddhist and Christian Dialogues.* Surrey: Curzon Press, 1999, pp. 157–205.

Knitter, Paul F., "Overcoming Greed: Buddhists and Christians in Consumerist Society." *Buddhist–Christian Studies* 24 (2004), pp. 65–72.

Loy, David, *The Great Awakening: A Buddhist Social Theory.* Boston: Wisdom, 2003.

McLeod, Melvin, ed., *Mindful Politics: A Buddhist Guide to Making the World a Better Place.* Boston: Wisdom, 2006.

Nhat Hanh, Thich, *Love in Action: Writings on Nonviolent Social Change.* Berkeley, CA: Parallax Press, 1993.

Queen, Christopher S., ed., *Engaged Buddhism in the West.* Boston: Wisdom, 2000.

—— and King, Sallie B., eds., *Engaged Buddhism: Buddhist Liberation Movements in Asia*. Albany, NY: S.U.N.Y., 1996.

CONCLUSION

Sources

On the complexities of double-belonging: Catherine Cornille, ed., *Many Mansions? Multiple Religious Belonging and Christian Identity*. Maryknoll, NY: Orbis, 2002. See Introduction.

On hybridity: Jeannine Hill Fletcher, *Monopoly of Salvation? A Feminist Approach to Religious Pluralism*. New York/London: Continuum, 2005.

On dialogue as a new way of being church: Thomas C. Fox, *Pentecost in Asia: A New Way of Being Church*. Maryknoll, NY: Orbis, 2002.

John Dunne on the spiritual adventure of our time: John Dunne, *The Way of All the Earth: Experiments in Truth and Religion*. New York: Macmillan, 1972. See Preface.

A NEW CONCLUSION

Sources

Drew, Rose, *Christian or Buddhist? An Exploration of Dual Religious Belonging*. New York: Routledge, 2011.

Thich Nhat Hanh, op cit. John Makransky, "How Contemporary Buddhist Practice Meets the Secular World in Its Search for a Deeper Grounding for Service and Social Action," published in the online journal *Dharma World*, March 2012.

Thich Nhat Hanh, *Being Peace* (Berkeley: Parallax Press, 1987); Aloysius Pieris, *Love Meets Wisdom: A Christian Experience of Buddhism* (Maryknoll: Orbis Books, 1988), pp. 110–36.

INDEX

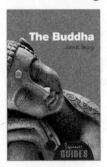

The Fifth Dimension
An Exploration of the
Spiritual Realm

John Hick

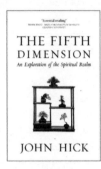

"Essential reading"
BRIAN HAYES · BRISTOL UNIVERSITY

THE FIFTH
DIMENSION
An Exploration of the Spiritual Realm

JOHN HICK

£10.99/$16.95
978-1-85168-991-0

Many of us today are all too willing
to accept a humanist and scientific
account of the universe which considers
human existence as a fleeting accident.
The triumph of John Hick's gripping
work is his exposure of the radical
insufficiency of this view. Drawing on
mystical and religious traditions ancient
and modern, and spiritual thinkers
as diverse as Julian of Norwich and
Mahatma Ghandi, he has produced a
tightly argued and thoroughly readable
case for a fuller understanding of our
reality, that appreciates the importance
of a fifth, spiritual dimension.

"Essential reading for anyone concerned
with spirituality in the modern world."
Professor Keith Ward – University of
Oxford

"Erudite, provocative, and deeply
moving." *Expository Times*

Find out more about this and other titles on our website:
www.oneworld-publications.com